# STREET SOLDIER

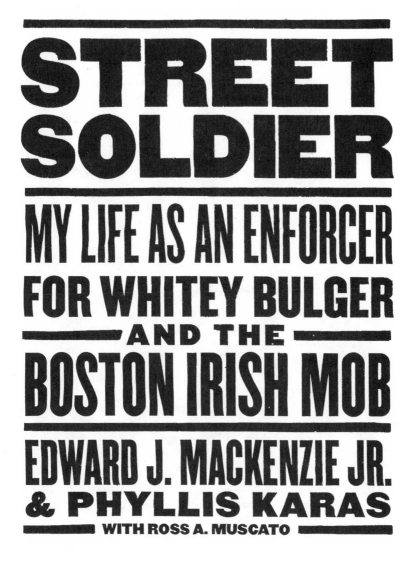

# STREET SOLDIER

## MY LIFE AS AN ENFORCER FOR WHITEY BULGER AND THE BOSTON IRISH MOB

### EDWARD J. MACKENZIE JR. & PHYLLIS KARAS

WITH ROSS A. MUSCATO

STEERFORTH PRESS • HANOVER, NEW HAMPSHIRE

*From Eddie*
For Courtney, Lauren, Devin, Kayla, Danny, and Brittany.
That was then and this is now. We all change in time,
but my love and devotion to you will never falter.

*From Phyllis*
For Adam and Amy and Josh and Chalese

For information about permission to reproduce
selections from this book, write to:
Steerforth Press L.C., 25 Lebanon Street
Hanover, New Hampshire 03755

The Library of Congress has cataloged the hardcover edition of this book as follows:
MacKenzie, Edward, 1958–
    Street soldier : my life as an enforcer for Whitey Bulger and the Boston Irish mob / Edward
MacKenzie, Jr., and Phyllis Karas with Ross Muscato. — 1st ed.
        p.   cm.
    ISBN 1-58642-063-1 (alk. paper)
1. MacKenzie, Edward, 1958– 2. Bulger, Whitey, 1929– 3. Gangsters—Massachusetts—Boston—Case
studies. 5. Irish Americans—Massachusetts—Boston—Social conditions. 6. South Boston (Boston,
Mass.)—Social conditions. I. Karas, Phyllis. II Muscato, Ross. III. Title.
HV6452.M4 M33 2003
364.1'092—dc21

                                                    2002154282

ISBN-10: 1-58642-076-3 (trade paperback)
ISBN-13: 978-1-58642-076-5 (trade paperback)

Some of the names in this book have been changed.

SECOND PRINTING

# Contents

# Foreword

It was a December afternoon in 1975, when I first heard about Eddie MacKenzie. Rosario "Rosie" La Monica was calling from his "place" at the Middlesex House of Correction, aka Billerica. Rosie had been my client for a few years. Predictably, he was calling for a favor. "Hey, Al, I gotta ask you for a little help on a matter," Rosie said. "I met this kid here; solid kid, young and not wise to the system. And he's getting screwed." Aren't they all?

Rosie told me that this kid, one Eddie MacKenzie, eighteen, was looking at a disposition for three nighttime felonies. His court-appointed attorney was offering eight to ten years at the state's maximum security facility at Walpole as a good deal. I told Rosie to have this Eddie Mac give me a call.

Eddie and I talked for a long time. Then I made a few calls to the authorities. I found out Eddie Mac was from South Boston, without family or identity, and had grown up knocking around not on the streets, but in the alleys, his brother in tow. After one of Eddie's friends dropped off a small "visit retainer," I headed to Billerica to meet the kid.

I must admit he looked the part of a burgeoning street soldier. Not tall, about 5'10", but built like a pit bull. He had these icy blue eyes and high cheekbones. Good looking in a menacing sort of way. He was very serious and all business. We got to talking, and I learned about his life. Eddie Mac had lived a brutal existence, including an early childhood of abuse and neglect. After I left the prison, I went to work. I determined early that Eddie was not ready for prime time — Walpole State Prison. He robbed at night, but there were no weapons involved and no one was home at the houses he hit.

By the time the case went to court, I was able to find the subtle defects in the indictments, and Ed walked out with time served (fifty-eight days). So began our nearly thirty-year relationship. I'd like to tell you that we have been merely friends all that time. But, of course, we've been lawyer and client for a good portion of this period. I am pleased to say that, during these years, Ed was never in jail, other than for bail and on the final disposition of the 1990 Whitey Bulger cocaine blast.

From the beginning I was intrigued by Eddie Mac's remarkable nature. I followed his career in the ring as a boxer and then as a champion kickboxer, and, out of the ring, as a loving father and failed husband. His gentleness with his daughters, whose number quickly grew to five, showed a doting father's sweet side and contrasted sharply with the vicious man in the ring and on the streets.

I watched, often awestruck, as Eddie the street soldier put his fighting ability to good use. One of my favorite stories happened the night a manager at Houlihan's, a Boston bar, called in Eddie because some Boston College football players were getting out of hand after their victory over Notre Dame. The college guys had started to separate beautiful women from men who weighed less than they did. Eddie had just won his second consecutive national kickboxing victory and was a fierce street fighter. "Now, let's all have a pleasant evening here," Eddie calmly suggested to the four BC linemen, each of whom weighed in at least 225 with no body fat.

One of the players made the nearly fatal error of mistaking Eddie's immense chest size for a flabby gut, calling out "Hey, Fattie," while his pal doubled the mistake by putting a hand on Eddie's shoulder and patting him as if he were a cocker spaniel. Suddenly, Eddie lifted his right foot and placed it on the first linebacker's temple, instantly knocking him out. Before the other three could react, Eddie had spun around with a heel kick and dropped the second. He then slipped under a punch thrown by the third and came up with a vicious left hook. In less than sixty seconds, three BC football players were out cold. Eddie looked at the sole remaining player and said, "Sorry, buddy, but I think it's time you get your friends and leave."

I also knew that Eddie used his fighting abilities in the seedy and dark side of life, as a mob legbreaker, a drug dealer, a scam artist, an intimidator, a "collector," and a lot of other things. But let me say that Eddie, while inextricably tied to the "other" side of society and easily seduced by the illegitimate deal, is also a good person and intensely loyal. He is a street soldier.

There were occasions when Eddie and I socialized together, which was a rarity for me with clients. But Eddie, who always called me "Boss," was articulate and respectful toward others, and I trusted him. Over the course of our relationship, he relayed to me in bits and pieces the tales of Whitey Bulger and rogue FBI agents John Connolly, H. Paul Rico, and John Morris. He knew what was going on. Connolly, now doing a prison stint for corrupting his position and his office, won't find *Street Soldier* enjoyable cell reading. He gets hit hard. The truth hurts.

That Eddie devoted so much time to young people never surprised me. The hell of his childhood was all the motivation he needed to do this good turn. He admits he peddled stuff that hurt kids, but today he's a fitness enthusiast who shuns drugs and booze. Today, when he tells kids that drugs and booze can destroy anything good they try to achieve, they listen. I've lost count of the number of kids who received free memberships to his boxing and martial arts gyms.

I do take a bow for urging him to attend UMass Boston, where he obtained his bachelor's degree and set an intercollegiate record: he was thrown out of seven consecutive games for unnecessary roughness as an impolite linebacker. He dedicated his graduation party to me.

And I'm proud that he had the guts to tell his story and offer a rare glimpse inside a troubling and unsettling world. It's shocking and entertaining and thought-provoking. I'm not so sure, like Eddie's life, it offers any conclusions or moral absolutes. And that's about right. Because I've known Eddie for over a quarter of a century and he still perplexes me. He has made too many mistakes to count, but he's also improved himself through hard work and overcome a heap of adversity.

I am proud to count Eddie Mac as my friend. And if I ever had to face an angry mob or battle an approaching army, Eddie Mac would be my first pick for comrade.

I'd want the ultimate street soldier.

ALFRED E. NUGENT, ESQUIRE
AUGUST 22, 2002

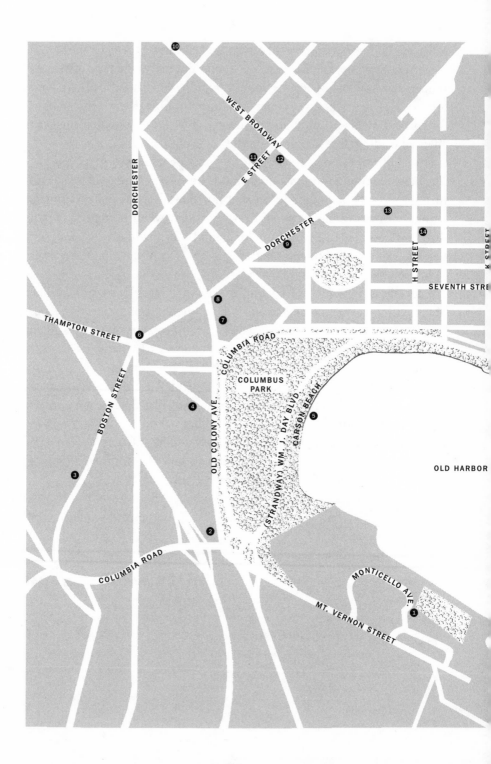

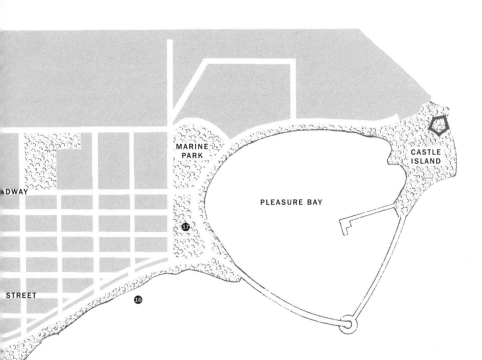

MARINE
PARK

CASTLE
ISLAND

DWAY

PLEASURE BAY

⑰

STREET

⑯

❶ Columbia Point Projects
❷ South Boston Liquor Mart (Whitey's headquarters)
❸ 30 Boston Street (first meeting with Whitey)
❹ Old Harbor Projects
❺ Carson Beach (race riots)
❻ Academy of Martial Arts (Andrew Square)
❼ Frankie McDonald's House, Old Colony Projects
❽ Mullen Club (Whitey's hangout)
❾ O'Brien's Funeral Home (site of Frankie's funeral)
❿ Triple O's Bar
⑪ 251 Gold Street
⑫ Connolly's Corner Café
⑬ McDonough Gym and Southie Courthouse
⑭ 4th & H (Teresa Stanley's house)
⑮ Norcross Place
⑯ South Boston Yacht Club
⑰ Marine Park (Southie Day)

# Danbury Federal Penitentiary

If you can't do the time, don't do the crime."

My lawyer Al Nugent used to say that to me every time I called him up with a new "problem." Not that this latest problem came as a grand shock in August 1990. We'd gotten the word from someone who worked at the Justice Department. Big drug sting coming up: South Boston dealers going down. And that was me, all right: big-time drug dealer for Whitey Bulger.

James "Whitey" Bulger, for those who haven't looked around the walls of their local post office lately, is presently on the FBI's Ten Most Wanted List. He was on the lam for four and a half years before the FBI decided he wasn't coming back on his own and, in August 1999, hung his picture right next to that of Osama bin Laden.

Whitey Bulger was head of the South Boston mob, a kind of Irish mafia that ran gambling rackets, extorted protection money, peddled black market products, pushed tons of pot and cocaine, and killed those who got in its way. He is being sought for extortion and RICO (Racketeering Influenced and Corrupt Organizations Act) charges, along with eighteen counts of murder. Yeah, that's my boss. And if you help find him, there's a million-dollar check waiting with your name on it.

Whitey is also, of course, the older brother of perhaps the most powerful and cutthroat politician in Massachusetts, the one and only William M. Bulger, who spent seventeen years as president of our state senate, and all his life in South Boston, which we call Southie. One brother a feared, brilliant, and ruthless outlaw, and the other brother a feared, brilliant, and ruthless politician; one a graduate of Alcatraz, the other of Boston College Law School; both setting up practice in Southie. A *Boston Magazine* article characterized the Brothers Bulger perfectly: "The yin and yang of absolute power." When Billy took over the reins of the Massachusetts Senate in 1978, the brothers began their evenly balanced control of South Boston.

1

But back then, Whitey controlled me. I tried to be careful, always following his orders, keeping a low profile, not talking on the telephone, staying far away from anyone we suspected of being a rat or wearing a wire. But we were all dirty and we knew we were dirty, so it was no surprise there'd be a heavy price to pay.

The life I was leading then was good. Me and Tommy Dixon, one of Whitey's top sellers, were roomies in a luxurious new apartment in Southie, raking in a ton of money, about $50,000 to $75,000 on a good week, less the $20,000 we paid in tribute to Whitey. This was our cut for spreading coke and marijuana throughout Southie and the Boston suburbs, and for making sure that Whitey's operation ran smoothly. When we weren't distributing drugs, we were breaking the legs of punks and deadbeats on Whitey's orders.

I was thirty-one, a criminal with a long record, a $320,000 Spanish colonial stucco house on a half acre of land in Milton, a spanking new Vanden Plas Jaguar, a Pathfinder, and three Rolex watches. My two daughters went to private parochial school and had everything their hearts desired. I ate at the most expensive restaurants and wore designer clothes whose names I couldn't pronounce. There was nothing I wanted that I couldn't buy.

Day in and day out, I did my job, satisfied with the way I felt when I woke up in the morning and the way I felt when I went to bed at night. For a tenth-grade dropout who'd spent his childhood bouncing from one hideous foster home to the next, I was living the life I'd only dreamed about when I was young. Working for Whitey was as good as it got. True, he was a homicidal psychopath. I'd known that from the first moment I met him. But he was *my* homicidal psychopath, *my* boss, the man I respected and feared and served with every bit of loyalty in my being. He told me to beat someone within an inch of his miserable life; I did it. He told me to burn down a house; I did it. He told me to avoid drugs; I did. He told me to respect the Code of Silence; I did. If Whitey, like Italian mobsters, had made me swear to put his needs before those of my children, I would have drawn the line there. But he never did. So, every word he spoke was my law.

One hot August morning, it all fell apart. I was outside my apartment on Gold Street in South Boston. It was 6 A.M., and I was heading out for coffee and then to Connolly's Corner Café — a bar of which I was the manager of record, when I noticed an undercover car slowly driving by with two cops inside. This must be the bust we'd heard about, I thought. The car crawled beside me for a few minutes before I said, "Hey, you guys looking for me?"

"Who are you?" a cop yelled back.

"Eddie MacKenzie," I said. "And if you want me, I ain't running from no one. So, here I am." They called on their radio and, sure enough, I was on their arrest list. They got out real nice, like we were friends, and cuffed me and put me in the back. This wasn't the first time I'd been arrested or sent away. My criminal record, which included attempted murder, assault with a deadly weapon, mayhem, breaking and entering, and rape, was nine pages long.

"We hope everybody gives up so easily," the driver said. We headed over to Connolly's Bar, where television crews from all the local stations were waiting, obviously having been informed exactly who was being picked up where. The federal Drug Task Force, which included the U.S. Attorney's office, the Drug Enforcement Agency, the state police, and the Boston police, had raided Connolly's a week earlier but found nothing. I'd been there when they searched the premises, looking for information on Whitey's empire, but I hadn't been interviewed by the task force. They spoke to no one, just came in with a warrant and searched for evidence. Nobody put a microphone in my face this time, but the cameras were all over me as the cops transferred me to an unmarked van. The police deliberately took their time, making me do the perp walk for the media as they put me in the van in front of my bar.

They ended up arresting quite a crew that day. A collection of fifty-one drug dealers, ranging in importance from scumbag drunks who were petty pushers to major lieutenants, like me and my roomie Dixon, who were running several millions of dollars a year in coke and pot and were the foundation of Whitey's drug empire. The van transported us, ten to a van, to the Coast Guard base in the North End of Boston. There, each of us was singled out for another perp walk by the media on our way to the cafeteria, which served as a holding area. The Drug Task Force held a press conference and answered a few questions for the press, but none of us perps was questioned. In the cafeteria, the DTF asked each one of us separately if we wanted to cooperate. Not one head nodded.

We were then transferred in groups of ten to the U.S. Courthouse in

downtown Boston for arraignment. While we were huddled in the holding cell in the courthouse, I called my lawyer, Al Nugent. I was shitting
bricks: the eighty-page indictment had so many charges on it that it
seemed as if I'd be going away for a hundred years. But, as Al patiently
explained to me, it was a group indictment and there were only two
charges against me: conspiracy to distribute cocaine and use of a tele-
phonic device — in my case, the telephone — in a drug transaction. The
first charge could put me away for twenty years; the second, four. It didn't
look great. Al told me that I should have done things differently. I should
never have given up so sweetly. Unlike most of the other drug dealers I'd
been arrested with, I'd set aside money for a time like this. I should have
avoided the cops, headed to Al's office, and, with him at my side, turned
myself in. Then I could have made bail and avoided some of this mess. But
I'd been stupid. And so I was stuck with the rest of the dummies.

As the bail hearings went on, those who were designated not dangerous,
or who posed no threat of flight, were sent home on personal recognizance to await trial. I wasn't that fortunate. With my record — coupled
with the level and extent of my involvement with Whitey and the drug
ring, and the fact that I was roommates with Tommy Dixon, the ringleader of the group — it was determined that I was going to be held for a
while in a government facility. I would not be heading back to Gold Street
that afternoon.

So, me, my buddy Dixon, and ten other guys were designated for transport to Danbury Federal Penitentiary in Connecticut, where we'd sit while
the powers that be determined whether we would make bail or be held
until trial. I knew that I was looking at a weekend in the can, no matter
what. The wheels of justice do not spin on weekends. The feds purposely
arrested us on a Friday, just to make us suffer a little more. You better
believe that on a Friday afternoon in August, no federal prison employee
is going to start any type of processing that might cause him to arrive even
a minute late at the beach.

When you hear that the feds are going to ship you somewhere, you get
nervous about something called diesel therapy. It's a tortuous system in
which prisoners are shackled in a plane or minivan and ferried around
aimlessly for about sixteen hours, then put in a holding cell for eight
hours, then back in transit for sixteen hours, and on and on. I once read
in the *Boston Herald* that the federal prison system is so overcrowded that

there are at least five thousand inmates in transit all over the country on any given day. The government claims this transit is necessary to prevent overcrowding of certain facilities, but don't believe it. It's actually a state-sanctioned form of torture. Mild torture, but still torture.

The worst part of diesel therapy is that you are completely cut off from the rest of the world. You never get to phone home, and your family has no idea where you are. Even your lawyer can't reach you. You can't read or write or watch television or exercise. It's a big deal if they unlock your hands to let you wipe yourself if they take you to a bathroom. You have no idea where you're going or when this punishment will end. Big deal, right? You're a prisoner. But guys say you lose your mind when you're shackled in a van or bus for sixteen hours a day. There's no doubt it's a deterrent though. If you're sitting next to a child molester or rapist in a medium- or minimum-security prison, you think twice about busting the prick's jaw when you know it could land you in diesel therapy. Luckily, I've never been slapped with diesel therapy.

Those of us selected for the Danbury trip were relatively fortunate. We were transported directly there, with one quick stop in Hartford. Even so, the trip was the closest thing to diesel therapy I'd ever experienced. It was a hot August day, and the long black van had tinted glass that didn't allow us to see outside. It didn't have any air conditioning and became an oven as it soaked up the heat from the sun and road. Both the driver and the guard seated next to him were U.S. marshals, carrying handguns. A partition made of thick chicken wire separated the prisoners from the marshals. We sat behind them, three to a row, three rows in all, with our hands shackled to our legs. There were no piss stops during the three-hour drive; the stench was overwhelming. The brutal heat and disgusting smells were making me sick, but there was nothing to do but suck it up. After all, we weren't on vacation.

The infamous Charlestown hoodlum Butchie Doe was transported in the same van. This guy was a lunatic. Even though he didn't work for Whitey, Butchie was involved in just about every illegal activity there was, including, from what we heard, killing more than one woman. He was a paunchy-looking Mick of a guy, early thirties like me, six feet tall, well over two hundred pounds, with this Baby Huey, beach-ball face.

It killed some of the boredom of the trip to taunt him, saying, "Hey, woman killer, you fucking piece of shit. How'd you like your jaw broken?"

And he had no choice but to sit there and take it. We were getting on him pretty good, until the driver told us that if we didn't shut up, we'd all be gagged.

Butchie was the reason we made the stop in Hartford, to drop him off at the maximum-security facility there. After that, we finally arrived at Danbury and were unloaded. It was like being back in boot camp. We were marched into this holding area inside the prison, a big colorless room with no windows. The shackles were removed at this point, thank God. Then, one at a time, they took us out of that room and sat us down so they could ask us questions and fill out paperwork, take our picture, our fingerprints, our weight and height. I'm surprised they didn't measure our dicks while they were at it.

After that, we had to trade in our clothes for a regulation orange jumpsuit. Not my favorite color, but it didn't look that great on anybody else either. We were each given a pillow and a blanket and sent to take a shower to be fumigated for crabs, lice, and who knows what else.

For three days we were kept in twenty-four–hour lockup, two men to a cell, not allowed out to shower or shit or eat. We stayed in the cell, with one toilet in the middle. We were filthy, sweating, stinking. It was a bit different than the lifestyle I'd gotten used to. No bars. No restaurants. No Jag. The one decent thing they did was give us books. Most of the guys ignored them, but I liked mine. It was called *Adrift* and was about a guy who spends more than seventy days at sea on a raft after his sailboat sinks. It was a real story of survival and I loved every word. On Monday morning, us boys from Southie were finally released from our cells and allowed to mingle with the general population while we waited to be processed. We were housed in one of those classic tiered prison setups, like you see in the movies. It sort of looked like the Alamo, with one fat wall and an electric barbed-wire fence surrounding it. The prison itself was three stories of gray poured concrete, each story consisting of about ten cells, two men to a cell. On the ground floor was a big, open recreation area, the size of a basketball court, filled with card tables and benches.

As we walked around, we tried to keep things in perspective. We could have been sent to a number of other federal facilities that were much worse than Danbury. Danbury was a level-two, medium-security pen, nowhere near the league of a Leavenworth, Kansas, or Marion, Illinois, which are level-six, maximum-security. Danbury had its bars and razor wire and gun towers, but was widely known as a "Club Fed" facility, a place where most of the inmates were nonviolent. The cells were occupied by drug pushers who had never carried weapons, dirty politicians and cops, and accountants and investment bankers who had gone a few steps too far.

Unlike Leavenworth, where most prisoners had no hope of ever getting out, Danbury was a short-timer's prison; nobody was in for more than fifteen or twenty years. Even though the middle-aged, paunchy white guys shuffling around Danbury weren't escape risks and weren't likely to overpower a guard or inmate and shank him, they demanded a whole different sort of special attention — and special treatment. These guys had the juice, the connections. There were the gangsters doing time for gambling and racketeering charges who had the power to commission hits. And the corrupt bank execs, real estate brokers, and politicians could hurt people on the outside, too. They didn't hurt them with a gun or a knife; instead, they used money and influence to make people's lives miserable. Perhaps the most dangerous of the lot at Danbury were the mob bosses and their lieutenants, guys who could reach you in lots of ways: with money, political connections, and all sorts of nasty physical violence.

Still, as far as prisons go, Danbury is considered a walk in the park. How many prisons offer international cuisine and multiple entrees with an all-you-can-eat salad bar?

On Tuesday, my second day in the general prison population, I thought for a second I was in the wrong place. It was a hot afternoon and Tommy Dixon and I were walking down to the softball field. As we got closer to the field, I couldn't believe what I was seeing. Were those girls sunning themselves?

I grabbed Dixon and said, "Tommy, what the fuck is this? Is this place coed? Look at those fine bitches." As we got closer, we had to do everything we could to keep from laughing out loud. Those weren't girls, but guys — guys that were all smooth and brown and wearing thongs right out in the middle of the prison yard. You'd have thought it was South Beach in Miami. The guys in the thongs were surrounded — protected, actually — by these huge black guys who had claimed them for their own enjoyment or would pimp them out in exchange for cigarettes and other goodies from the canteen.

But not every bitch in that joint was wearing a thong, as Dixon and I discovered in the weight room. Here we met Tyrone, this massive black guy, jacked out of his tree and cut to shreds — juiced on steroids and without an ounce of body fat — who was doing time for selling steroids. And let me tell you, he was his own best customer. We were lifting with him, and he pointed over to this other guy and said, "Look at that punk bitch. That boy is a faggot, man."

"How do you know that guy is sweet?" I asked.

"'Cause I fucked that bitch last night," he answered.

Talk about jailhouse mentality. If you're giving, you're straight; if you're receiving, you're a fag. We steered clear of Tyrone after that.

I'll never forget another scene I witnessed in the weight room. I was working out when this kid with a twenty-pound dumbbell walked up to a guy lying on a weight bench and with one swing crushed his skull. What a shot. It put the guy into a permanent vegetative state. I heard later that the recently demolished had been the kid's cellmate, and the night before had raped him in their cell. It's tough to find fault with a kid who responds this way to being forcibly ass-fucked. I imagine even a mild-mannered accountant could be moved to this type of payback. Word was that part of the kid's punishment was a nice long session of diesel therapy.

Experiences like these leave their mark on you, sure, but there was one event during my two-week stay at Danbury that changed my life. That day, four of us — me, Tommy "Speedy" Dixon, Paul "Polecat" Moore, and Kevin "Andre the Giant" MacDonald (if you were from South Boston, you had a nickname; I was "Eddie Mac") — were stretching our legs in the prison yard. Like everybody else, we were decked out in our bright orange jumpsuits. Danbury wasn't Southie, but the rule of the streets still applied: watch each other's back. We kept to ourselves. We weren't interested in making friends.

I'd been outside ten minutes when I saw two of Danbury's most notorious guests, a pair of "celebrity" inmates, standing by a wall: Raymond J. "Junior" Patriarca, the Providence-based godfather of the New England Mafia, and his soldier, Carmen Tortora, a newly made member of La Cosa Nostra. Tortora was a stand-up guy, well-liked by both inmates and authorities. His family came to see him every weekend. A year earlier, in 1989, the FBI, after a tip from underworld informants, had scored a historic coup when it bugged an induction ceremony of the New England Mob in the Boston suburb of Medford. For federal authorities, the recording was pure gold, providing the ammunition for three major Mob prosecutions, including the indictments of Patriarca and Tortora. Both were awaiting trial on racketeering charges.

That day, they were standing together, smiling slightly and looking at my crew. Patriarca made a motion with his head for us to walk over to him. We did as we were instructed. You don't ignore the request of a Mafia godfather. Not even if he's wearing a bright orange jumpsuit. Patriarca and Tortora were both on the shortish side, five-six or five-seven. Both had olive skin, Roman noses, and fat bellies; prison food agreed with them. There were no hellos, no pleasantries. Patriarca, still smiling, asked, "You know why you're here, don't you?" Without waiting for our response, he dropped the bomb. "You're here because you got ratted out by your boy Whitey. We've known for years he was a canary."

No one spoke. We didn't know what to say to Junior Patriarca, a quintessential Mafia don, no rocket scientist but still a lot wiser to the ways of the street than any of us. Even if we didn't believe him, it wouldn't have been the smartest thing to tell him he was full of it.

I didn't believe him right away. More than anything, it was a shock to hear something like that come from someone so powerful, the don of New England organized crime. We'd all suspected that Whitey had been paying off the feds for years, but this. . . . Suddenly, I felt a deep pain inside that was nothing like fear. Fear I'd learned to deal with years ago. Yeah, I was in jail and I might be going down for ten or fifteen years. But that didn't shake me up like this was beginning to do. Had I actually been shanked by my boss?

"He's been snitching for years," Patriarca continued. "We've known it. Not Stevie, though." (Stephen "The Rifleman" Flemmi was one of Whitey's top lieutenants.) "Stevie's good. But Whitey," and he started to shake his finger as if to scold a young boy, "he's no good."

*Whitey?* My mind kept racing back and forth. *Could Whitey give us up?* What about his code of silence, a code he constantly preached? No one ever rats out anyone. No one. How many times had I been seated next to Whitey, listening to him rant that no matter what, you never rat on an associate? If you have to go to jail, you go like a man. This code of silence was a mantra, an ethical doctrine, if indeed a mobster can possess such a thing, that seemed central to Whitey's being. So it was central to all of our beings as well. Whitey was my hero, the guy I would have taken a bullet for. He was fearless, a bad ass, and I respected him for that.

I was in Danbury, I had thought, because "Dem dat plays pays." Some of the other guys were crying in their cells, but not me. If it was necessary for me to go away for Whitey, I would have been proud to do time for my mentor. It would have been my honor.

But now, certain things began to make sense. We'd wondered how Whitey avoided indictment all these years. Selling out supposed friends and fellow bad guys to the feds can work wonders. Snap to it, Eddie Mac, I ordered myself. How can you act so surprised? After all, through the years I'd seen plenty of Whitey's "friends" end up dead, under his orders. What made us any different?

As we learned later, Junior Patriarca wasn't talking nonsense. The reason that he and Tortora — as well as me, Dixon, Polecat, and Andre — were behind bars that afternoon was because of the same guy: Whitey. Whitey had sent us all there. By 1990, the FBI suspected Whitey was responsible for close to thirty murders — and more charges would be added in the years to come. It would be another five years before they came after him, but the stage was being set. He'd offered them a bone — all told, fifty-one of us — to hold off the dogs. Sooner or later, they'd be after his hide. But at that moment, he was on the outside of a jail cell, and we were deep inside.

For me, that meeting with a pair of hardened mobsters was a flash point. It would take some time before I could fully accept it, but on that day in Danbury, I began to come to grips with the reality that Whitey had trained us, mentored us, been our partner in crime — and then sold us out.

Put a lousy Band-Aid on your wound, I told myself. It was time to start to get a handle on the mess I'd made of my life. I look back now and call Danbury my epiphany. Don't get me wrong. There was no cosmic and immediate transformation. Life isn't that easy. Nor is redemption. But, at Danbury, I began to see the light, even if at the time it was nothing more than a dim, far-off flicker.

And that flicker, tiny as it was, made me realize that my life had been a series of sorry decisions. Like dropping out of school, committing armed robbery, stealing, swindling, kidnapping, arson, intimidating, mugging, dealing drugs, beating people up, inciting others to violence, and helping to make people, let's just say, disappear permanently.

I realized finally that my choices in life had jeopardized the future of my two young daughters, Courtney and Lauren, six and four years old at the time, who were living with my ex-wife Carolyn. Carolyn was doing her job, but I wasn't doing mine. Until my arrest, even though she and I no longer lived together, we were able to work together to give our kids plenty of love and attention. And I had been able to rationalize that it was all right for Daddy to be a drug dealer, because the heavy money he was making in the cocaine trade financed the parochial school education, the clothes, the trips to Florida.

Talk about an inability to see the bigger picture. Life was great as long as Daddy remained a free man. But a Daddy behind bars was no Daddy at all. It was amazing how that simple statement about betrayal changed my life. Now that I'd been ratted out, the playing field had been irrevocably altered. I'd played with the idea many times of trying to go legit. At the time I was arrested, I even had a plan in development to work with a Medellin drug cartel to move so much powder through Boston that I would have about five million stashed away in a year's time. Once that score was safe and secure, I planned to retire from my life of crime. I know this particular plan is not most people's idea of going legitimate, but, then again, everything is relative.

But that was in the past. Right then I was a guest of Uncle Sam. I began to think that maybe it was time to abandon my allegiance to the destructive codes that had been preached to me by all the wrong people, including the high priest of screwed-up values, Whitey Bulger.

After all, Whitey wasn't the only one who had information that the government might find of interest. If Whitey had indeed been an informant, and if he was the one who helped the government take down all fifty-one of us, then I had every reason to rethink my vow never to talk. Particularly if I could buy freedom by releasing some useful information.

Within a few days, I had a plan. Because of the major Colombian contact I had, I could deliver to the FBI some powerful international drug dealers, all without hurting my boys from Southie — including Whitey. I was going to talk all right, but unlike our fearless leader, whom I'd still protect, I was going to do it without selling out my friends and teammates, still clinging to the unwritten code of not ratting. It had been drummed into me for as long as I could remember, and I wasn't ready to discard it. Plus, there was this small voice in the back of my head telling me maybe Patriarca was full of shit. Anyway, I had another ace. I could get out of the can using the Colombians, not the boys of Southie. After years of bad decisions, maybe it was time to start making some good ones.

That day, I resolved to embark on a long, tough journey to clean up my life. My children were not going to have a father they visited only in prison waiting rooms. I wanted to be a father they could be proud of, who could take care of all their problems because he didn't call a jail cell home. I was never going to be a choirboy, but maybe I could take that first step in the right direction.

But, before looking forward, I was going to have to take a long, hard look back.

# Ward of the State

If it weren't for my brother Ronnie I would know next to nothing about my family and my early life before I was placed in a series of foster homes. In the spring of 1990, Ronnie wrote to the Department of Social Services in Boston, requesting any information they had on the MacKenzie family. The DSS assigned Sheila Frankel to the case, who took all his phone calls and hunted down important records. After completing her research, on December 12, 1990, Ms. Frankel sent a letter describing a bleak family history. I came, as I had already suspected, from shit stock.

The letter told me some of what I already knew, but filled in a few of the gaps. Charlotte Kimble, my mother — and I use that term very, very loosely — was tall and attractive, and made it through the seventh grade before she quit school in Somerville and went to work. Her father died when she was young, her mother remarried, and she had two younger half brothers. Her childhood was pretty lousy, too, and she put in her own time in foster care, residential treatment, and an orphanage.

Charlotte had seven kids from 1955 to 1964. Pretty busy lady for those nine years. DSS got to know Charlotte five months after she became a mother, when she put her first kid Leonard in a boarding home and decided not to pay for his care. As a result, Leonard was put in foster care in 1956 and she was arrested for child neglect, but was given a suspended sentence. A month later, she was put in jail for some other unspecified crime. Once released, she got busy doing the only thing she did well, and she had Ronnie in 1957 and me a year later. Three months later, at twenty-one, she married my dad — another real loose term — seventeen-year-old Edward James MacKenzie Jr. On my birth certificate, it states that Charlotte was twenty-one when I was born and Ed was sixteen. That means he had to be fifteen when Ronnie was born. I guess I'm more like my mother than my father in that every girl I've ever been involved with has always been at least eight years younger than me.

Ed was also the father of my other full brother, Robert, born in 1961, but since I barely knew Charlotte's other kids — Leonard, born in 1955, Dennis in 1961 (for all I know Robert and Dennis may have been twins), Sandra in 1963, and Tammy in 1964 — I have no idea who their fathers were. According to Ms. Frankel's report, Ed was about 5' 8", stocky, in good health, and had been in special education classes in public school. His employment history was pretty spotty, but when he did decide to work, he was an okay worker. He had an older brother and two younger sisters. His parents were divorced and had both remarried.

While Ed and Charlotte were together, we did a little traveling as a family. Right after I was born, Ed and Charlotte and Ronnie and me moved to California, but the happy family was back in Somerville four months later. Charlotte didn't do much better taking care of me and Ronnie than she had of Leonard, and when I was two, a neighbor complained that we were left alone and the home was filthy. Charlotte would get depressed and ignore us kids; Ed would stay home from his painting job to help out, and then get fired. Not that he did much at home, since he was pretty much a drunken slob. The Massachusetts Society for the Prevention of Cruelty to Children and the Department of Public Welfare (DPW), which later became the DSS, got involved, and all five of us kids — me, Ronnie, Robert, Dennis, and Sandra — were committed to the DPW on May 13, 1963.

Ronnie has this perfect memory of men in suits coming into our apartment to take all five of us away that day. We lived in the projects on Mount Vernon Street in Somerville. He was six, and I was a month away from my fifth birthday. Dennis and Bobby were still in diapers, as was Sandra, who was not more than five or six months old. Ronnie remembers our mother saying she was going out to get us each ten cents for candy. But she never came back. The men in suits took us to a big room where we stayed for a little while. Then Ronnie, Bobby, and me were sent to a foster home in Revere. Sandra went with Charlotte's mother, and Charlotte's brother and sister-in-law took in Dennis and later adopted him.

Poor Charlotte said she didn't visit us boys in foster care because she couldn't bear to leave us. In 1964, Ed was arrested for falling behind in child support payments. To make matters even better, Charlotte had Tammy in 1964, who also became a ward of the state. The charges against Ed were eventually dropped, and his child support payments were lowered.

The file said Charlotte visited me and Ronnie twice in 1964. But at the end of 1965, Ed stopped paying any child support and he and Charlotte took off for Florida so he wouldn't be arrested again. A year later, they returned to Massachusetts together. Lots of the information about our family was confusing, because, as the social worker told Ronnie, part of our file was lost in a fire in the Cambridge Area Office of the DSS. For me, it was more than I ever wanted to know. I had no desire to find out who my father was.

Ronnie and I did learn, on our own, that our mother died of uterine cancer in 1992. She was in her mid-fifties. It was a nasty way to go, following a life of almost constant depression and hardship. Around the same time, we heard that our brother Dennis was living over in Somerville and was emotionally messed up. I think he spent some time in a mental hospital a while back. Big surprise, huh?

As for our father, well, the last I heard he is still alive and living down in Florida, in Kissimmee, doing nothing or next to nothing. In 1989, Ronnie, through DSS, located him in the Sunshine State. Ronnie wanted to meet our old man face to face, so I gave him a couple grand and he flew down there to find Pops doing part-time roofing and living in a run-down shack. Figures. Ronnie called me from Kissimmee and put my old man on the phone. "You got a million bucks?" I asked him. "Do you have any money stashed away?"

And he said, "Nah, I don't have any money. But I was thinking of coming up in a few months to see you."

See me? "Hey, listen," I told him, "if you don't have at least a million bucks to compensate me for the thirty-plus years of neglect and hell you put me through, then don't bother coming up to see me. Send a picture. Screw you."

My reaction horrified Ronnie because he really wanted to see our so-called father and try to forge something of a relationship with him. So much for the family reunion. I did get a picture, though, and he looked just like me. I did some checking up on him and learned that years before he'd been one of the toughest guys in Somerville. The Winter Hill area, actually. Winter Hill as in Whitey's Winter Hill Gang, before Whitey moved his base to Southie in the late seventies. Ed used to clean out barrooms. Like father, like son, I guess.

While Ronnie was down in Florida, he was also able to find Tammy, that last sister of ours that neither of us had ever met. She was twenty-five, divorced from some Cuban guy, and trying to take care of a few kids she had with him. I tell you, the pattern is hard to break.

In May of 1963, we said goodbye once and for all to those loving folks, Mom and Dad. The DPW brought me, Ronnie, and Bobby to a home in Revere where we lived with a witch of a woman and her husband, who was usually drunk. There were no other kids there. We hadn't been in that place more than ten minutes when the two of them smacked Bobby around because he shit in his diaper. Ronnie knew right then and there that this was going to be a horror show. And the old lady hadn't even started in with her belt yet. That place was bad. It wasn't only the wife who used to hit us; her drunk husband used to whack us around as well. He'd come home smashed and begin arguing with his wife. Strange thing was, he didn't share a bedroom with her. He had a bed in the same room with us. Ronnie and I shared a bunk bed. Bobby had a crib. And the husband had his own bed. Nothing ever happened, but, still, talk about weird.

People wonder how adults get away with child abuse. The simple answer is fear. The kids are afraid to talk. Sure, the state caseworkers used to check up on the homes where we stayed and talk to our foster parents and then talk with us. But do you really think we were going to take the chance and tell them what was going on in the house? This is why child-abusers are the lowest of the low. They pick on those who can't fight back.

Bobby, who was only two when we were placed in the home in Revere, was taken away by the DPW not long after we arrived. We came home one day and there was no Bobby. I guess you could say that the state was not too delicate when it came to separation issues. Eventually, we were told that Bobby was sent off to live with another family. The state must have decided it was bad enough that our foster parents were treating Ronnie and me like shit, but it was nothing short of obscene that Bobby, who was just a toddler, was being mistreated. It was a smart move getting Bobby out of there. I later found out he was sent to Wakefield, Massachusetts, where he was treated well by a family who later adopted him. Today, Bobby works as a shop steward at Boston Molasses Company. He represents the union and goes around the company to make sure that all the union rules are abided by. He's a regular, hard-working guy, taking good care of his family. He lives in Dorchester with his wife and kids, a girl and a boy. Bobby caught a break. He didn't grow up like Ronnie and me. That family in Wakefield took such good care of him.

Ronnie and I were removed from the Revere foster home a year after Bobby left. The teachers at our school must have reported that we were showing up on a regular basis with the types of bruises you don't routinely pick up in good old, youthful roughhousing. Whatever the reason, the next stop for Ronnie and me was a home in Ashland, a small town about twenty miles west of Boston.

Things didn't get any better in our new home. The authorities could have saved themselves the time and effort and left us in Revere. This next horror movie featured a demented she-wolf named Mrs. Fazio. I'll never forget her or that home, no matter how hard I try. Mrs. Fazio was a small, dark-haired, paunchy-looking Italian. She was out of her mind. As far as I remember there was no husband around, though she did have two teenage daughters and a son who was in Vietnam. And there was also this vicious Rottweiler with sharp teeth and the worst breath, that we had to pacify or else he'd bite whatever skin he could sink his fangs into.

Accommodations weren't top-shelf, to say the least. Mrs. Fazio used to pull a mattress out from under her bed in the master bedroom for us to sleep on. We were never allowed to sit on the furniture. She had plastic on the couches and chairs, and we spent 90 percent of the time on the floor. We weren't even allowed to eat with her and her daughters. We ate only after they finished.

But the hell with the neglect; Mrs. Fazio really outdid herself when it came to direct punishment. I wonder what blows life dealt her to turn her into such a sadist. She would punish us by sending us down to the cellar, alone, in the pitch blackness, often for the night. That was my first experience with holding cells. And we'd still get hit. Tough love, you understand. And when I say getting hit, I'm not talking about spankings or slaps on the hand, but beatings. You never knew what would trigger them. Looking at her wrong, sitting on her furniture, taking a piece of bread from the counter. She'd whack us with wooden spoons and belts. One time, she hit me so hard with the belt that I had to go to the hospital for stitches. She told the doctors and nurses I got the cut from falling down. No one questioned her explanation.

I've come to the conclusion that many of those foster parents were in it for the money. I don't know how much they got paid, but I bet a lot of them were figuring all sorts of ways to sock away the state money instead of spending it on their foster kids. I'll tell you that Mrs. Fazio must have made out with our clothing allowances. Our clothes never fit. They were all too big. We looked like clowns in some of those outfits. Now, Ashland was not Beverly Hills, but it was a middle-class community. So Ronnie and I stood out. The kids at school used to call us the "ragamuffins." You know, "Look, here come the foster kids."

One time, my mother and father came to visit. To us, they were just hazy memories, some people who used to take care of us. We didn't have the concept of Mom and Dad like most kids do. I can't say the meeting was big on emotion. I do remember they brought presents for us. Fire trucks, dinosaurs, some plastic animals. That was a big deal. But we didn't get to keep those presents, because the minute our parents left, Mrs. Fazio took them, figuring that she and her daughters could use them more than me and Ronnie.

If there was a beginning to our delinquent behavior, it had to have been in Ashland. It's possible that we inherited these belligerent genes from our parents, but it was not until we were in Ashland, when I was around seven, that we started to act up.

We began to devise little schemes. We were always hungry, so Ronnie and I used to sneak to the refrigerator at night to steal extra food. One of us would alert the other if anyone was coming by making a few light taps. And, of course, we had to contend with the dog. Most of the time, we had to cut him in so he didn't go nuts on us.

We also stole money. Our favorite hit was Mrs. Fazio's pocketbook. We'd pinch a buck here and a buck there. I think our biggest score was when Ronnie got away with ten dollars. Mrs. Fazio never found out we were ripping her off, and I can't imagine what she would have done to us if she had. One of the daughters caught us. But she didn't tell. Instead, she shook us down for a few bucks in exchange for silence.

We were only seven and six, but we began to notice girls in a new sort of way. There were these two girls who lived next door; they were probably eleven or twelve. From our bedroom, Ronnie used to actually watch them get undressed in the bathroom before they took showers. We also played games with them in the backyard, behind some trees. You show me yours and I'll show you mine. They were willing participants. And the four of us showed plenty.

It took a while, about two years, but the authorities finally caught on to the fact that we were being mistreated again. The last straw was when Mrs.

Fazio went after me with a broomstick. When I put up my arms to fend off the blows, she slammed my right arm with such force I hit the floor. She continued to slam me with the broom, screaming like a crazy woman, and when she finally stopped, I knew something was really wrong with my arm. Finally after two days of me crying all the time and being unable to go to school because of the pain and the swelling, she took me to the hospital. She'd beaten me so badly that she'd broken my arm. I don't think the hospital bought Mrs. Fazio's story that time. And I don't know if she was ever arrested for child abuse, but, at the very least, I hope there were no other foster kids placed in her care. Ronnie and I were pulled out of the house and were on our way to yet another foster home, this one in the Jamaica Plain section of Boston, known as JP. I was only a grade-schooler, but for the first time I would know the streets of Boston.

# Jamaica Plain

In 1966, Ronnie and I were placed in the Edith Fox Home, which was part of a foster-care organization called Volunteers of America. It was our third foster home in less than four years. A stable home life was not something we knew.

The house was a beautiful, old, well-maintained Georgian colonial with a half-acre of land out back. Jamaica Plain was a nice neighborhood that had parks, a beautiful pond, and a zoo, as well as an internationally renowned greenhouse, the Arnold Arboretum, which was owned by Harvard University. A trolley ran through JP as well as an elevated train track that girdled Washington Street, the major thoroughfare connecting JP to the rest of the city. When we arrived in JP, the neighborhood was still largely an Irish-Catholic enclave, but there were a few public housing projects that were more racially and ethnically diverse.

There was good and bad at the Fox Home. More good than bad. Besides me and Ronnie, there were seven other kids at the house, all around the same age, three boys and four girls. Most of the time, we were afforded the care and protection you might expect society would extend us. Case workers visited once a year, if we were lucky, to make sure we were free of excessive bruises and hadn't made frequent visits to the hospital. The physical environment was nice, but the parenting and caretaking was less than ideal.

During the week, we had a couple real beauts who took care of us, a husband-and-wife team, Rich and Betty Jean, who basically didn't give a shit. They were young, probably in their late twenties, and really in tune with the times — long-haired, scrawny, hippie freaks. In some ways, it was a trade-up because we weren't getting beaten and we were never hungry. But, then again, we weren't being properly supervised. They didn't care what we did, nor did they keep proper tabs on what we were doing. They were probably baked and tripping half the time.

But things were different on the weekends, because that's when Mom and Pops stayed over. Mom and Pops Cossitt were a married couple in their late forties who drew Friday-night-through-Sunday-night duty. Pops was actually Colonel George H. Cossitt, retired from the U.S. Marine Corp and a combat veteran of World War II and Korea. He and his wife, Margaret, were godsends and the closest to caring parents that Ronnie, me, and probably most of the other kids who came through the Fox Home ever knew.

Pops was tall and real skinny, and bald, with a bit of a hawk nose. Mom had a matronly look about her, silver hair piled on top of her head. They both smiled a lot. Mom's eyes showed you how she really felt, even when she was trying to make you believe that she felt differently. Unlike Betty Jean and Rich, Mom and Pops talked and played with us and genuinely seemed interested in who we were. And they used to take us places on weekends, like to a cottage they owned in Damariscotta, Maine, and on camping trips up to Nova Scotia. You couldn't help falling in love with them.

It seemed impossible to make Mom or Pops mad. Mostly they laughed at our antics. When they were around, we were less likely to act like problem children. Mischievous kids? Sure. But problem children? No. Well, at least not all of us.

Of all the kids in the Fox, Eddie Chisholm was the most twisted. He was one of those kids who went beyond mischievous behavior and started to show signs of becoming a serious problem to society. He was a year older than me, real gaunt, with these big round eyes that would fix on you for a second or so before he pivoted his head like an owl and stared at something else. He just kept to himself, never said much, and rarely smiled. He was strange, and he unsettled me.

By the time he was twelve, Chisholm had already crossed the law several times, and had run away a few times as well. One night, during one of his periods of prolonged absence, I was woken up by Ronnie. "Hey, you gotta check this out," he said, pulling on my arm. "C'mon. Just keep quiet."

I crawled out of bed and followed Ronnie into the hallway. The moon was shining through the windows. I could see the other kids, silently looking over the balustrade to the foyer below. Pops was in his pajamas, holding open the front door, and looking back inside the house toward a figure I couldn't quite make out. What I could make out was a big knife glinting in the shadows. My heart was racing. I could hear the other kids breathing.

In a calm voice, Pops said, "Now, Eddie, just put that knife down and get the hell out of here. There's no need for any problems here. Just walk away. I'll forget about it. You forget about it. Let's avoid trouble, all of us."

Chisholm didn't say anything. Pops just stood there, holding the door open. Twenty to thirty seconds of terrifying silence passed, and then Eddie shrugged, walked over to a little table and laid the knife on it. Without saying a word, he walked past Pops and out the door for good. Pops looked after him and said, "Eddie, take care of yourself."

Pops softly shut the door. Then he looked up at us and said, "Okay, kids, back in bed. The show's over." We jumped to it and were all back under the covers in seconds.

Eddie must have been on some whacked-out drug trip. He probably didn't even know where he was. As scary as it was for all of us, it wasn't until three years later that I was able to understand just how potentially dangerous Eddie's surprise visit had been. That was when I cracked open the Boston Herald and read about Eddie's newest exploits.

Apparently, Eddie was hitchhiking one night in a small town about twenty-five miles south of Boston. Some guy in his early forties gave him a lift. From what I gather, the guy was cruising for sex. Eddie must have figured it out quickly enough and used it as an opportunity to get the poor prick alone in a hotel room. I don't know what set Eddie off when that hotel room door closed, but whatever it was, he became Eddie the Ripper. He beat the guy senseless and stole his wallet, watch, and anything else of value. But he did much worse. The autopsy performed on the victim's body the next day revealed sixteen stab wounds.

Eddie might have managed to avoid justice had he not, with blood stains on his clothes, taken the victim's car and driven to a Chinese restaurant, where he bought himself a meal on the recently deceased's charge card. The cops arrived before he could get to his fortune cookie.

His claim of self-defense was lost on the jury. One particularly alarming piece of evidence was the fact that, in addition to the sixteen stab wounds in the body, there were thirty-two stab wounds in the floor. Eddie Chisholm was sent to prison for life. Last time I checked, he was doing his gig at Massachusetts Correctional Institution at Cedar Junction, one of the state's maximum-security prisons.

If Pops had not been so cool and calm under pressure that night, I wonder whether Eddie Chisholm might have carved a few of us up.

The only black kid with us at the home was Jimmy Wornum. His race wasn't an issue. We were still too young and naïve to understand that if someone looked different from you, you were supposed to treat him differently. Unlike Chisholm, Wornum was fun-loving, witty, smart, and well-liked. And he caused enough trouble to be one of us. Except for one bad decision and a bad break, Wornum might have made it and done something meaningful with his life.

His problems began one afternoon when he pulled a fire alarm downtown. Not smart. But for most thirteen-year-olds who do something stupid like that and get caught, the punishment is just a fine and some community service. And that's probably what Wornum would have been assessed had not one of the firemen, who was responding to the call, fallen off the ladder of the fire truck and died. Wornum was arrested, tried, and sentenced to a juvenile facility until he was eighteen.

When Wornum was seventeen, he escaped. No matter how smart you are — and Wornum was smart — there is a tendency to return to the neighborhood, even when running from the cops. That's just what he did. And while visiting, he ripped off the Pond Spa Café in JP. Soon after he did the job, I was walking down Center Street with my buddy Paul Donnelly. Cop cars went screaming by, sirens blaring and blue lights flashing. I didn't know what was up. Then I heard someone say, "Eddie. . . . Hey, Eddie."

Paul and I looked around. We couldn't see anyone.

"Eddie, over here. In the bushes."

I looked toward some tall green bushes covering the entrance to a small alley. Surprise. There was Jimmy Wornum, face covered in sweat, peering out at me from between two shrubs.

"Hey, Jimmy, long time no see," I said with a laugh, looking around to make sure no cops were in the vicinity. "They looking for you?"

"You got it. I just scored the Pond Spa."

Paul continued along the street, head down, trying not to give Jimmy away. "Well, Jimmy, good to see you," I said. "Stay low, and I'll see if I can get them off the scent. Be cool."

"Thanks, man."

"You'd do the same for me."

I quickly caught up to Paul. About a block later at an intersection, a cop car with its lights flashing pulled in front of us. I immediately did my thing. "Officer, officer, a bunch of officers just ran by chasing some black guy down that street," I said, pointing away from where Wornum was hiding. The cops thanked me and floored it after their suspect.

Unfortunately, Jimmy was back in custody by nightfall. He ended up serving some time and finally got out of prison in 1980. It wasn't long before he ended up back in the can again for armed robbery. And about twenty-five years after pulling that fire alarm, that's where he's living today.

We all missed Jimmy when he left the home. Things seemed less fun. But everything else continued as before. Both our groovy foster parents and Mom and Pops had their residences downstairs. During the week, the hippies rarely bothered to make the climb to the second story to find out what the racket was all about. On the weekends, Pops usually managed to calm us down without acting like too much of a drill sergeant.

Meanwhile, Ronnie and I started school in JP at the Bowditch Elementary School. The first day we showed up for class, I thought I was on a photo shoot for *National Geographic.* Outside of books and magazines, I had never seen more than a handful of black and brown kids. But at Bowditch, kids of color were as plentiful as us white kids. And most of these kids had no more money and no better clothes than me and Ronnie. It was culture shock.

But, you know something? Most of us got along. We played and hung out together. We were all poor, and that was our bond. Some claim that class division is a bigger problem for this nation than differences in skin color, religion, or ancestry. Well, a nice little petri dish for all those social scientists would have been Bowditch.

Ronnie and I were classic middle-of-the-pack students. We didn't win any awards, but we didn't have teachers calling home or requesting special conferences to talk about how we were doing. Not that the hippies would have shown much interest, anyway. And neither of us was spending much time in the principal's office or in after-school detention.

Considering where I had come from, things were looking up. Maybe I was going to be all right. After all, those sickos in Revere and Ashland couldn't touch me now. I wasn't bruised. I wasn't hungry. The kids at school seemed to be more on my level. And, yeah, sure, no one was really looking after me, but truth be told, I was beginning to like it that way.

After all I had been through, I dared to think that maybe my luck was changing. The worst might be over.

I was wrong.

# Violated

t all started innocently. Betty Jean and Rich said we would be getting a tutor to help us with our homework. This seemed like a smart idea. Not that any of us were on the honor society track. A few days later, this guy shows up. He was in his mid-thirties or so; I was nine. He seemed nice enough. He was tall and thin and reminded me, in a good way, of one of my teachers at school, a decent guy who paid attention to me. He said he'd help us with whatever homework we had. Sounded pretty good to me, since I'd never bothered to do any homework before. He visited once a week and almost all of us met with him. The tutoring sessions were one-on-one, conducted behind closed doors, usually for about half an hour.

After a couple of weeks, though, I was getting more than a half-hour of his time. He appeared to really like me. The third time he met with me, he stood behind me and began rubbing against me. I just stood there, too frightened and confused to move. I never said anything about it to the other kids, not even Ronnie, and certainly not to our freaky caretakers, who had brought this mistake into our home. I didn't know what was right and wrong about his behavior, but I was damn sure that the way he rubbed his crotch against me didn't feel good.

At our fourth meeting, which I'd been dreading all week, the tutor decided to take his relationship with me to the next level. We were both sitting on chairs that were pulled up to a desk, studying. Suddenly, he pushed back his chair and turned it a bit so that he was facing the side of my chair, his legs wide open. "Hey, Eddie, why don't you just stand up for a second," he said. "Come over here."

I kept my head down and pretended to read my lesson. I was trembling inside. He reached out and grabbed my arm lightly. "Come on, come on. Just stand up for a second. Stand right here in front of me. I'm your teacher. Everything is all right." I didn't think I had any options other than to do what he asked. So I stood up and took a step toward him. I kept my head down.

"Hey, don't worry about a thing," he said with a smile as, still seated, he grabbed hold of the waist of my pants and began to claw at the elastic band of my BVDs. I was beside myself with fear, but I had no idea what to do. That sick bastard practically fell out of his seat with excitement as he leaned forward to look inside at my prepubescent penis. Then he smiled. I was shaking like a rag doll.

And that's what that scumbag did for the next two weeks, not actually touching my penis, but just smiling and looking at it. Then, one day, he decided to touch it. He did it lightly and gave it these caresses, all the while smiling at me and asking if I liked it. I told him I didn't know what I felt. But I did know what I felt, and I felt something wasn't right.

He told me that the reason he was doing these things to me was because we were "special friends," better friends than he was with the other kids. He also told me that our time together and the things we did were "our secret" and no one could be told about it. Special friends need to keep secrets, he said. One of the other secrets I needed to keep was how he sat me on his lap and ground against me while he reached inside my pants.

What my tutor was doing scared the hell out of me. The minute he left, I was overcome with relief. But that feeling never lasted long as I knew he'd come back. I had no idea what to do, but I knew I had to do something.

The following week, when he started messing with me again, I told him I had to go to the bathroom. As soon as I left the room, I ran outside the house and stayed away until I was sure he was gone. That night, I told Betty Jean and Rich what happened. I told them that he was doing "funny things" to me and that he touched my "wee-wee." A lot. They just laughed and told me that I was making up stories. They also said that if I were to repeat any of those stories, I would be put on punishment for a week. That meant no snacks, no TV, no playing outside after school. Just sitting in my room, doing nothing.

The next week, he came back and didn't mention anything about me bolting our previous session. As always, I was the last kid tutored. But before we began, he called down the hall for Rich. My foster father, the Haight-Ashbury reject, came toddling down to the room. My tutor said that since I had been doing a great job with my lessons, he wanted to take me out for an ice cream as a reward. My maggot guardian said sure. Just like that he surrendered me to this pervert. Okay, I was just a foster kid. I wasn't even related to him. But he was in charge of me. He was supposed to protect me.

I was scared shitless that afternoon, but I didn't think I had any recourse but to go along. We got into his car and headed out for our ice cream. I was only nine, but I think I had a good inkling of the type of reward I was in for. We were driving along when he told me that we had to stop at his house so he could get some money. We pulled up to his place and he said to me, "C'mon in for a second, buddy. I'll show you my place."

We went into what I guess was the living room of his apartment. There was a couch in there and a TV and a stereo. It was a lot neater than the Fox Home, but it had a weird smell, like he had just disinfected the place. My tutor told me to sit on the couch and then started repeating his mantra: we were special friends and we needed to keep secrets. Up to that point, I'd been pretty sure he was going to mess with me again, but those key words, "special" and "secret," made it official. He told me that he had a big "surprise" for me and that I should close my eyes and wait for my prize. He repeated that I had to keep my eyes closed or the surprise would be ruined. He must have said this three or four times.

"I have a nice, big lollipop for you," he said. "Now keep your eyes closed. Don't open them. Don't open them. Now open up your mouth real wide."

I did as I was told. Don't ask me why. All I knew was that I was too paralyzed with fear and dread to do anything but what he told me.

"Keep those eyes closed," he reminded me.

I felt something enter my mouth. And it didn't feel or taste like any type of lollipop I knew. It went to the back of my throat and I gagged. Then I felt hands clasp the side of my head. I opened up my eyes to find this guy inches in front of me, attached to me by his erect penis. I tried to pull back, but he pulled me toward him.

"Everything is going to be all right," he said, grunting. "It's our special game. Our special secret."

I was crying now, but he kept force-feeding his dick to me for another few minutes. Back and forth in my mouth he went. I was so traumatized I couldn't even think.

Finally he stopped. But there was more to come. He grabbed me by the shoulders and began to turn me around. I struggled. "What are you doing?" I asked. "Please, please, let's just go home."

"Hey, everything is going to be all right," he said breathlessly, starting to get violent as he overpowered my resistance. He threw me forward onto the couch and grabbed at my pants. I was kicking and clawing at the couch, doing anything to get out of his arms. But he was too strong. "This is our secret," he kept repeating. "We're special friends."

Within seconds, he had my pants down. I was bent forward with my knees resting on the edge of the seat cushions and my hands holding onto the back of the couch. I must have known that I couldn't get away because I remember that I stopped fighting. From behind, he put his arm around my waist and pulled me toward him. Then he entered me. The pain was like nothing I'd ever experienced before. Not even with the worst beatings. Through tears, I was screaming, "What are you doing? You're hurting me! Please, please, stop!"

"Don't worry," he said. He was panting. "I won't put it in too far."

"Please, please, don't!"

I don't know how long that pervert sodomized me. It seemed like forever.

I didn't know then what it was called, but today I can tell you that he came, because he left me with a "present." He was nice enough to clean me up with a towel. And then he told me to pull up my pants because it was time to get an ice cream.

We got that ice cream, although I don't think I took more than one lick. I was just focused on making it home. When we were in the driveway, I jumped out of his car and ran for the door. I ran by my bewildered foster brothers and sisters and straight to the bathroom. I threw the melting ice-cream cone into the toilet. Then, I started to scrub myself with a burning hot wet towel. There was a lot of blood coming out of my rear, and it terrified me as I tried to clean it up with the towel. I was still hurting badly.

I didn't tell anyone what happened to me, because I didn't want to go on punishment. But that molester never got at me again, because I made sure I was not at the home when he came around. I started running away in the afternoon on the days he tutored. Oh, sure, I ended up going on punishment anyway, but at least I wasn't getting diddled anymore. If he had touched me again, I would have killed him.

# The Streets

stayed in the Edith Fox Home for another three years, but nothing was ever the same for me after that day. Before the rape I'd experienced pain, but it always came and went. I never felt all that different after a beating or being hungry or being teased by other kids. But after the rape, that changed. Something awful had happened and no food or game or story could make it better. I was only nine, but I felt old and sad and frightened and angry. Living at the Edith Fox Home had almost convinced me there might be decent adults in the world. The rape set me back, solidifying my earlier conviction that no one gave a shit about me.

So many times I wanted to tell Pops what had happened to me, but I couldn't even begin to get the words out. I've never mentioned it to a single human being before now.

Eventually Betty Jean and Rich took off, and a series of new people came in to fill their role. After a year of lots of different faces, Mom and Pops started coming in during the week and staying with us pretty much fulltime.

It was great having Mom and Pops there so much of the time, but they were busier than ever keeping things under control. With so many kids in the house, it often seemed like a cross between a party and a zoo. Lots of horseplay and laughter. All the boys shared one big bedroom and the girls another. We were always running up and down the hall, spying on each other and sneaking into one another's rooms after lights were supposed to be out.

By the time I was eleven, I was interested in only one thing after the lights went out. I had quite a system worked out. I'd wait till everyone was asleep. Then I'd go sneaking into the girls' room and crawl up to their beds and pull their undies down inch by inch so I could check for any sign of a growing bush. I would then touch them very lightly and just stare at their snatches. They started to catch on and woke up screaming, "Mom, Pops, he's doing it again!" When the Colonel found out what I was doing, he called me a little scumbag, but I could see that he did everything he could to keep from laughing. Pretty much all I thought about was how to get into these girls' panties. That helped me stop thinking the bad thoughts. I guess I was a sick little bastard.

Everything changed one night when our baby-sitter, a twenty-one-year-old chick named Susan, who was even weirder than me, let me and another resident, Donna, stay up later than the others. Donna was also eleven, and pretty, with long brown hair and the body of a grown woman. Big tits and all. Susan had a joint and she had us try some. Suddenly, we were all relaxed and feeling real strange, and before I knew what was happening, we were talking about doing it, going all the way. Donna said she'd take her clothes off if Susan would take hers off, too. I was in my glory, trying to make sense of what was about to happen. Susan finally said she'd take her shirt off and, man, two seconds later, she did.

I nearly shit in my pants as I stared at her tits. I'd spent months of my life trying to get a tiny peek and here was the whole deal. Staring right back at me. Before I could catch my breath, Susan instructed me and Donna to get naked. Next, Susan moved me to the top position and literally lined up my Johnson and stuck it in the girl's hole. I had no idea what was happening, but Susan kept telling me to start pushing it in and out. I did this for a few minutes, and then Donna and I both got scared and stopped. It wasn't a complete job, but it was enough to get me interested in finishing it up a lot better the next time.

For a year after that, finishing it up a lot better became my mission in life. I had sexual encounters with every girl in the home: Darlene, Geraldine, Mary; everyone who slept in a bed there. Nearly every night, I'd sneak into one of their bedrooms and do my thing. I don't know what was wrong with me, but I just couldn't get enough pussy. I'm not sure but I've often thought that the rape made me more aware of sex because of how that pervert used my body.

Ronnie was thirteen and spending more time on the streets than at the Fox Home. Mom and Pops tried to work with him, but he was becoming too much of a problem. He started experimenting with booze and drugs and hanging out with a bunch of hippy acid freaks. He was rarely in school. In the eighth grade, he walked away from school forever. I know the law says that you have to stay in school until you're sixteen. But that's only on paper. I never heard of a truant officer bringing anyone in. That was for the suburbs. In the city, kids quit school regularly in eighth and ninth grade, and no one came looking for them. No surprise. No one gave a shit.

Ronnie began to live large when he was on the streets. I remember him at fourteen, pulling up in front of the Mary Curley School in JP, where I spent grades seven, eight, and nine. We'd be getting out of classes and he'd be sitting behind the wheel of a brand spanking new Lincoln Mark IV he'd just ripped off, a pair of sunglasses on, a big smile on his face. I looked up to him and started running away, too.

Around this time I had my first brush with the Department of Youth Services, or DYS. Ronnie was really going crazy, stealing and drugging and drinking. One night, he ripped off this big boat of a Malibu sedan. I was standing in front of the Fox Home when he pulled up in the car and jumped out. He tossed me the keys with a big grin and said, "Eddie, why don't you take this rig for a ride? It's time you learned how to drive."

I took those keys and jumped in behind the wheel and slammed the door shut. Ronnie was standing outside the car, arms folded, happy for his twelve-year-old brother. I pushed on the gas and the car leaped forward. Whoa! It gave me a scare — but what the hell. I accelerated and drove away. The first hundred yards or so were fine. The road was straight. But then I came to a curve, and the trouble began.

I didn't know how to steer, and I sideswiped a car trying to make the curve. To make matters worse, I didn't do such a good job of straightening the car out. It went right across the street and smashed into the back end of another car, putting a big old dent in it. I would have done a lot more damage had the Boston police not cut in front of me within five minutes. Incredibly, I managed to brake the Malibu before hitting the cruiser.

It sure didn't look good. I was arrested for driving a stolen car without a license, malicious destruction of property, leaving the scene of an accident, and a few other things as well. I was remanded to Mom and Pops until the local juvenile authorities could figure out what to do with me. A month after my spin around the block, the judge in the juvenile division of West Roxbury Court decided it would be good for me to go to a DYS facility in West Roxbury for three months. I was scared a little, but not out of my mind, because it was right down the street and Mom and Pops said they would visit me every week. And they did.

All in all, it wasn't a bad twelve weeks. Fifty or sixty of us, guys around the same age, were housed in this barracks with barbed-wire fence around it. It was clean and we were well supervised. We had school during the day and some recreation, and there was study hall at night. The more I think about it, maybe it's not a bad solution for a lot of troubled kids. They're not free to roam the streets at night and commit more serious crimes. For a short period of time they're in a controlled atmosphere with few temptations and a lot of structure. For some kids, it could lead to a better way of life. Not for me, though.

When I returned home after my quick hitch, all my foster brothers and sisters were hungry for news about my detention. I told incredible lies about how I was beaten and tortured and how I beat people up. I got a big kick out of their shocked faces. I didn't bullshit Ronnie, though. He could always tell when I was on the level.

Soon after that, we kids received another jolt. The Fox Home was closing. Mom and Pops were leaving. We were devastated. Just further confirmation that life was designed to screw you, and there was nothing you could do about it. The day that Mom and Pop said good-bye was hideous. We tried to be tough, but it was useless. We all cried, and so did Mom and Pops. They hugged us and gave us the phone number and address of the house they were buying in JP and told us all to visit as often as we liked. We were supposed to wait around at the home with Mom and Pops until the authorities came to take us to our new homes, but Ronnie and I bolted before the cars showed up. We weren't going to be abused by the system anymore.

With Mom and Pops gone, and our foster brothers and sisters scattered, it was down to just me and Ronnie. I probably would have died without him. We were fortunate in having a network of friends who came from homes that were only slightly dysfunctional. These kids had it made: at least one biological parent at home, regular meals, brothers and sisters who looked out for one another, and their own beds with clean linen. If there wasn't enough money coming in from a breadwinner, there was a public-assistance check showing up in the mailbox.

Ronnie and I were home-hoppers for our first two years on the streets. We mostly slept outdoors, especially on warm nights, but we were almost always able to crash at someone's house if we needed to. We rarely hung at the same place together. In the first four years on the streets, I still went to school, mostly because of the teachers. Some of them, like Mr. White, my shop teacher, or the principal, Mr. Kearns, or Mr. Sarno, my English teacher, talked to me and paid attention to what I said. I missed a lot of classes, but I finished seventh, eighth, and ninth grade at the Curley School, managing to convince the authorities that I was still living at the Fox Home. The system kept promoting me until I began tenth grade at Jamaica Plain High School. I stayed for half of that year, but then dropped out. I had too many other things to do and there seemed no sense in wasting time going to school any more.

Ronnie and I managed. Even if we didn't find a couch or extra bed or space on the floor, we'd have a spot on a porch or a cellar. At that time, people in JP and Southie were big on clotheslines, and that's where I did my shopping. I'd pull freshly washed sheets and blankets off the lines and make myself a bed in someone's yard or porch till an adult shooed me away. Nearly every piece of clothing I owned came from those clotheslines. Even when I wasn't eating at someone's table, my friends brought me food, so I rarely went hungry. It was all pretty exciting. Here I was, thirteen years old, and I was living on my own. In many ways, I felt safer than I ever had before. I wasn't worried about anybody beating me or coming home drunk or humiliating me.

And I was developing important new skills. I became a junior criminal, a senior thief. I started shoplifting and, when that got boring, I broke into homes and businesses. I found it easier to break into someone's house when no one was around and grab the goods than walk into a store, with all eyes on me, and pocket the stuff. Soon I was walking around with wads of cash in my pocket that I'd either found in the houses or gotten from selling stolen merchandise picked up in the B&Es. Now I dressed better than kids in the suburbs. Me, Ronnie, and a couple of other boys established a nice fencing operation, selling TVs, radios, stereos, jewelry, appliances; you name it. We were budding capitalists of the first order, real entrepreneurs. Our customers ranged from scum-of-the-earth druggies, who got a break on nice merchandise, to the so-called law-abiding "legitimate" folks who couldn't resist a bargain. We even had cops and detectives buying things like coin collections and jewelry and Hummels — those kitschy, hand-painted, porcelain figurines from Germany — knowing full well that the goods were stolen. It was real weird to sell a Hummel to a cop who would arrest me the next week for stealing something else. But I never took it personally. He was just doing his job. And so was I.

Even though I was a year younger than Ronnie, I did the fighting for him. It didn't bother me when I lost, because I knew that I'd win later. My brother was not the type to go one-on-one with you, but he would grab a bat and split your head open without batting an eyelash. He never went anywhere without a knife or a sword and became known as the Mad Stabber. But Ronnie wasn't as good as me with his fists, so I took care of things for him.

I started getting into fights on a regular basis. When you're poor and there aren't many people looking out for you, you understand quickly that you fight or you fall to the bottom of the heap. You take care of yourself so no one can hurt you.

When I was fourteen, Ronnie got us an apartment on Cheshire Street in JP. He had an older guy pay the rent, which we had no trouble supplying from the profits from our B&Es, as well as another little business venture — selling pot. We hung out with the local kids, who were all dealing, and started out selling half-ounces of pot with no problem. We got a nice little basement apartment and furnished it pretty damn good with stolen items, from the furniture to the hanging plants, the rugs, and the great TVs and stereos. A real home.

On and off, over the next couple years, I did five to six more months in DYS facilities. One time, because I'd roughed up a kid pretty bad, I was sent away for a four-week stint to a DYS forestry camp south of Boston. As the van of juvenile troublemakers pulled closer to the camp, I realized we were going to the same place that Mom and Pops took the Fox Home kids for camping trips during the summer. Same place, different purpose.

My feeling of nostalgia didn't last long. It was the middle of winter, and I froze my ass off cutting down trees and clearing shrubs. One of the other kids was Ricky Salemme, the nephew of New England Mafia soldier "Cadillac" Frank Salemme. One afternoon, Ricky and I decided to make a break for it.

We split up at the nearest paved road. Ricky was out only two to three hours before he was apprehended. I did better, catching rides all the way to JP. At suppertime I showed up at the McManuses, a big Irish brood that included four boys Ronnie and I chummed with. Everyone was happy to see me, even Mrs. McManus. She fed me, told me what a stupid move I'd pulled, then called the cops. By ten o'clock bed check, I was back in camp.

# Frankie

**W**hether in school, on the streets, in a detention center or in jail, Frankie "The Tank" MacDonald was my best friend. I don't think I would have survived childhood without him. I loved Frankie from the first day I met him on the playground at the Mary E. Curley School in Jamaica Plain. I don't know why, but being with Frankie made lots of the hurt go away. He was someone I could trust completely. Ronnie was my blood, the only relative I had in my life, and I loved him. But Frankie was something different. He could break down the wall I'd built around myself. So many people had hurt me, but I knew Frankie never would. And he was so much like me that I called him my shadow. It felt like we were the same person, with the same thoughts. He was as tough and ruthless as me. I knew that, like me, he'd never back down from anybody or anything.

But Frankie had something I've never stopped wanting: a family. It wasn't a perfect family, by any means. There sure as hell wasn't any dad around. His family was big and wild and crazy, but above all else, close-knit and loyal. And there was a mother, who often appeared down one quart of oil and looking for a tune-up, but she was a real mother who loved each one of her kids fiercely. That, alone, was something to be envied.

Frankie and I did everything together, including getting into a shitload of trouble. By the time we were in junior high, we were regularly pulling jobs together, including a ton of B&Es. Mostly we worked in Newton and Brookline, the wealthier suburbs where the money was, not in our own backyard. After all, we ate and slept there. We didn't want to run into people whose stereos we'd just ripped off a couple of hours earlier. Usually we operated in groups of two or three, working up to four times a week. Paul Donnelly, another great B&E partner, was a junkie with a bad heroin habit by the time he was thirteen. I would shoot him up when he was too shaky to do it himself, and he'd offer me some. But, for some reason I never quite understood, I never tried it. Maybe Pops at the Fox Home planted a seed when he told me I was a good boy, a special boy, and someday I could have a normal family. Or maybe it was just that I never wanted to try anything that made me lose control of my mind.

Me and Frankie and Ronnie committed too many B&Es for me to remember them all, but one stands out. We got together at this thirty-room redbrick mansion on a couple of acres of land in Chestnut Hill, a Boston suburb. Frankie and Ronnie were loading TVs and Oriental rugs into the car, while I made the bed in the master bedroom with my usual surprise under the pillow.

You see, I always got nervous during the B&Es, and in the middle of the whole thing I'd have to take a dump. It drove Frankie and Ronnie up the wall. But I stopped worrying about it and just used it to my advantage. I'd imagine the people whose house we'd just robbed finishing up dealing with the police, having gone over the list of all their valuables which they knew they'd most likely never see again. They'd be worn out and exhausted and finally, when everything was over, they'd hit the bed. And that's where I'd plant my gift. I'd neatly make up the bed so they'd never suspect anyone had been there. They'd lie down on their expensive silk sheets and feel something awful, and the next thing they knew they were covered with shit. Just a little present from me to them. I'd drop dead laughing just imagining their faces when it hit them.

So that night, I did my thing and came downstairs. As I hit the last stair, I saw through the window two Greek Orthodox priests with long black robes and even longer black beards approaching the front door. When they opened the door and saw me, I screamed, "Frankie, Ronnie, time to get the fuck out of here!"

One of the priests opened the coat closet and pulled out a machete. He started toward me, shouting, "I'm going to cut you into little pieces, you thief!" Frankie and Ronnie had already jumped off the back porch and were heading for the woods. I raced to the porch, did a somersault and landed on my feet like a gymnast. I reached the edge of the woods with this guy five feet behind me slicing the air with the machete, getting closer to my ass every second. I thought it was all over, that I would be mince-meat in another moment, but out came Frankie with this huge tree limb. He cracked the priest right across the head and beat the hell out of him with it. My best bud saved me.

Frankie was a great partner in crime, but, more than anything, he was a

fighter. A great fighter on the streets and, later, when we both took to boxing, inside the ring as well. He was better than me. And I was good.
Frankie would work his way inside you and pound your body with ferocious punches. I have never to this day seen anyone hit the body as well as
Frankie. For at least six years, every couple weeks, he would fight in a local
hall or armory or wherever a fight had been arranged. I went to every one
of them, except when I was detained in jail or was in the Army Reserves or
the Marines. Frankie wasn't just a slugger. He understood the sweet science of boxing. Nearly every day, from the time we were fourteen, Frankie
and I sparred at the McDonough Gym, nicknamed the Muni, since it was
in the Municipal Building in Southie, which also housed my second home,
the South Boston Courthouse. The way me and Frankie went at it, you'd
have thought we hated each other. In the ring, we never held back. He
broke my nose three times.

It meant everything to me that Frankie was loyal. He was the one I
wanted guarding my back in a B&E. No matter what happened to me,
good or bad, it hadn't really happened until I told Frankie about it. Mom
and Pops had given me parental guidance, and I had thought that meant
we loved each other, but I wasn't all that sure what love really was. All I
knew was that Frankie was the most important person in my world.

When I first met Frankie, he was living in JP, but in the summer of 1973,
when we were both fifteen, his mom moved Frankie and his seven siblings
into the Old Colony Project in South Boston. Since I was practically a
member of the MacDonald family, I felt like I'd moved into Southie, too.
Not unexpectedly, Frankie had problems with the local kids when he
moved there. They didn't know Frankie and they didn't like him. One day,
twenty kids began beating on Frankie and me in front of his building. Not
a good idea. The kids were white kids who had lived in the project for a
long time and were testing the new family on the block to see whether
they were cowards or had balls.

Two of Frankie's older brothers, Johnny and Joe, got wind of what was
happening and came to our rescue in the nick of time. Johnny, who was
6'1" and 240 pounds, picked up kids and threw them up in the air like rag
dolls. Frankie and Joe and I were banging people, throwing punches
everywhere and landing them perfectly. We were definitely winning the
battle, which had been going on for a good ten minutes, a long time for a
street fight, when one of the kids from the projects announced he was

going home for a gun. Frankie said, "I wouldn't do that if I were you," and then pointed up to the window of the third floor at 8 Patterson Way. Ma MacDonald was standing there, waving a shotgun out the window.

"If anyone goes after one of my kids with any weapon," she shouted down to us, "I'll blow their brains out. Nobody's scaring us out of our home." The neighborhood kids took one look at her and bolted. But we'd earned our bones that day. From then on, the project kids left Frankie and me alone.

I couldn't help but respect Frankie's mom, Helen MacDonald. But there were times when both Frankie and I, along with Ronnie, didn't get her. Like the night several years later when Frankie, his mother, and I attended a banquet at the Sheraton Boston. We were celebrating Ronnie's graduation from a special culinary arts program that was a joint venture between the hotel and the Department of Corrections. It was a chance for someone like Ronnie, who'd already done jail time and was on parole, to learn a trade. He'd spent two and a half years in Deer Island prison — which really wasn't an island — in Winthrop, Massachusetts, for possession of burglary tools and was trying to change his ways. He turned out to be a pretty good cook, loved the program, and graduated with honors.

What a feast they had that night. The only time a bunch of poor people from Southie got to see a spread like this was on television. You can imagine our excitement as we plowed into this food. When it came time for the main course, a waiter came to our table with a big platter of filet mignons, maybe twenty in all. Helen, Frankie, Ronnie, and I had been putting on quite an eating show, but when we saw the filet mignons, we knew that everything till then had just been a warm-up. There were three other people at our table, also guests of the graduates, and they were watching us eat with one of those "Where-the-fuck-did-these-animals-come-from?" looks. Of course, they were smart enough to keep their mouths shut. When the filet mignons hit the table, we wasted little time in forking a pair apiece onto our plates.

Ronnie had been cool about us until then. Actually, he'd been every bit as active with his fork and knife as we were. But when he saw our assault on the steaks, he suddenly became self-conscious. He did his best to tell us diplomatically to slow down, not act so ravenous. He should have saved his energy. After we'd grabbed our share, the other people at the table each took one. Now there were six filet mignons left on the platter. And you just had to see what Helen did next. She casually pulled the platter over and swept all the remaining steaks into her big pocketbook. She hadn't even wrapped them. She just calmly clicked the bag closed and gave us a smile and a matter-of-fact look.

Ronnie's jaw nearly hit the table. Frankie and I were astonished, and you had to do something off the wall to astonish us. As for the other people at the table, forget about it. They were sure that this was all part of some *Candid Camera* episode. But the Southie gang wasn't done for the evening. Dinner was still going on when Frankie got up from the table and motioned for me to come along. He'd planned a little shopping excursion. We went directly to the coatroom where we traded up our Southie barracuda coats (navy or tan coats with elastic waistbands and plaid linings, worn with collars turned up to show we were from Southie) for something a little nicer. Both of us were on the lookout for some full-length coats, or maxis as we called them in Southie; something good for concealing a shotgun. Frankie grabbed this beautiful black leather number, and I took an expensive cashmere coat. Poor Ronnie. He didn't think any of it was funny. I guess we ruined his graduation. But we sure had a great time for ourselves.

Frankie's family always felt like mine. Especially his older brother Johnny. Man, did we idolize him. John MacDonald graduated from the elite Boston Latin School, where you have to have a razor-sharp mind to get in the front door, and went on to Tufts University, where he was a middle linebacker for the football team. We'd go to his games and scream till our voices gave out. Johnny ended up in the Navy Seals, the toughest outfit in the world, and came out a lieutenant commander. But that poor family endured more than its share of tragedy. Frankie's oldest brother David killed himself at twenty-three by jumping off the roof in the projects. Another brother, Kevin, hanged himself at twenty-two. His sister, Kathy, got shitfaced one night in 1981, fell off a roof, and was left a cripple at nineteen. I don't know or, out of respect for the family, wish to speculate why David and Kevin ended their own lives. And what finally happened to Frankie years later was, for me, the biggest tragedy of all.

# Rage: Summer of '75

**W**ay before the final black days, Frankie and I were doing our own dance, listening to our own inner song of fury. In the two years after Frankie and his family moved to South Boston, I hopped back and forth between wherever I was living in JP and the MacDonald clan's quarters in the Old Colony Projects. Between JP and Southie, Frankie and I were stealing, brawling, mugging, and getting into a mess of trouble. We were developing into full-blown predators. And our anger was soon directed at a particular problem, and a particular group of people. It was the summer of '75, and the world outside Southie was pushing into our own little world, forcing me and Frankie to rock and roll with the frenzy.

Boston was burning with racial tension, fueled by forced busing that had started in September 1974. Boston School Committee member Louise Day Hicks was still riling up the city with her antibusing rhetoric. And Judge W. Arthur Garrity was using the Racial Imbalance Law to "desegregate" Boston public schools and force busing on Southie. Judge Garrity was Irish, but a product of the affluent suburb of Wellesley, and Harvard Law School, and therefore not Boston Irish. Garrity ordered Southie kids to be bused from their good schools in what was the city's safest community to crappy schools in Roxbury, a predominantly black community and Boston's highest crime area. And vice versa. Little Southie, a city low in income and rich in traditions, became the symbol of resistance to busing. Louise Day Hicks didn't care who she took on. She was keeping Southie kids in Southie schools. The busing supporters gave her constant shit, calling her a vicious, violent racist, but she never backed down.

Black kids were bused into white neighborhoods, and white kids were bused into black neighborhoods. Frankie and I were the embodiment of white rage: two white, racist assholes who beat up on blacks. We had our counterparts in the black community. But the media didn't do nearly as good a job in showing black rage as it did white rage, focusing almost

exclusively on the Frankie MacDonalds and Eddie MacKenzies. The ignorant, white, racist micks.

Guys like us made the media's job easy. Frankie and I were the rock-
throwing punks who smashed the windows of the buses filled with black
kids coming in from Roxbury and Dorchester. We stoned the buses so
often that the authorities had to change the route. We taunted the black
students on their way up the steps of South Boston High School. They
were outsiders, who didn't belong in our community, being forced on our
community. Everyone around us was angry at what was happening to
poor Southie. Keeping these outsiders away from Southie was the thing to
do, so we did it the only way we knew how. If you look at the old news-
reels, you could probably spot us assaulting black kids and wrestling with
cops. But the worst things we did, the most violent, racist acts, were not
caught on tape. We did a lot of damage and hurt a lot of people.

We thought we were doing Southie a favor.

On an unforgettable hot summer night in '75, when we were seventeen,
Frankie suggested we do a drive-by in the Columbia Point Housing
Projects, a black public housing project two miles away in Dorchester, at
the tip of a peninsula that extends into the Atlantic Ocean. Instead of a
classic drive-by — that is, single some guy out and mow him down — we
were merely going to do some blasting at windows and doorways. And if
anyone got hurt or killed, even if it was a child, well, it was unintentional.
We were ignorant and filled with hate, evil even.

We jumped in Frankie's beat-to-shit '68 Chevelle, and with Frankie driving and me riding shotgun, we headed out. Frankie had a .357 Magnum. I
had a .380-caliber Walther PPK pistol. I didn't have a license to carry, but
I'd learned to shoot in the streets and in local rod-and-gun clubs. This was
far from my first weapon. I'd been using guns since I was twelve, when I'd
buy them hot on the streets or pick them up during B&Es.

To get to the projects that night, me and Frankie drove along Morrissey
Boulevard, the shoreline route, with fetid Boston Harbor on our left. (The
start of the federal cleanup of the harbor was about ten years away. When
I think about breathing in those noxious fumes, I'm not surprised that the
blacks and whites who lived near the harbor were at each other's throats.)

There was only one road into the projects and only one road out.
Rumor had it that was so the projects could be easily sealed off in the
event of rioting, so we understood that we'd be running a gauntlet. We

cruised into the projects without too many problems. It was a hot night, but there weren't many people outside. We were spotted driving in, but I guess most of the blacks figured if we were stupid enough to enter the projects at night, we had a reason to feel secure. Maybe we were junior cops on some undercover gig. Frankie drove to the end of the street and turned the car around and we drove a hundred yards back toward the entrance.

We were now in front of a brick building five or six stories high. Half of the buildings in the project were boarded up and looked vacant. All were dilapidated, covered with graffiti, surrounded by garbage piles. We checked to make sure there weren't too many people within striking distance. We'd brought a limited amount of ammo, not enough to protect ourselves if we got into real trouble. Frankie threw the car into park and we jumped out. We pointed our guns at the buildings and squeezed the triggers. We were screaming at the top of our lungs, "Niggers suck! . . . Fuck you, you niggers! . . . Southie rules!"

We blasted away, hollering and laughing, humming with testosterone, adrenaline, hatred, and loads of stupidity. It took ten seconds for me to empty my nine-round clip and Frankie to pump his six bullets: a short thrill, but a huge charge, kind of like blowing your load. Windows shattered. Bullets ricocheted. The project came alive. Lights came on; lights went off. Yelling and screaming; absolute madness. A good time to exit. We jumped back in the car and Frankie floored it. The car hiccuped and sputtered, but, thank God, it started moving.

We saw a group of ten guys running after the car, swearing and shouting. Soaked in sweat, I screamed for Frankie to do anything to get that piece-of-shit car moving faster. Rocks hit the side of the car. At last the car picked up speed and we put some distance between us and our would-be executioners. I looked back and saw a bunch of these guys shouting and waving their fists and giving us the finger. Relieved, we both began to laugh and I started slapping the inside roof of the car. Not exactly a clean getaway, but a getaway nonetheless.

Or so we thought. I told you that car was a piece of shit.

We were within a hundred and fifty yards of Columbia Road and sanctuary when . . . kerplunk . . . kerplunk. The car just died. And I knew we were dead along with it. "Fuck! Ahhhhhh fuck!" Frankie shouted, turning the ignition and pumping the gas for all he was worth.

"What the fuck happened!" I screamed, looking back at our send-off party, which now saw that we were stranded.

"Motherfuckers!" they yelled. "You piece of shit!" Translation: we were both going to die a terrible death. I looked back and saw the black guys breaking into a run again. But they were still about three hundred yards behind us.

Meanwhile, Frankie jumped out of the car and threw up the hood. I hung out of the passenger window and screamed, "Fuck the car! Let's get the fuck out of here!"

We had no bullets left. I jumped out and did a quick assessment of the mob, now sprinting full-tilt and screaming loud enough to wake the dead. This was not good. I yelled to Frankie that we should just take our chances on foot. But as soon as I said that, Frankie shouted out, "Aha! . . . That's it. . . . It's in there! Let's go!"

I looked at Frankie with astonishment, but he'd already headed for the driver's seat. There isn't an Indy pit crew who could have done what he did that night. I turned tail toward the passenger side just as a rock ricocheted off the back windshield. The guys leading the pack, about four or five abreast, were seventy-five yards back and closing fast. Vegas would have given us even odds on survival.

Frankie gave the gas pedal a gentle nudge and it responded. Two more rocks hit the roof and the back windshield. Frankie had one hand on the wheel while the other rolled up his window. I rolled up mine. That piece of shit car wasn't sounding so good, but it was moving. And just in time. Because now we were getting heavy hail. Whoomp! . . . Whack! . . . Whoomp! . . . Whoomp! Columbia Road was directly ahead.

But our troubles weren't over. Not yet. Now there were ten guys ahead of us, closer to the exit, who'd just figured out what was going on. They picked up rocks and bottles and started running toward us. Just as we were outdistancing fire from the rear, we had incoming shit from the front and sides.

The final sprint to Columbia Road was nasty. By the time we made it out of there, nearly all the car's windows were broken. Guys were within a few feet of us, throwing strikes at our heads. Glass was flying. Miraculously, we survived, even though justice would have been better served if Frankie's shitbox had broken down again and we were beaten to death right there.

But Frankie and I weren't done for the summer. A month after our assault on Columbia Point, we were involved in another horror show, complete with guns, hate, and a near-death experience.

Southie Day was supposed to be a showcase for community pride. It was organized by a great guy named Whitey McGrail and held every August at Marine Park, down by the South Boston waterfront. McGrail was a prominent South Boston community activist who owned a bar on Broadway called Whitey's Place.

At least two thousand people came to Southie Day, usually wearing something green, like a shamrock, to show Irish pride. Lots of people in shorts and T-shirts and shades. There were all sorts of things to do, like games for kids and free hot dogs and burgers and balloons. McGrail had set up a boxing ring and was inviting all comers to take a chance with whoever else was brave enough to jump in. It was a pretty tame affair. You had head gear and these big puffy gloves.

When I heard Whitey recruiting boxers, I ran toward the ring, yelling that I'd take on anyone in the park. McGrail pulled me into the ring and asked the crowd if anybody was willing to take me on. This guy named Jackie Callahan came forward, about my size and eager to go at it. McGrail sized both of us up and figured he had an even match.

Whitey and the referee helped us put on our gloves and headgear. Then, they brought us together in the middle of the ring and made a point of telling us to have fun. But I wasn't in it for fun. And Callahan, who was grunting and snorting, didn't look like he was in it for fun, either.

We went to our corners to await the sound of the bell and then raced forward to do battle at the center of the ring. This was brawling, not pugilism. Initially, Callahan took command. He was tough and I was drunk, and I was getting it handed to me. I was so shattered that I threw two punches that completely missed *him,* but sent *me* reeling to the canvas. The crowd thought it was hilarious, but I was getting pissed. So, no surprise, I lost my cool. I got Callahan in a headlock and started windmilling him. The referee moved in to break it up, but before he could get there, I threw Callahan down on the canvas and punted him in the head with my sneakers. All hell was breaking loose. It took the ref and someone else to separate us.

The crowd was hollering. McGrail said that was the end of our match, and we were both winners. But Callahan was none too happy about the way I treated him in the ring. Three guys held him back, and they had their hands full. He swore and vowed revenge. I paid no attention.

As I made my way through the crowd around the ring, I saw these cra-zies making their way toward me. Callahan's four brothers, all bad news. They were going to jump me, but it never came to that. You see, Frankie, my man, suddenly showed up and moved into their path, calmly opening up his jacket to reveal a gleaming .357 he'd holstered. That's a big hand-gun. Frankie's little demonstration discouraged them from coming after me. That was not, however, the end of an eventful afternoon.

After everyone's tempers cooled, McGrail had a little ceremony and handed out awards to the participants. I received a T-shirt that said SOUTHIE DAY BOXING CHAMP. I thanked McGrail, shook his hand, took the shirt, and then grabbed the microphone he was holding. I turned to the crowd and bellowed into the mike, "I want to thank all the niggers in Boston for keeping me in shape!" It was as if all South Boston fell silent. My voice carried nicely over the public address system. You probably could have heard me in the financial district.

McGrail was horrified and, despite what you hear about South Boston, most of the crowd was horrified as well. All the faces looked like they'd just seen a dead body, and it was me. McGrail tried to grab the mike, but I danced away from him, shouting, "Let's all march on Columbia Point!"

Someone killed the sound system. Three cops ran up on the stage, grabbed me by the arms and pulled me off the stage, muttering, "You're outta here." I was shitfaced and offered no struggle at all. They detained me for a few minutes, mulling over whether they were going to charge me with attempting to incite a riot. They finally let me walk. Frankie grabbed me and we got the hell out of there. Once again, it was a miracle no black guy killed us on the spot.

But, years later, no miracle saved Whitey McGrail, who did so much for the community. One day a couple punks who'd just gotten out of prison came into his bar and caused trouble. Whitey threw them out. They came back later and shot him dead. Of course, when the cops came around to question those who were in the bar at the time of the shooting, they found out that either everyone was playing pool or in the bathroom or having such an interesting conversation that they didn't notice two guys commit-ting homicide.

Meanwhile, the summer of '75 rolled on. Before busing, during the early seventies, us kids used to hit the beaches along Boston Harbor. We even went swimming off those beaches, totally oblivious to how filthy the water was. One of the places we went was Carson Beach, a municipal beach that started in Southie, ran into Dorchester, and kissed the edge of the Columbia Point Project. It had long been established that Carson Beach was a white area, at least on the Southie side. On hot days the beach was packed, but us pale-skins stayed on "our" side. Blacks hung out on the Dorchester side, near the projects, but not in the same numbers as the whites in the Southie area. There was a stretch of no-man's-land, a quarter-mile long, that was observed as a buffer zone between whites and blacks. There were no problems. We did our thing. They did their thing. It wasn't a great example of cultural diversity, but we didn't want to socialize with each other anyway. That was the way it was before busing. (Today, Carson Beach is no longer segregated. Everyone, black and white, sits together.) But when busing started, neither blacks nor whites should have been surprised when know-it-all liberals zoned in on Carson Beach and started shoving both groups into each other's path, all but insuring major trouble. By the summer of '75, for the first time ever, blacks started massing on Carson Beach and spreading their towels along the area that used to be no-man's-land. The blacks moved closer to our side, and us whites moved closer to their side. Conflict ensued: fist fights, verbal assaults, blacks dunking whites, whites dunking blacks, and rocks and bottles thrown back and forth.

It got so bad that the city assigned the Tactical Police Force (TPF) to patrol the area. On weekends, the TPF attempted to separate the races by forming a human chain that stretched from the parking lot up to the edge of the water. Bringing in the TPF actually gave blacks and whites a common outlet for our anger and frustration. The TPF was taking shit from both sides. Talk about a lose-lose situation.

Me and Frankie and the boys were right in the middle of everything down at the beach, stirring up unrest. One nice summer afternoon, Frankie, his big brother Johnny, and a few other live wires were right up against the cops and shouting at the blacks on the other side of the line, who were giving as good as they got. The cops had no qualms about pushing us and butting us with nightsticks to keep us back. It had become a police state on the coast. Anyway, I had a nice new set of darts with me. Competition darts, precisely balanced and weighted. I was wearing these baggy Bermuda shorts with two deep and wide front pockets, each of which held three darts.

Naturally, the cops couldn't keep their eyes on everyone, and I used the breaks in surveillance to slip a dart out of my pocket and fling it at the blacks. I was a decent dart player, and that day I was in a zone. I was five-for-six. I was on. I hit four people in either the arms or legs, and one of my throws connected nicely to the forehead of some poor prick. The cops were going bananas trying to figure out who was tossing the darts.

After I'd spent my ammo, Johnny figured he had to do his share. Johnny would be starting his sophomore year at Tufts in the fall. As I've already told you, a future Seal: tough-nosed, superb athlete, and one hell of a swimmer. That afternoon, Johnny swam out about seventy-five yards, then paddled over into the black area. There weren't any blacks swimming that far out, but Johnny just treaded water and smiled and looked at everyone. He was just trying to piss off the cops and the black people.

After no more than a minute, the cops figured that Johnny couldn't stay out there. One arrogant lieutenant, a scrawny gestapo-type with mirror shades, stood at the edge of the water, blaring away on his whistle and waving Johnny in. Johnny took his sweet-ass time returning to port. He did a slow breaststroke toward the shore, smiling all the way. The cop went apeshit, screaming for Johnny to pick it up. And Johnny, even when he got to the point where he could just stand up and wade in, continued to paddle slowly. He must have been only fifteen yards out, still smiling, and basically crawling on the sand beneath the water, when the cop lost it.

"I told you, motherfucker, to get your goddamn ass in here!" he yelled, striding into the surf. Decked out in his police suit and hat and mirror shades, he looked a bit like MacArthur in that famous picture, except he was going in the opposite direction. He'd taken no more than four splashing strides into the water when Johnny, now twenty feet away, finally stood up and sauntered forward, grinning from ear to ear. MacArthur stood there, up to the top of his boots in water, red as a beet, veins standing out in his neck, screaming like a banshee. Johnny finally got within reach of the cop, and then the cop did something really stupid. He grabbed Johnny by the shoulder and tried to throw him down. I could've told him that wasn't going to work. No sooner had that cop put his hands on him, than Johnny's grin faded and he grabbed the cop like Hulk Hogan would grab an opponent, turning him horizontal and balancing him on a knee. The cop's hat and sunglasses fell into the water, and Johnny made like an Olympic powerlifter as he hoisted the cop shoulder-high, then pressed him over his head. We all stood on the beach, awe-struck, watching this brazen display of strength and lunacy.

The lieutenant was gasping, "Put me down, you motherfucker!" when Johnny, still holding his prize above his head, spun toward the ocean, did a semi-crouch, and then half heaved, half pushed the cop about six feet out. He hit the water sideways, arms and legs flailing. He splashed for a second or so before he managed to get upright. Everyone watching was still stunned. But not Johnny. He was already doing a full-speed crawl back out into the ocean.

"Aw, fuck, Johnny's done it now," said Frankie. I couldn't disagree.

The cop stood there, soaked, hair matted to his head, screaming at the departing Johnny, vowing personal revenge and all sorts of legal consequences. About ten other cops ran down to the water and called out to Johnny, demanding that he come back in immediately. Even if they weren't in full uniform, it was obvious that there wasn't an officer there with any hope of swimming him down. There were no police boats assigned to the beach, and no cop wanted to be the one to call in a vessel to hunt down one wise-ass swimmer.

While the cops stood along the shore, stamping their feet, yelling, screaming, and pointing at Johnny, he casually backstroked about a hundred yards out, periodically giving the cops the finger and sticking out his tongue. By now, the people on the beach — blacks and whites both — were cheering Johnny on. It was hysterical.

After fifteen minutes of swimming off Carson Beach, Johnny gave us all a wave and started toward South Boston, stroking like Mark Spitz. We just stood there, watching him get further and further away. The cops followed him along the beach for about a quarter mile before they gave up and convinced themselves they were happy to be done with him. We had no worries. Johnny could swim ten miles if he had to. He pulled himself ashore about a mile down the coast. He filled us in on the swim as we sat around Ma MacDonald's dinner table that night.

# Prison

The wild summer of 1975 may have ended, but my own rage continued unabated. I went from one problem and confrontation to another. No sooner had I vented the fury than it began to build again, and boil and bubble and explode in yet another exercise in violence and stupidity. I sensed that I was out of control, but I had no idea how to stop myself. I see now that I was aimless, with no hold on my life and no plans for the future, no self-confidence, no positive role models, and no solid stake in a community. Lacking purposeful direction, I embraced the bitterness and anger all around me, eager to make their acquaintance.

I remember one September night at Kilgariff's, a dance club in JP. Gus, the owner, had a convertible Cadillac Eldorado and lived in a house adjacent to the club's parking lot. He was a tough, no-nonsense loudmouth who liked to keep a tight rein on the crowd at the club and wouldn't hesitate to knock a few of the neighborhood punks around. That night me and a bunch of my buddies were acting up, breaking up tables, roughing up the other customers, and causing major damage. When things got out of control, Gus suckered me, hitting me from behind in the head with a blackjack. As I turned around, stunned, he split the brow over my eye wide open. I was dazed and bleeding badly, blinded in one eye from all the blood, and plotting revenge as I staggered out of the club.

Within a half hour, I had gathered armfuls of newspaper and shoved them inside Gus's Eldorado. I poured a gallon of gasoline over the paper and set fire to it with a match. Man, that car went up fast. I was laughing like a maniac, loving every tiny flame I'd created. *Ah, payback's a bitch,* I was thinking. With the car in flames, I ran over to the front of the club and told someone to get Gus. He came out, looking around to see if he was going to get jumped. He didn't know I'd already taken care of him. "Hey, tough guy!" I shouted. "Do you want some fucking marshmallows for your car?"

In total shock, Gus ran back to the car. Too late. It was totaled. But he was able to notify the fire department in enough time to save his house, which had caught fire as well. This was a pretty serious case of arson. But the case never went to court; it was a matter of his word against mine, and since neither was credible, the cops and the courts didn't pursue the matter. I got a walk.

Later that night, I went over to Frankie's place in Southie. We sat down and I started replaying the incident, and we were laughing our balls off. Well, we talked too loud and Frankie's mother overheard us. She flipped out, and for me it was back to JP for the night.

A few weeks later, I was in Boston's South End, which shouldn't be confused with South Boston. They are separate places, separate worlds, even though they're only a few miles apart. (Today, the South End is one of Boston's most affluent sections, noted for its handsome brownstones and tree-lined streets. In the 1970s, though, it was decrepit: the brownstones run down, their windows broken and boarded up, the streets littered with bottles and trash. It wasn't until the gays and yuppies started moving in that the turnaround began.)

I was walking down the street when two cops came up to me and said I was under arrest for arson. I was dumbfounded. After all, this had happened two weeks earlier, and Gus had decided not to press charges. When I got to the station, I was told there was a witness who was going to testify against me. I couldn't believe anyone would have something to gain by fingering me, but they sure as hell would have a lot to lose. I was released on personal recognizance and went back to living with friends, shuttling from apartment to apartment.

Ten days later, I was with Frankie in court and we were both itching to find out who the rat was. The door opened and both of us nearly shit ourselves. It was Frankie's mother!

Poor Frankie had had no idea. We would find out later that Helen figured that if I was in jail then I wouldn't be with Frankie, dragging him into a heap of trouble. She had called the arson squad and offered herself as a witness. Smart thinking, actually.

But not smart enough. As soon as Frankie saw her, he pulled her away for a short conference in which he told her that if she testified, he would move out and never speak to her again. Poor Helen thought it over for a second or two and decided she wasn't sure what I'd been talking about after all and that she couldn't really testify. The DA was ripshit. He thought he had me. Well, not without a witness. The state had to rethink its case.

"What do you want me to do, Edzo?" Frankie said as we walked out of the courtroom together. "She's my mother."

"I know, bro," I told him. "No problem."

A week later, I was back sleeping over at Frankie's house like nothing had happened. I couldn't blame her. Maybe if I'd had a mother, she would have done the same thing.

As it turned out, Helen MacDonald got her wish — for a little while, anyhow. The DA decided there was still probable cause to go ahead with a trial. I stupidly didn't turn up for the first court appearance and got picked up for default. I was considered a flight risk, so the judge revoked my bail and had me locked up on the spot. I was given a shit-ass public defender who tried to get me to cop out to seven-to-ten years in the medium security arm of Walpole State Prison.

I'm no Einstein, but I figured I could do better than that. I didn't have any priors — none I'd been convicted for, anyhow. And this genius didn't think he could score me anything better than seven to ten, even if it was in a medium security prison! But, then again, what were my alternatives? Go to trial with this weak prick as my counsel, the same one who wanted me to plead, and try to beat the matter?

It didn't look good. Finally, the prick brokered a deal in which I'd get twenty years in the Massachusetts Correctional Institution at Concord, a medium-security facility in which I'd serve eighteen months and then spend the rest on parole, which was insane. I rejected all his ideas and spent six months in prison, awaiting trial, jumping back and forth between the Charles Street Jail in Boston and the Middlesex House of Correction.

I'd like to tell you that I wasn't afraid to go to prison, that Charles Street Jail didn't scare me at all. But that would be bullshit. I was terrified as they transported me in shackles to that pit. I'd heard the stories about Charles Street, the maximum-security detention center where prisoners were held awaiting trial. I'd heard about the rats and the backed-up plumbing and the filthy conditions. I'd heard how the prisoners ran the place. I'd heard how they threw everyone in together, the druggies and the child molesters, the murderers and the rapists. It had been built in 1850 and was a fun-house for sociopaths.

Charles Street was situated on three acres of land next to the Charles River, which separates Boston and Cambridge. What a weird place for a jail. Here you had a holding center for the scum of the universe located in the shadow of Harvard and MIT, and a stone's throw away from the Boston Museum of Science, Massachusetts General Hospital, and the tony neighborhood of Beacon Hill. Two totally different societies, separated only by walls and wire. I just read that some hotshot Boston developer is planning to transform the jail, which closed for business in 1990, into a 305-room, four-star hotel. More power to him. I couldn't care less what they do with the place.

Charles Street Jail was not only scary, it was depressing. Poured gray concrete and steel, the place smelled of urine and floor cleaner. Hardly one ray of natural light ever entered the building. It was one of those multi-tiered facilities, five stories high, with two wings located directly across from each other. Each story contained ten single-person cells that abutted each other and were separated by a foot of concrete. The cells couldn't have been any larger than seven feet by twelve. The ceilings were ten feet high and the door to each cell consisted of iron bars, top to bottom. It wasn't until a few inmates and guards got tossed off some of the upper tiers, resulting in serious injury and even death, that special steel bars replaced the four-and-half-foot-high guardrails that had previously lined the edges of the tiers. The new bars were being installed when I got there.

I'd only been there a few days when some guy got tossed off the fifth-story tier. I heard a scream, a thud, then a lot of laughter and yelling. The only cell that poor prick was going to was six feet down.

Charles Street was, as intended, a dehumanizing experience. If you ever doubted that you were an animal in a zoo, all you had to do was stand at the bars of your cell and look over to the wing directly opposite, to see the other animals bolted in tight. What most affected me was not seeing an inmate acting violent in his cell or standing there cursing like a devil, but seeing someone caged and without emotion, someone who had given up, who had been so beaten down that he had no will. You can't send a small-time criminal into a den of hardened murderers and expect to rehabilitate him. If he wasn't already a well-conditioned sociopath when tossed into prison, the guy would inevitably become one, with no sense of right from wrong.

The whole place, the entire scene, freaked me out. I felt like a scared nine-year-old all over again, and I had to fight hard to swallow that terror. I was a brawler and loudmouth on the outside, experienced in youth detention centers, but I was a terrified eighteen-year-old in jail. No one was going to mess with me, and I wasn't going to take anyone's shit, but that didn't stop me from being scared. I used to call Ronnie, sometimes crying like a bitch. Ronnie had already done time at Deer Island House of Corrections, which made Charles Street look like Miami Beach, and he kept me strong and sane. Just like when we were kids, Ronnie helped me survive.

I soon learned that you had to look out for yourself. You couldn't rely on the guards or authorities. And if you couldn't stand up for yourself, you had to figure out something quick. Some of the poor pricks who couldn't handle themselves ended up becoming some tough guy's girl-friend in exchange for protection. Not ideal, but consider the alternative. Fortunately, I was big, mean, and trained to fight. I didn't hesitate to visit damage on anyone who messed with me.

One of the worst things about Charles Street was that you were locked down twenty-two hours a day, like you were doing time in the hole. The only time you weren't locked down was when you were eating or when you were let out of your cell for an hour of recreation. It made me even meaner and nastier — and more scared.

In the late seventies, Charles Street was a hotbed of racial tension and segregation, a powerful breeding ground for racists, no matter if they were white, black, brown, yellow, or purple. Whites hung with whites, blacks with blacks. Arguments and physical fights, many involving weapons, broke out frequently, usually because one guy's skin color was different from another guy's.

Whites and blacks didn't sit down and chow together pleasantly. The cafeteria was only large enough to accommodate about ten six-person tables, so we ate in shifts, one wing at a time. In a textbook example of horrendous design planning, the cafeteria was located on the ground floor. While half the jail was eating, the other half was in its cells, over-looking the dining area. The guys eating were sitting ducks for any half-decent marksman who could fire something from his cell.

I remember once I'd just sat down to eat lunch. I was shoveling in the food, my face practically in my tray — this wasn't a place to practice Emily Post tips on etiquette — when I heard hooting and screaming. I looked up and saw a bunch of guys at an all-white table tossing their lunch trays on the floor, while other inmates were standing and pointing at the upper tiers. "You motherfucking nigger!" one of the white guys yelled. "Show your face! You're fucking dead!"

I scanned the wing where the prisoners were in lockdown. Most of them were at the bars of their cells, yelling and screaming. But the black guys were not only yelling, they were laughing as well.

Then I saw something coming down from the upper tiers. Someone had thrown what looked like a clump of mud. Guys who'd been sitting a few tables over were in the path of this muddy meteor, and they started running for cover.

The clump landed two tables over, on the edge of some guy's tray. It splattered in all directions, hitting three inmates, who jumped like they'd stepped on a hornet nest. Uttering every racist epitaph known to man, and some they'd just made up, they danced and shook their bodies, like they'd just come in from a rainstorm. But they weren't shaking off water.

Being shat on while you ate was just one of the dehumanizing experiences a prisoner typically endured. There was also the strip search. There you are, naked, and some miserable screw, or guard, who most likely is getting turned on sexually, is groping you with a gloved hand. Often the strip search takes place in front of other inmates. Depending on who you are, and your recent conduct, you may be subject to a cavity search. In a cavity search, the screw, who is wearing gloves, pokes inside your rectum to make sure you aren't hiding anything there.

Once, I saw an inmate turn the tables on the screw. This black guy was being strip-searched in full view of a group of us who were on lockdown. A rookie guard had the man stand on a table and take off all his clothes. The guard then walked to the edge of the table in front of the guy and started inspecting his boots and clothes. The guy is standing there naked and you can see that he has a cock close to a foot long. While this geek rookie is inspecting his clothes, the guy rotates his hips so his cock smacks right against the guard's head, making him stumble backward in shock. Man, we were laughing like hell; slapstick comedy at its best. Too bad the guards didn't share our amusement. They maced that guy good, beat the hell out of him, and then tossed him in the hole.

About two months into my stay, I went to make a call. But the phone was being used by some big black guy who just kept talking and ignored me. Finally, I said, "Hey, bro, how about being fair and giving me a chance to make a call before lockup?"

Keeping his back to me, he spoke over his shoulder. "Go fuck yourself, cracker."

That wasn't nice. Too bad for him. I walked to my cell, grabbed a pencil, and walked back to the telephone, where this guy was still gabbing away. I drove that pencil through his cheek and into his tongue. He dropped the phone, screaming, and buried his head in his hands before falling to his knees, moaning in pain. I casually walked away. And I didn't make my phone call.

I should've known I wouldn't get away with it. A few mornings later, at six A.M., a guard came into my cell and told me to pack. He said they knew I stabbed the black guy, but that he wouldn't testify against me. The authorities didn't want us in the same jail, so I would be shipped off to the Billerica House of Corrections, twenty miles north of Boston. If I'd known how good Billerica was going to be, I would've stabbed that guy sooner. No Club Fed, but a hell of a lot better than Charles Street.

The Billerica House of Corrections was another detention center, like Charles Street. But, in addition to holding prisoners awaiting trial, it also housed convicted prisoners serving their sentences. The three-story prison was newer, cleaner, and had a lot more windows than Charles Street. It was also much bigger, with close to one thousand prisoners. My section was divided into two sides: the I&J cells, where I was housed, and the K&L cells. Other sections were designated by different letters of the alphabet. The cells were wider than those at Charles Street and, unlike Charles Street, the door to the cell was made from solid metal, not iron bars. Each door had a barred window, or open porthole, about one foot square. The fewer bars, the better you could see.

What was especially nice about Billerica was the schedule. You were out of your cell for up to six hours a day to play hoops or lift weights or play cards, among other things. Everybody was out for two hours in the morning and two hours in the afternoon. At night, each side of the facility would be out for two hours, while the other side was in lockdown. But even when you were locked in your cell, the guys from the other side could come over and talk to you through the window of the door to your cell.

Which ended up coming in handy one time. There was a guy named Keith, a big black kid who was the captain of our prison basketball team. He was liked and respected by everyone; he had free reign and you didn't mess with him. Until the day he smart-mouthed one of the guards and the guard decided to get Keith back.

The guard gave us a newspaper article that made for interesting reading.

Keith had told us that he was in for armed robbery; but that's not what the article said. I hadn't yet learned that what a guy is in for, and what he says he's in for, are often two very different things. Keith, the article explained, was in jail for a savage sexual assault. He and two of his brothers had tied up a white girl, sodomized and raped her with a soda bottle, and then burned her with cigarettes before leaving her to die. But she lived to tell the story. We were horrified and formed a plan to mess up Keith real good.

Keith was housed on the K&L side, so in the evening he'd be locked down while us guys on the I&J side were out. One night, me and a few other guys began conversing with him through the open window of his cell door. He had his face right up in the window, just talking away. He didn't realize that hugging the wall outside his cell was a fellow conspirator carrying a cup of boiling ammonia. The guy had heated the ammonia with one of those "stinger" coils we were allowed to keep in our cells for warming up cups of soup. We'd convinced one of the trusties to give us a cleaning product containing ammonia, supposedly to clean our cells. Keith never saw it coming.

At the last second, we stepped away and this guy let Keith have it. You should've heard that bastard squeal. His face looked like a black T-shirt that had been bleached white. He was blinded instantly, though temporarily. We calmly and quickly walked away from the area. One guy was charged for mayhem for his participation in the attack, but he ended up beating it.

Billerica wasn't a problem for me because I had balls, knew how to fight, and made the right friends. I was the type of friend a guy could count on. I remember a buddy had a problem with some punk and he asked me to serve as physical cover for him when he sought payback. On the way to our weekly Sunday movie, I acted as a shield so that the guards couldn't see my buddy stick a foot-long Plexiglas knife, which he'd made by smashing the window in his cell, into this guy's back. (These windows were covered by bars, but prisoners routinely broke the Plexiglas, placing their bottles of juice and milk outdoors in the winter to keep them cold.) He drove the knife in above the kidney so hard that the tip came through on the other side right below the rib cage. That poor slob was in intensive care for weeks. No one ratted on my buddy. He got away clean.

Unfortunately, I eventually got bagged for a TV scam that sent me back to Charles Street. I'd sell a TV to some weak prick, who had to send a money order to Ronnie. When Ronnie received the payment, I would take my TV back and resell it to another prisoner. If anyone complained, I'd threaten him with a knifing or beating.

Two weeks before I was sent packing from Billerica, however, I made a connection that would spare me a lot of grief through the years, someone who remains one of my closest friends. I was talking to Rosario "Rosie" LaMonica, a one-armed habitual criminal who was awaiting trial on an armed robbery charge. I told him I'd been in jail for almost six months and my trial still hadn't come up. I explained that my court-appointed lawyer was advising me to plead out and he thought he could score me a seven-to-ten.

LaMonica was beside himself. "You gotta be shitting me."

"What other options do I have?" I asked. "I can't afford a private attorney. I'm stuck with this deal."

"Listen," LaMonica said. "Give my attorney a call. Al Nugent. This guy is the fucking best. He knows the system inside and out."

"I can't afford it," I said. "He's big bucks, right?"

"Maybe. Just call him, anyway. That plea is fucking ridiculous. You shouldn't see one more day of jail. You've been jumping between here and Charles Street for close to half a year. And that dick defender wants you to plead so you can get seven to ten? You're out of your mind."

I got Al Nugent's number and gave him a call. Al told me that if I could find some way to get five hundred dollars to his office, he'd come out and see me. Even in the late seventies, five hundred dollars was not a big fee for an experienced and accomplished counsel.

I made a number of phone calls, and leaned on my brother Ronnie. One way or another, the money was scared up and dropped off at Al's office. Two days before I was carted back to Charles Street, Al came to check me out in person and review my case.

The case never went to trial. Al took a look at the indictment and saw something was wrong with the state's case. It had screwed up a technicality. Al zoned in on the mistake, got the case dismissed, and less than two weeks after I'd landed back in Charles Street, I walked out the door a free man.

# '78

onnie had rounded up the money to get me out of jail, but, unintentionally, he put me back within the reaches of the long arm of the law. In 1978, his drug habit didn't appear out of control. He seemed like a regular kid, wanting to get high and make some bucks selling pot. I'd been making good money doing B&Es and flimflams, like selling hot TVs and scamming hot credit cards, so when Ronnie asked me to front him nine hundred bucks to buy a couple pounds of pot, I said okay. I've never been that smart with money.

Two hours later, Ronnie came back, his face swollen and covered with welts and scratches, evidence of a good, solid shit-kicking. Plus he had neither a dime nor a thimbleful of pot on him. Yep, he'd been beaten for the drugs and the money, and the only thing he'd been given in return was a vicious mugging. Time for payback. These suckers were going to pay, big time.

Ronnie took off, and I called one of my trusted sidekicks, a tough guy who dealt well with fear. I filled him in and told him to meet me at my place at four-thirty the next morning. We were going to give these shitheads one screaming wake-up call.

We rendezvoused at my apartment at the appointed time and went over our plan. I loaded my twelve-gauge Mossberg shotgun, a beautiful pump-action firearm that was, and remains, a favorite of the military and law enforcement, especially antiriot cops and government narcotics units. We jumped into my dust-gray '73 Eldorado and headed out.

It was five-thirty when we arrived in Brighton, a section of Boston known for its student population. I jumped out of the car and my buddy slid behind the wheel to handle getaway duties. Wearing a full-length leather maxi coat, its pockets jammed with a pair of handcuffs and a roll of duct tape, I walked to the three-story apartment complex where the druggies lived. I made it to the second-floor landing and carefully stepped through the swinging door, which led into the main hallway. As instructed by Ronnie, I turned right, crept up to the specified door and listened intently. All quiet inside. Slowly and very delicately I tried the doorknob. No surprise, it was locked. I gave it a few hard knocks with my knuckles and then jumped a few feet down the hall and pressed my back against the wall, sinking into a slight crouch, ready to pounce. The big cat on the prowl thing.

Someone was moving in the apartment. "Who the fuck is it?" asked a groggy male voice, probably a druggie who'd been sleeping off a high. I didn't say a word. Whoever was moving was shuffling toward the door.

Again the voice. "What the fuck . . . don't fuck around." Then, and I didn't have time to be stunned by this guy's stupidity, the doorknob turned. The door swung open. It took just a millisecond to jam the gun barrel in that guy's face, the tip of the barrel grazing his teeth. Talk about a wake-up call. That shaggy-haired druggie was ripped out of his stupor in no time. "Please don't shoot!" he gasped, wide-eyed with fear. He stepped backward into the apartment and put his hands up, palms facing me in a show of surrender.

"Shhhhhh," I whispered as I pushed him backward, shoving him in the chest with the butt of the shotgun. "Do as you're told or I'm going to blow your fucking head right off. You got that?"

"Yeah . . . yeah . . . yeah . . . j-j-j-just please don't shoot," he stammered.

Just then another door in the apartment opened to my left. Another spaced-out, medium-built druggie in boxer shorts stumbled out to the front room. It probably wasn't necessary — from a brief glimpse of his face, he didn't appear to know what planet he was on — but I quickly eliminated him by slamming him upside the head with the butt of the rifle. He let out a weak yelp and crumpled to the floor, bleeding. I stepped back and waved the gun at both of them. "I'm here to collect my brother's money. And I am leaving here with every fucking penny or I'm leaving here with both of you dead."

"Yeah, yeah, sure. We got it all here," said the first druggie. "Let me get it." He started to back up.

"Don't move another inch, motherfucker," I said. "We'll get the money together." He stopped still as a statue. I looked down at the guy I'd just slammed. "You too, get up." I booted him in the side. He groaned but managed to crawl and get up on his feet.

With the two of them facing me, hands up, I said, "Okay, we're gonna do this slowly and right. Let's get my money, and not one false move. Nothing stupid, 'cause, so me help me God, I'll put holes through both of you."

As he jerked his head toward the rear of the apartment, the guy I'd surprised at the front door said, "It's-s-s-s . . . it's-s-s-s . . . down here. All of it."

"Okay, let's go," I said, motioning with the shotgun. Keeping their hands up, they nervously turned and walked toward another room in the apartment where a door was open. Clothes and all sorts of junk were strewn everywhere, and the smell of grass was pungent and overpowering. As I moved inside the room, I saw a girl, wearing nothing but panties, lying face down on the bed. Even though she was zoned-out on who-knows-what, she sensed us and rolled her head toward us. She wasn't bad looking. When she saw us, she became lucid real fast. She scrambled on her hands and knees toward the end of the bed in an attempt to find a sheet to pull over herself, screeching, "Oh my god! What the hell is going on?"

"Shut the hell up, you cunt," I snapped. The two druggies said nothing. Unable to locate a sheet or blanket, the girl swung her legs over the side of the bed and sat up, doing her best to cover her tits with her arms. I quickly scanned the room. In a corner, I saw one of those green military-type duffel bags, obviously full of something.

"What's in the bag?" I asked.

"Nothing," the bleeding guy said.

"Fuck you, you maggot. Go over and open that bag. And do it slowly."

No one was talking, but the bleeding guy gave me a bad-ass look before walking over to the bag and dragging it toward the center of the room. He pulled the top open; it was full of pot. Already I was ahead. "Where's the cash?" I asked.

The first druggie said, "It's in this dresser over here. I'll get it, but can my girlfriend please put her shirt on?"

"Fuck, no, your girlfriend can't put her shirt on. You're lucky I don't make her blow me in front of you. Now get my fucking money."

I grabbed the first druggie by the back of his neck and walked him toward the dresser, keeping an eye on the girl and the second druggie, ready to start blasting if necessary. There was no gun in the drawer. But there was plenty of cash, a stash of around seven thousand dollars. I started laughing. "This is just about right for beating my brother out of a grand and slapping him around. The cash and the pot are going to make us even."

The bitch sitting on the bed began to yap, "You gotta be fucking kidding me. No fucking way. You're not going to fucking get away with — "

"Shut the fuck up!" I yelled, pointing the gun at her. "You're fucking lucky I haven't blown you all away!" That shut her up. The guys, who had less balls than she did, didn't say a word. I made the guys lie down on the floor and used my handcuffs to cuff one of the guy's wrists to the other guy's ankle. Then I used duct tape to tape the girl's arms behind her back.

I took off my maxi and laid it out on the floor. I shoveled all the money onto it, rolled it up tight, and placed the bundle under my left arm. Then, keeping the trigger and barrel of the shotgun firmly controlled in my right hand, I used my left hand to hoist the bag of pot over my right shoulder. I backed toward the bedroom door with the gun leveled on the two guys, now Siamese twins. "Listen good," I said. "If you try to follow me, I'll blow your fucking brains all over and up and down and all the fuck around." After a quick check of the hallway, I scooted out into the hall, feeling like Santa Claus on Christmas Eve.

I made it to a door that led to a fire escape. Without looking, I got to the landing and pivoted to run down the stairs and . . . Shit!

Right in my path, about ten steps away, were two uniformed police officers on their way up the stairs. They hadn't even moved for their guns, but the Mossberg was in my hand, and I could have blown them away. But I was frozen. And so were they. We stood there, motionless, for about two seconds. Then I made one of the smartest decisions in my life. I wasn't going to shoot any cops. "Hey, fellas, it's not worth it. I give up," I said, letting the bag fall off my shoulder. I slowly turned the shotgun sideways in my hand, holding it out in front of me, as I crouched and placed it on the landing. I then stood up and put my arms in the air.

You should have seen the relief on their faces. They slapped the cuffs on me. One cop dragged me down three flights of stairs and out to the cruiser, while the other checked the apartment I'd just visited. On my way to the station, the cops, who'd been called to the scene by a concerned neighbor, told me that because I'd done the right thing on that fire escape, and, because I was still a kid, just nineteen, they'd do the right thing by me with the charges: not push too hard.

They were true to their word. When the case was arraigned the next day, they weighed in on my behalf. They didn't mention anything about the money, and they pinned the pot on the druggies in the apartment. As for the armed home invasion, they couldn't help me with that, other than to explain to the judge that it was all part of a street dispute. I was licensed for possession of the shotgun, so no problem there.

With the cops' and the judge's help, I was able to get out on bail, awaiting trial. My second appearance in court was set for two months later. I knew I had to scramble. I needed a plan to stay out of jail. I hitched my fate to an option that many young crooks and many judges have agreed on for years: the military. Uncle Sam and me were going to become tight. Five weeks after my arrest, I visited the recruiting station of the Army Reserves in downtown Boston. I said I needed to see a recruiter. I was quickly led into an office where a staff sergeant named David James was standing behind a desk.

Sergeant James was in his late twenties, about 6' 1" and in good shape, with a full head of dark hair. He listened to a story he'd heard many times before: a young man who'd screwed up and needed a bargaining chip to stay out of the slammer. A Vietnam combat veteran himself, Sergeant James explained that no matter how committed I was to the military, there was no guarantee my enlistment would enable me to beat jail time. But he offered to do what he could to help.

The first step to induction was to take the basic entrance exam. A week after our first meeting, I took it. I failed, but Sergeant James fixed it so that my score was pulled up to a passing grade. At the time I thought he was just being nice to me. Then, he appeared with me in front of a judge to add strength to my petition, which was also supported by the Brighton cops who had arrested me, asking that I be released on probation, on the condition that I would enlist in the Army Reserves. The judge had his reservations, but he went along with the recommendation of the cops and Sergeant James. I wasn't going back to jail. Not yet, at least.

Before I became an enlisted man, I decided to get married to a girl I'd been seeing. Joyce Jollimore and I met when we were kids at the Mary E. Curley School in JP. I liked her a lot, and even thought I loved her. I was her first, and she thought she loved me, too. She was a small-framed girl, an average looker with short, dirty blond hair. We were both nineteen. I was a weak little prick who wanted a security pussy. Since I was going to be away for a couple of months, and then maybe, who knows, even a couple of years, I figured if we were married she wouldn't go out with anyone else while I was away. It was pretty selfish of me, but it was fine with her. I got the money for an engagement ring, hired a justice of the peace, and married Joyce in a three-decker house in JP. We were two poor kids, but we invited one hundred of our friends, along with her mother, and had a great celebration. Lots of booze, loud music, a typical low-income party.

Over the next few months, as I moved steadily toward induction, I hung around more with my new buddy, Sergeant James, than I did with my new wife. It was a guy thing, spending time with a buddy, rather than sitting in the Green Street apartment in JP with Joyce. We went out drinking together and hit the rifle range together. A week before I was to report to Fort Dix in New Jersey, Sergeant James suggested we drive down together and go out and grab some pussy. A last hurrah of sorts before eight weeks of boot camp. We left Boston the day before my induction. Just before I left, Frankie came by to wish me well. I told him to watch out for Joyce, and he promised he would. The drive took about five hours. We got a motel room in a town called Wrightville, a few miles away from Fort Dix. We both got shattered, but were not successful in dragging any women back with us. I did make it back to the motel room, covering the final few feet to my bed with my arm draped around the shoulder of Sergeant James. I remember him dropping me onto the bed. Then things got screwed up.

I was dreaming this gorgeous woman was doing a kamikaze dive on my joy stick, giving me the best blow-job of all time. I entered that weird space between dreaming and consciousness, and I was thinking, This is so real. I soon realized I wasn't dreaming, and although groggy, I knew I was awake and that someone was between my legs, mouth on my cock. I was half-paralyzed by the booze, but focused enough to realize that Sergeant James was blowing me. I recoiled in horror, my body driving back toward the headboard of the bed. "You dirty sick motherfucker!" I yelled. "You fucking sick homo piece of shit!"

This was far beyond anything I could comprehend; I had no idea what to do. I was frozen against the headboard, holding my knees against my chest, my body tense and shaking. Sergeant James jumped up and started to ramble, his words spilling over one another. "I . . . I . . . don't know what the fuck I was doing. . . . I can't believe this. . . . I must be totally fucking gone. . . . this isn't me." For thirty seconds I didn't say a word as he stood at the end of the bed, his arms and hands in front of him in a form of pleading, as if he were saying, "Come on, please, buddy, come on."

Then I shouted, "How the fuck could you do this! You were my friend! My recruiter! I trusted you! You sick fuck!"

Sergeant James continued to apologize. I told him to shut his mouth, to get away from me. I couldn't decide whether to remain in a guarded position at the end of bed or run out the door or snap his neck. I decided to stay on the bed. But if he'd moved even an inch toward me, I would have killed him.

After ten minutes of begging forgiveness, Sergeant James walked out the door. I sat curled up at the end of the bed, like a child. I felt even worse than I did when I was raped at nine. Because this time I knew it was wrong. For years I'd been on the street, living on my own, proving that I was the toughest of the tough. And then this guy, this pervert, this Vietnam vet who I respected and who'd helped me, had gotten me drunk and molested me. And once again, I was powerless. I'd just turned nineteen and I was as helpless as I'd been at nine. What the hell could I do? Was I, a kid with no family or support, going to file a report against a respected sergeant in the Army? Would I ever want to reveal to others what had happened to me? No way. The only choice I had was Fort Dix or Walpole.

Three hours later, Sergeant James came back to the room. I had my stuff packed and was ready to head over to the base. We didn't say a word to one another. I threw my gear in the back seat of his car. I thought about getting in the back, but decided I'd look pretty stupid so I got in the passenger seat, and he drove us to Fort Dix. I was still hung over and stunned by what had happened. More horrified than angry, I no longer had any desire to beat the shit out of him. Maybe I'd been to blame for what had happened. Maybe I'd done or said something to make him think I'd wanted it. I was too scared and sick to try and figure that out. From the quick glance I gave him, I could see that Sergeant James was embarrassed, unable to look me in the face either. After a wordless fifteen-minute drive, we were waved through the entrance post to Fort Dix. I grabbed my belongings from the backseat and walked briskly away, not daring to look back.

But it wasn't that easy to leave it behind. For weeks afterward I was ashamed and traumatized by what had happened in that motel room. I knew something had gone terribly wrong that night and I struggled to convince myself that I had done nothing to bring it about. I spent the eight weeks of boot camp barely aware of what was going on around me. Every time I saw a guy in uniform, I thought of Sergeant James and got sick all over again.

I found out quickly that I arrived at Fort Dix with a couple of strikes against me. One was that I was from South Boston, and several of the drill instructors were black. My first up-close encounter with a black DI had me shaking in my boots. We were standing at attention, and he got right in my face, doing his best to push all the right buttons. "You from South Boston, boy, aren't you?" he shouted. "You don't like me, do you? You don't like black people, do you? Well, let me tell you something, boy. There may come a time when this black man may have to save your life." I didn't doubt him for a second. But I wanted him to know that there were some folks in Southie who weren't racist and that the liberals who had shoved desegregation down our throats had caused all the problems. But I knew this wasn't the time for a philosophical discussion about blacks and whites, so I kept my mouth shut and did as I was told.

As it turned out, that DI was tough with me, but he never went overboard. He dished out what I deserved, no more, and we soon became tight, running long distances, performing exercise routines and everyday operations side by side. Military life has a way of making one blind to color, religion, or ethnic background. The DI, like any good leader, led through example in order to gain the respect of his men.

Another strike against me was that the DIs all knew that I, like others in my group, was trying to escape jail time by joining the Reserves. They'd give us a hard time, saying things like, "Hey, we know why you're here, recruit." It didn't make me angry when they said that, just scared that they would send me back to jail.

To make matters even worse, I had a lot of personal problems while I was there. I had a very new wife back home who, in my head, was tapping everything in sight. Joyce wrote me a few times and I wrote back, telling her how much I loved her and how I wanted to spend my whole life with her and have kids with her. I didn't tell her about Sergeant James. About four weeks after I left, Frankie called and confirmed my suspicions that Joyce was feathering out on her own. She'd hooked up with this guy named Scott. When he asked if I wanted him to do anything about it, I told him to forget about it. Soon I began banging girls whenever I met them. I didn't give a shit about Joyce. When I got out, Joyce and I decided to separate. Neither one of us was interested in getting a divorce until four years later when she decided to remarry.

More important, my brother Ronnie was back in the Deer Island prison and had nobody but me for support. When I'd been in the Charles Street Jail, he'd been there for me, easing my fears every time I called him. Now he was in again, his drug habit worse than ever, and I couldn't be there for him. He'd been in and out of Deer Island for two and a half years, in for five or six months, then out for a month or two, then right back in again. This time he'd stolen the car of an FBI agent who was arresting a suspect who lived near us in JP. The agent walked out of the house, suspect in hand, and found his car heading off down the street. The entire Boston police force ended up charging down our street to get Ronnie. He was pinched in about five minutes, but not before he slammed into three cruisers. The FBI and police were a little concerned during the chase because there were machine guns in the trunk. Good thing Ronnie didn't know about them.

My worries about Ronnie only intensified while I was at Fort Dix. He needed me and I couldn't even visit him in jail. And you couldn't just pick up the phone and call someone in jail. They can only call you when they're able to get access to a phone. Since I had even less access to a phone than Ronnie, it was impossible for us to talk.

For eight weeks, the DIs did nothing but scream at me and order me around, which did nothing to improve my attitude. Basic training finally ended and it looked like I was going to be heading to advanced infantry training, which could last for four months. I knew I had to get out of there. When a second medical exam just before AIT revealed that I had flat feet, I felt relief, the first positive emotion I'd experienced since the recruiter molested me. I was out of there. Headed home to Southie.

# Tiger Crane

A brief stint in the Marine Corps took me out of Southie one last time, but it didn't take long until I was given an honorable discharge. Even in uniform, my insatiable thirst for a good fight had remained potent, and once I was back in civilian clothes my fists only got itchier. Fighting was as natural and crucial to me as breathing or eating.

I'd learned that when they called me a ragamuffin foster kid, the only way to shut their mouths, and make the hurt go away, was with my fists. I never felt bad when someone was lying on his back, begging for mercy, begging me to stop. If he'd made me mad, he deserved it. By the time I entered my teens, kids understood that a fight with MacKenzie was no easy match. Fighting provided me with my greatest pleasure and wiped away my deepest pain.

After the Army Reserves and Marines, I was meaner and tougher than ever. I had wrongs to avenge. It was nothing to go up to some guy who had beaten me or Ronnie when we were kids and knock him out cold. Before he hit the ground, though, he always heard the same message: "You were a lot tougher when Ronnie and I were little, weren't you, asshole?"

It didn't take long for another message to spread: when you get knocked out by MacKenzie, the real fun begins. Once my victim was sprawled across the sidewalk, out cold, I'd go over his body with as much precision as a surgeon in the operating room. First, I'd probe with my feet, kicking each rib, feeling a high every time I heard one snap beneath my sneaker. Then, with one or two swift heel kicks, I'd attack the leg bones. Then I'd lift up the arms, one at a time, and *smash,* there went the ribs underneath, broken as easily as sticks underfoot. I worked methodically until the body had been pummeled to my satisfaction. Sometimes I even used my teeth, biting off an ear and spitting it back at the body: a farewell present for my victim when he opened his bloodied, swollen eyes. Once, I went for a finger instead and actually swallowed it. Made me a little sick, but nowhere as pained as the poor bastard that had to go through the rest of his life with nine fingers.

I was as vicious as they come, a monster. Violence was my drug. When I beat someone, it was better than the high any druggie pulled from a speed-ball. The more hurt I put on someone, the more fear I created, the bigger my reputation. And I knew that every time I showed my prowess as a vicious and merciless fighter, I saved myself ten more fights down the line. My reputation was growing. No one was going to render me powerless ever again.

The martial arts added to my repertoire of personal weapons. I was twenty when I started exploring them. I couldn't get over the respect people on the street gave a guy named Freddy Weichel, a judo expert who held classes at the Tynan Community School in Southie. He was ruthless and mean, with the mental toughness and skill to grab you, toss you flat, and choke the consciousness out of you in ten seconds flat. He worked a hell of a lot less hard than I did putting away a victim. All the more impressive was the fact that Freddy wasn't very tall and weighed no more than 160 pounds. Unlike me, he didn't fight just for the sake of brawling. He was committed to judo. To him, it was a form of athletics, discipline, and self-defense, not a way to dispense violence. I kept going down to Tynan Community School to watch him teach. I couldn't get enough.

Finally, in 1979, after months of watching from the sidelines, Frankie and I approached Weichel about learning a few tricks of his trade. By then, I was a formidable street brawler and a veteran of Charles Street Jail. Judo would make me untouchable. While Frankie watched, I told Freddy I wanted him to show me some "good stuff." He sized me up and immediately saw I was clueless. He told me to get on the mat and come at him with any type of move, to take him out any way I wanted. He readied himself in a crouch, like a cornerback facing a wide receiver before the ball is snapped. I laughed inwardly and launched a full-bore charge. I hit the guy with enough force to budge a school bus. But it didn't do much good because, within ten seconds, Freddy was behind me, his arms locked around my windpipe. I flailed my arms for a few seconds, trying to grab hold of him to work some sort of reverse. It was useless; I was cooked. Just before I went to sleep, I had the presence of mind to "tap out" — to offer an "I give up" signal by tapping the mat with the palm of your hand. When I tapped, Freddy released his hold and I fell sideways onto the mat, gasping for air and believing for a few seconds that I had seen God.

Freddy taught me a lesson the hard way. Despite my bruised pride, I respected him enough to thank him for knocking me down a few pegs. Because I knew I would have a solid new weapon as a result.

I learned some things from Freddy, but it never felt satisfying. Judo was a system of grappling and throws and holds. It looked clunky and didn't feel as complete as real fighting. Frankie and I wanted to get into a ring and punch and draw blood, not just wrestle someone to the ground. After a few months, we quit, convinced there was something else out there for us. It didn't take long to find it. I wandered into Chinatown with a buddy, Paul Blair, to scout out some of the dojos, or martial arts gyms. Like any other American guy in the late seventies, I felt that the slant eyes had it over round eyes in the martial arts department. We ended up signing on at a place called the Academy of Chinese Martial Arts.

Ironically, the primary instructor was Tony Iantosca, a white guy who looked, at least to our narrow minds, no more like any of our martial arts movie heroes than we did. Iantosca taught a form of kung fu called Tiger Crane. It always amazed me that something so lethal was invented two thousand years ago by peaceful Buddhist monks. I liked kung fu because it offered complete, direct, and effective combat applications. You used the entire skill set: grappling, punches, blocks, throws, and kicks. Compared to other forms of martial arts, such as judo, kung fu was more graceful and fluid. The Tiger Crane style was more oriented toward hands and punching than the other forms of kung fu. I wanted something that made me look good while I drove my fist or foot into somebody.

Tony Iantosca was maybe a year younger than me, twenty-one when I first met him. He was one of the best instructors, and, if necessary, a very, very dangerous fighter. Tony was tall and solid, about a hundred and eighty pounds. He demanded attention and commitment, and if you intended to be one of his students, you had better give both. Paul and I did. We paid $40 a month for the classes and bought the black satin pants, black sash, and black shirt uniform.

Not only did we learn the moves and exercises, but we became cardio-vascular nuts as well, banging out five-mile runs at least four times a week along the waterfront in South Boston. We fell in love with kung fu and quickly became proficient. Paul and I were built for this martial art: me at 5' 10" and Paul at 5' 6", both broad-shouldered and relatively short-limbed. We had low centers of gravity, a major advantage in pivoting and moving sideways, backward, and forward.

But Paul and I were not good, let's say, ambassadors for the discipline. Iantosca would have kicked our asses soundly had he known that four months into our lessons we were using our newfound abilities to start fights in the streets and raise hell in bars. We deliberately gave out a hundred bad looks a day, looking for any opportunity to whoop up on people. We had a long stretch when we were pounding poor pricks without even breaking a sweat. I'm sure what Paul and I did was not what those monks had in mind two thousand years ago.

We'd been studying for about six months when Tony brought in from China a legendary master, Lee Yat Ming. Ming was probably sixty years old, five feet tall, and maybe a hundred and twenty pounds. But he was lethal. Even Tony couldn't take him. Master Ming had the "chi kung" going for him, a mysterious harnessing and channeling of energy that can make a pile driver out of an arm and fist. Master Ming was amazing. Tony and Master Ming had some sort of falling out, and Ming left the school to open his own studio in Chinatown. Paul and I followed him and soon learned that he liked American pussy. This made a nice business arrangement for me: I delivered a few Southie skanks to his door and he gave me free lessons. One day in 1982, Master Ming was found dead at the bottom of a long staircase. The medical examiner's report said it was a heart attack. But word on the street was he got involved in nefarious Chinatown activities, mixed it up with the wrong people, and was murdered.

I also began to participate in ultimate, or underground, fights, held in kung fu schools in Chinatown. It's similar to American combat karate. Anything goes in these fights, except blows to the throat or eye. You can be killed if you disobey that rule. You do battle until someone taps out or is knocked out.

Learning how to tap out can save your life. You start with a single tap, then two or three more in succession, until the other guy notices that you're quitting. A fighter can tap out at any time and end the match. That's important because, even with a knowledgeable referee (and in some illegal fights there is no referee), you can get caught in a type of chokehold or leg- or armlock from which there is no escape. If the guy with the advantage so chooses, he can break his opponent's arm or leg. Even a careful referee might not jump in on a limb lock, so it is up to the fighter in distress not to play the hero and to tap on the mat to end the match and prevent a broken bone.

These underground fights were very controlled, however. If you tried to continue after an opponent tapped out, the Chinese Tong would threaten to kill you: a promise guaranteed to make you stop. I won one fight and lost another. The average fee for fighting was a thousand bucks, winner take all. The audience was mostly Chinese businessmen who would bet big money on the fights. Sometimes ten or twenty grand. The few Americans who did come talked too much.

As for form, ultimate fighting is whatever works for the individual. If a guy is a great brawler and puncher and has success against a karate expert, then he uses that. Many participants get their limbs broken in these fights. The sound of human bone breaking is pretty sensual. It gave me a hard-on to see some poor prick who wasn't smart enough to tap out get his arm snapped in half. But I found this hobby too dangerous even for me. Two matches were more than enough.

So Paul Blair and I found other amusements. We'd jump into my car and head over to some dojo in Boston, or in the suburbs. We'd show up right before a class and walk in wearing sweats and acting stupid, asking to spar. We'd say we'd been training for a few months and thought we were getting pretty good and should start looking around for a test.

Usually the students would call on one of their top studs to take us on. Often, they'd set it up as an exhibition. You know, throw one of us to the slaughter for teaching purposes. There we'd be, squared off on the center mat against one of the anointed killers of Joe's Neighborhood Academy of the Lethal Fist. All the awe-struck young doo-bees in their immaculately pressed baker outfits and sashes would sit cross-legged, Indian-style, around the mat, mouths hanging open in anticipation of the beating their hero was about to dish out.

We played it perfectly, right up until the moment of truth. I can remember facing my opponent, doing my best to exhibit uncertainty and confusion. Sometimes the other guy even felt sorry for me. That was a mistake. The signal was given, and we'd go at it. Sometimes I'd play around for a minute or so, maybe even let my opponent score some shots. But, whether I let it go two minutes or ten seconds, the result was the same. With a clumsy stance and movement, I'd sucker the unsuspecting prick into letting his guard down, and WHAM! I'd connect with a punch or kick to the head, midsection, or ribs that would send him to the mat, sometimes unconscious, for a five-minute count. When the guy hit the mat, you'd hear a gasp. And then, dead silence. Paul and I had it timed so that, as CPR was being administered, we'd quietly and discreetly beat a retreat.

As spring approached, Paul and I found a new outlet for our aggression. On warm nights, we'd cruise down to the esplanade on the Boston side of the Charles River, where a decent-sized gay population hung out. We figured we'd use our martial arts skills to do some high-octane gay bashing. I didn't, and don't, give a shit about anyone's sexual orientation. We just identified the gays who hung out along the Charles as a minority on the fringe who had no real support or backing. Perfect victims for a couple of gutless dirtbags.

For five nights straight, it was easy pickings and great fun. Paul and I concealed ourselves in the darkness, moving quietly, ducking behind trees, acting like guerrilla warriors. We'd move in and start shooting the shit with some of the guys. We'd play it cool for a while, but not for too long. We didn't want to start thinking of these guys as humans. Once everybody started to relax, we'd pounce, blindsiding a few queer bears and dropping off a few heroes who came to the aid of their friends. We tried out all the new moves we'd been taught, plus a few we made up. Once we started kicking, it was bedlam: the rapid-fire staccato of fist or boot connecting, and then the yelling and moaning. We'd give ourselves a good two to three minutes of fun and then run like hell before the cops arrived.

Paul and I made sure we never struck the same place twice. We thought we were covering our bases. We didn't know that time was running out. We also didn't know that a block away from the esplanade, serious and dangerous talent, most of it gay, trained at this dojo called the Mattson Academy of Martial Arts.

It was a weekday night, the first week in June. Beautiful, warm, cloudless. Paul and I were on the hunt. We zoned in on a group of ten guys standing next to the water. I noticed that these guys seemed taller and wider than the men we'd encountered in our previous forays, but we were so confident of our abilities that we feared no one.

We crouched, moving slowly, stealthily, all the while getting closer to the clearing. This time, no small talk. We were going to run these faggots down and kick the shit out of them. We stayed on the edge of the field for ten minutes, gearing up, whispering to each other and pointing: "Okay, you take that one." "I got that motherfucker." "Let's hit that queer together."

We were in sync. We gave each other the nod, then sprang across that field like two players on a kickoff return team. We were twenty yards away, stride for stride, when our boys turned around to face us. We knew in the next second — when, in a relaxed manner, they all slipped into a classic kung fu stance — that this drill was going to be different. We were running headfirst into a gang of recruits from the Mattson Academy of Martial Arts.

We knew we had a problem, but there was no way I was going to puss out. Neither was Paul. Not yet, anyway. I went after a guy out front, a guy built like me, broad-shouldered, but two inches taller. That arrogant prick was waving me on. And I was coming: twenty feet, ten feet, five feet, and then, BAM! I didn't know what he hit me with because it happened so quickly. I don't know if I got caught with a fist, foot, a baseball bat, or all three. I do know that I saw a bright light and felt an intense, piercing, vibrating pain that reverberated throughout my head and body. I didn't go down, though. I always could take a punch. I stumbled backwards and tried to regain my senses. And I did, just in time for my opponent to take out my legs with a perfectly executed kick.

This prick was tough — and good. I bounced up, dancing on my feet and screaming, "C'mon, you motherfucking cocksucker!" I always had more guts than brains. Just before I stepped up for more punishment, I looked to my right. To my horror, Paul was running away.

I was in deep shit. I have to give those guys credit, though. I was outnumbered ten to one, but it was left to me and the guy who'd just rocked me to resolve the issue. Then again, I think his buddies had figured that I was going to get my ass kicked without their help. I hadn't come to the same conclusion. I was hurt and tingling, but I was pissed, and stupid enough to think I could still pull out a victory. I danced around for ten more seconds, giving myself time to shake off the stars and the ringing and the pain. The truth was I had no idea how I was going to get out of it without becoming the poor prick who loses an ear or a finger.

I'm not sure if it was my anger, fear, adrenaline overload, or all of it together, but I then did something that would have caused Tony Iantosca to deny he ever knew me, never mind taught me. I dispensed with all discipline, with all consideration of balance and leverage, and became a Southie street brawler. I executed a combination lunge-and-flying-tackle at my opponent's waist. Of course, this stroke of brilliance resulted in further distress. I remember a knee connecting to the bridge of my nose and the instantaneous crack of cartilage and bone, and blood pouring out of my nose and into my mouth.

And then I was on my back. The guy straddled me, his knees pinning my shoulders to the ground. He bent forward, his face six inches from mine. My face was throbbing and my head was in a fog, but all I could worry about was that he was going to try to kiss me. Nope, he was just getting close enough so that I could hear what he had to say. I couldn't see much of his face, but I did notice that he was smiling.

"Okay, you stupid fuck," he said calmly, not a shade out of breath. "Do you give?"

I had little choice. "Yeah, yeah, sure, I give," I said.

"Okay, now get the fuck out of here. And I don't ever want to see you here again. Not you. Not anyone who looks like you. You got it?"

"Yeah, sure. Just let me up. Please."

He didn't say anything as he stood up and took a step back. I scrambled to my feet and turned toward Storrow Drive, making like I was heading out. But then I spun around and tried to land a haymaker. The only thing I landed was on my back, as my target deftly slipped the knockout punch and turned my momentum against me, grabbing my shoulders and executing a perfect body toss. I could hear the air punch out of my diaphragm as my body slapped the earth.

Again, he straddled me. Through the moon beams and lightning bolts dancing in front of my eyes, I could see his face. He wasn't smiling now. "I'm going to make this very clear," he said slowly. "If I let you up again, and you come back at me, I'm going to pull your pants down and fuck you up the ass."

I don't think I need to tell you that, at that moment, my days of gay bashing came to an end.

# Whitey

On a late January afternoon in 1980, Whitey Bulger stepped out of the shadows. I was working out in my second-floor apartment on Boston Street in South Boston's Andrew Square, preparing for the Eastern United States Kickboxing Championships. I'd been into serious kickboxing for more than a year and was in prime shape, throwing two to three hundred kicks a day. I wore my karate pants and my black belt, wrapped around my midsection. As always when I was working out, the door to my apartment was open so my buddies could walk in.

I was throwing kicks and studying my form in a full-length mirror when I saw a reflection of four guys in the doorway. They gave me a look like they owned the place. "What the fuck are you doing here?" I yelled. Two of them walked right in. The other two stayed at the door. I started toward them, ready to separate their heads from their bodies. "Anyone ever teach you to knock, assholes?"

One of those assholes had icy, blue-gray eyes and receding close-cropped silver hair, brushed straight back. He was maybe forty or fifty. With his barracuda jacket, jeans, and leather sneakers, he had the casual Southie look, or rather the Boston docks gangster look. It wasn't just the glacial stare; this guy's whole being was ice cold. I was twenty-two and one tough shit myself, but something made me hesitate. I knew the guy in front of me was someone you didn't mess with.

"My name is Jimmy Bulger," he said. The name didn't register with me, which he seemed to realize. "Most people call me Whitey." Whitey Bulger. Now that was a name I knew. Bulger pointed to the other man. "This is my friend, Stevie. Stevie Flemmi." Stevie "The Rifleman" Flemmi. I knew that name, too. Whitey didn't introduce the other two.

Standing in my apartment, I now realized with a rush, was a stone-cold killer, the most feared and notorious gangster in Boston. Next to him was Stevie Flemmi, born and bred in Roxbury, not Southie, but still the most feared man in Boston's underworld after Bulger.

Whitey Bulger was an institution unto himself. Brilliant. Ruthless. Murderous. Lucifer personified. If the word on the street was to be believed — and what other word could I rely on? — Whitey Bulger could kill you and your dog, fuck your wife, burn down your house, and walk away clean. I realized this probably wasn't a visit to say hello.

When Whitey spoke again, his voice was so soft I had to lean closer just to hear him. I learned later that he kept his voice low to avoid being recorded by surveillance devices. The trouble, he explained, was $10,000 worth of Hummels me and a buddy had stolen from some guy's house. What we hadn't known was that this guy was in the mob. What we had known was the guy's niece. We took turns banging her upstairs, while the other one was downstairs ripping off the place. Whitey wanted the Hummels returned. Unfortunately, they were long gone. We'd sold them.

I did the only thing I could do and began to explain exactly what happened. "Whitey, we — "

He cut me off. "I prefer to be called Jimmy."

"Jimmy, " I said, "we did take the Hummels. I don't know how much they were worth. But they were fenced two weeks ago. I don't know where they are, and I don't think we can get them back. But, out of respect for you and Stevie, I'll do whatever is necessary to make things right."

Whitey listened intently, all his attention focused on me. "I'm working at the Boston Rose Sub Shop in Boston," I continued. "I can make payments every week or whatever to clear this thing up. Shit, I didn't even know the girl was connected."

Whitey looked at me for a couple of seconds and then asked, "Who did you do the score with?"

I gave him the only answer I could, even though I knew it might be signing my death certificate. "Jimmy, I can't say who I did it with. I'm in this on my own."

His eyes hardened. "What the fuck do you mean you can't tell me?" he said, his voice edged, though still barely audible. "This guy is going to kill you. You don't understand the rules. No one shits in my backyard without getting my permission."

"Jimmy, I respect you and Stevie, and I hear what you're asking, but I'll have to take the weight myself. I can't give this guy up." All the while I was thinking that if this guy is going to kill me, then if I give up my buddy's name, he's going to get whacked, too. It sounded like an insane reason to die, but it was my code. I honored very little in the world, but the code of not ratting on my buddy was on the top of my list.

That appeared to strike a chord with Bulger. He smiled slightly. "Okay, I respect that. I respect you won't give up your buddy." Then he leaned back and thought, looking at me all the while. After a few seconds, he said, "Listen, I'm going to cut you a favor. You're all set. No one is going to come after you. I'll take care of everything." A wave of relief swept over me. I was in the clear.

Whitey extended his hand, which I gratefully shook and offered profuse thanks. "You won't be hearing from us for a while," he said. "But, down the road, I may need a favor, all right?"

"Jimmy, that won't be a problem." Whitey looked at me for a couple of seconds, always that icy stare, before he turned toward the door. He still had that slight smile. Flemmi and the two other guys stepped aside to let Whitey take the lead. They didn't take their eyes off me or turn around until their boss had passed them.

My heart was still racing as I heard them walk down the stairs. For a minute there, I'd thought I was living my last day on earth. But I knew I wasn't done with Whitey Bulger. I'd learned enough of the ways of the street, and the way mob bosses earned and maintained their power, to understand that he would call me on that favor.

Meeting Whitey Bulger that January afternoon seemed to be the defining moment in my life. I'd spent so much time proving I was the toughest of the tough. But once I met Whitey, I understood that all my toughness would somehow be laid at his feet. A new phase of my life was beginning, one that would make earlier scenes of violence look like child's play. I was headed into the big time, about to devote my street smarts and fighting skills to the service of the one man worthy of these gifts.

# The Bulgers' Boston

I knew that Whitey Bulger was king, but what I'd heard until then was a mixture of reality and folklore. After my exhilarating in-person experience with Jimmy Blue Eyes, I started to ask questions, do research.

It intrigued me that he was absolutely feared, yet also held in high regard. I heard he killed with no remorse. And if he was in a good mood when he sought revenge, he merely had one of his strong-arms beat the offender to within an inch of his life. I also heard he was something of a Robin Hood, a gangster who robbed, killed, and controlled the streets and drug sales of South Boston with ruthless authority, yet paid the rent for a penniless old woman and bought candy for the neighborhood kids. I heard he kept the streets clean of heroin and angel dust, as well as any drug dealers who weren't working for him, a public service that included, if necessary, making dealers who broke his rules disappear permanently.

And, of course, there was no ignoring his younger brother Billy, the president of the Massachusetts senate. Billy was said to be ruthless in his own right. If you messed with him, especially if you were a political opponent, he'd send you to a political graveyard. Many of the old-timers in the neighborhood, who had known both brothers since they were kids, felt that of the two, Whitey was the smarter.

Jimmy and Billy had grown up in the Old Harbor Housing Projects in South Boston, which means they grew up poor. There were six kids in the family. Jean was the oldest, followed by Jimmy in 1929, Billy in 1934, then Sheila, Jack, and Carol. Jimmy, who got the nickname "Whitey" because of his platinum-blond hair, became a troublemaker early on, running with gangs and brawling and getting into all sorts of mischief. Billy went in another direction just as early, becoming a star student and altar boy, winning the notice and approval of both the young and the old in the neighborhood with his fine manners and bright mind. As Whitey became a more committed delinquent, Billy became a more committed student, even something of a classics scholar, studying Latin at Boston College. By 1953, Whitey had graduated to hijacking and bank holdups, and Billy had graduated from Boston College.

In 1956, as Billy was finishing up a two-year hitch in the army, Whitey, in hiding with his hair dyed black, was dragged out of a Boston nightclub and arrested for robbing banks in Massachusetts, Rhode Island, and Indiana. He always enjoyed traveling and got to do plenty when he was convicted and began a nine-year tour of federal penitentiaries, including Alcatraz. During his stay in an Atlanta prison, he received brownie points and years off his sentence for volunteering to enter a risky, month-long CIA experiment to study the effects of LSD. He got into so many fights in Atlanta that he spent ninety days in the hole. Convinced he was working on an escape plan, the authorities sent him to Alcatraz, the toughest of maximum-security federal prisons. When Whitey returned to Boston in 1965, his kid brother Billy was already married with four kids, a graduate of Boston College Law School, and a member of the Massachusetts House of Representatives.

Following their reunion in 1965, the Brothers Bulger continued on their paths to becoming the best and the baddest in their respective pursuits. It was a path that for one would lead one to the presidency of the Massachusetts senate and then the presidency of the University of Massachusetts. For the other brother, the path included deceit, drug-dealing, mayhem, murder — and a top spot on the FBI's Ten Most Wanted List.

It's a story that could have played itself out only in the movies or a novel — or in the insular and incestuous world of South Boston. It's been said that Boston excels in two things: politics and revenge. If this is true of Boston, then it's doubly true of South Boston, a place unique for its ethnic tribalism, fierce parochialism, and partisan politics.

There are only three ways into the South Boston peninsula: the Broadway Bridge, the Summer Street Bridge, and Day Boulevard. This geographical isolation, which separated Southie from the rest of Boston and the rest of the world, no doubt enticed the Irish to settle there. We might have chosen this spot because of the prejudice we met elsewhere. Or it might just have been chance that landed so many of us in what became an almost exclusively Irish enclave.

Skyscrapers never flourished in Southie. The tall buildings were situated a couple miles away in Boston's financial district. Today, if you were to drive from the land of the traders, brokers, and venture capitalists into Southie, you would pass South Station, a commuter hub, and then head across a bridge and over a channel of water. You'd drive through a few blocks of brick warehouses that were used for storage, meatpacking, and light industry when I first moved to the neighborhood. Now, many of them are occupied by all sorts of dot-com and other upstart companies. Some of them have been turned into artists' lofts. The area looks great, but you'd have a tough time getting some of the old-timers to concede this. To them, the new kids who live, work, and play in the buildings are interlopers.

Wharves and long rows of warehouses hug the northern tip of the peninsula, which also boasts the World Trade Center, a gigantic exhibition hall and office complex. The wharves and docks are a kind of blue collar Wall Street, a hotbed of commerce during the day, but a ghost town at night.

The heart of Southie is the grid of alphabetical and numbered streets, probably arranged that way initially because the Irish knew their alphabets and numbers, today lined with well-maintained triple-deckers, or three-family buildings. This area was once almost all Irish, Catholic, and lower-to-middle class, but things have changed in the past ten years. A surge of minorities has given the city some diversity, while infiltrating yuppies have raised the average income substantially. Some of the triple-deckers and schools and other buildings in Southie have been converted to nice condominiums and other types of housing, like townhouses and Victorian-style bungalows, affordable only by professionals making big pay.

Toward the southern part of Southie are the projects, including Old Harbor, where Whitey and Billy grew up. Block after block of two-story, redbrick apartments. From 1938, when the Bulger Boys moved in, until 1961, when Billy left, at age twenty-seven, to get married, the projects were all white. And the black projects, like Columbia Point, were in neighboring Dorchester. Today, black, brown, and white all live together in Southie, but almost exclusively in the projects. The crime statistics have risen sharply. The projects used to be safe enough to leave your doors open, but try that today and you could come home to an empty house.

There are also long commercially zoned boulevards, lined with buildings no taller than three stories, many of them stores and bars. The facades of these establishments, for the most part, look poor and uninviting. Many of the bars are dark, dingy, and shadowy: classic buckets-of-blood. They reek of thousands of days and nights of heavy smoking and boozing and of men and women who almost never feel the fresh air and sunshine. A bar like the L Street Tavern, made semi-famous in the movie *Good Will Hunting*, provides a look inside the nicer "Irish-type" taverns and neighborhood establishments that are favorites of the recently relocated and more genteel crowd.

But the treasure of Southie is its coastline, which includes seven miles of beaches. A seawall and combination bike-running-walking path runs along most of the waterfront. If you live in Southie, you've probably used it at some point. If you were to start at the northernmost point, you'd be at Castle Island, a peninsula off a peninsula actually, which faces a massive earthen and stone fortress, Fort Independence. The fort, which looks like a castle, saw action during the Revolution when its soldiers fended off the British trying to get into Boston Harbor. Today, Castle Island is a community haven. No matter the weather, people use the paths that lead out to and around the peninsula. On nice days, the place is maybe the hottest spot in Boston. Everyone is there: old, young, priests, mobsters, hustlers, attorneys, doctors, homeless, slim, fat, fit, out-of-shape. Whitey loved walking along the water in South Boston. He especially loved Castle Island.

But to know Southie, especially "my" Southie, is to understand something about the Irish and all that they have endured. To know Southie, you have to know something about the parochial, stubborn, proud, and fiercely loyal character of the Irish.

The Irish were once known as the "niggers of Europe," the low-lives of the continent. As for me, I have no idea what generation American I am. Eddie MacKenzie Senior was Scottish. He was born in Malden. That's all I know. Us MacKenzies fit right in, though, because Boston is the most Irish of American cities. And South Boston is the most Irish of Boston neighborhoods. It's mind-boggling that so many Micks parked their asses in this city, especially since, in the mid-to-late nineteenth century, the period of the real mass exodus from Ireland to America, Boston, with its tight-knit WASP aristocracy, was the last place an Irish person was welcome. But the Irish came anyway, and started to tear down the old guard by banging away at the three Ps of opportunity: police, politics, and the priesthood.

The Irish did it their way. In some respects, their methods were noble, but they were also crude, loud, bigoted, and sometimes violent. Still, they succeeded, without apology. Their success was fueled by extraordinary courage and by love of God, country, neighbor, and family. Big families were a key to their success. James Michael Curley, who served four terms as mayor of Boston between 1914 and 1949, once said to a Boston blue blood power broker: "We are going to out-fuck you now, and out-vote you later." I think that many in South Boston forgot the prejudice and exclusion the Irish suffered when they first came; they so easily turned around and did the same thing to other people, choosing not to remember the signs that read IRISH NEED NOT APPLY. When the Irish gained control, they weren't giving anything back.

The South Boston I knew so well from the mid-seventies through 1990 fairly dripped with Irish pride, love for neighbor, resistance to outsiders, and a desire to run its own show. It was the perfect place for a guy like Whitey Bulger to build a massive criminal enterprise and earn a reputation as a gentleman bandit and legendary street warrior. It was also the perfect place for a politician like Billy Bulger to build power. I believe that Billy Bulger, who never forgot his people, was, and remains, one of Southie's best assets. I also believe he orchestrated corruption and helped run interference for his brother against law enforcement. During the busing crisis, and in many other fights vital to the welfare of his constituents, he stood on the front line, advancing and protecting their interests. But Billy had to have known what his brother Whitey was up to. He knew how bad Whitey was. Through the years, I heard guys who worked for Whitey say that Billy enabled the killing, drug-dealing, and all the other crimes by either directly protecting Whitey, or by turning his back on the evidence that was in front of him. But then again, Billy was only protecting another one of his constituents, another representative of the people.

Whitey was never directly involved in defending or advocating for his brother. It could only hurt Billy. But I once heard a story about a local newspaper reporter who had a history of being critical of Billy Bulger. The guy was sitting at Ames Plow, a bar at Faneuil Hall, a national historic site and tourist attraction in downtown Boston, when a man with menacing blue eyes sat down beside him. The reporter must have shit himself when he saw who it was. The newly arrived patron looked squarely at the reporter and said, "Listen, I'm Whitey Bulger. I kill people. You better watch what you write." And then the man with the scary eyes was gone. Big brother looking after little brother.

For a young kid, who couldn't imagine winning in life the legitimate way, Southie was its own world with its own rules. Why ever leave? There was always a hustle or deal to make, cheap rent or even a slot in the housing projects to score, and a bar on every corner where you had friends to share the booze, the fun, the stories. And, if you wanted to go legit, there was always a city counselor or ward boss or hack who could put you in touch with the right government job. A phone call and a promise of a campaign contribution and, a few Mondays later, you were at the parks and recreation department, housing department, water department, or some other bureaucratic hole in the wall where you could feed at the public trough for as long as you wanted.

All most of us needed was Southie, and nothing else. It was especially easy if you were a tough, self-reliant hooligan and big-time, moneymaking drug dealer. I was all of that. Me and the boys had our drug-running, our working out, our fighting, and, yeah, our fucking. Oh, how we fucked. It's hilarious, but to most of the girls in South Boston, we were it: fit, tough, self-reliant, and usually holding a thick roll of cash. What else could a girl want? Well, what else could a Southie girl want? I had four hat tricks during my time in South Boston. A hat trick in hockey means scoring three times in one game, but in Southie, it meant screwing three sisters in the same family — though not at the same time, of course. After all, I had my morals. And I had four hat tricks.

Something of a vigilante mentality operated in the neighborhood. One of my most memorable, and definitely most enjoyable, fights was against the Guardian Angels, a quasi-volunteer community policing — in other words, "vigilante" — group. The majority of the Angels are black and Hispanic, but even so, none of the black, brown, or white neighborhoods in Boston warmed to their presence.

One hot July night in 1984, eight Guardian Angels decided to do a walk through South Boston, wearing their stupid-looking red berets, white T-shirts with red-winged logos, and black combat boots, for no other reason than to act macho and cause problems. They didn't get far before they got their asses kicked.

That should have ended it. In terms of violent crime, Southie was maybe the safest neighborhood in the city. We didn't want the Guardian Angels there, but they decided to come back the very next night – thirty strong. We knew they were coming. Me and Frankie and the boys weren't interested in diplomacy or negotiating. We were just going to ambush them to send our message home.

They arrived by subway. All black and brown, with maybe a couple yellows thrown in for good measure. They were joined by an army of Boston's finest, about one cop for every marcher. Twenty of us were hanging around below the stairs that connected the train platform to the street. Without a word, the Angels fell into formation, five rows of six across, like drum majorettes. The cops lined up to the left and right of the formation.

The Guardian Angel dick in charge raised his fist, and, flanked by the police, they started marching down Gallivan Boulevard, into the heart of Southie. Our plan was simple. We'd wait until this little parade made it into the projects. Then we'd attack. If we did it right, the police would be forced to chase us, thereby leaving the Angels without protection and vulnerable.

When the parade turned onto South Broadway, someone threw a bottle and the yelling started. "Get the fuck out of our neighborhood!" "Motherfuckers, go home!" "Cocksuckers." The cops gave chase and broke ranks. The Angels kept moving forward, maintaining their stoic, hard-ass act.

I zoned in on one marcher, under orders not to break formation, and hauled off with a dope slap. He never saw me coming. Some cops ran over to attend to him. But the Angels kept coming. By this time, the police escort was no more. I teed-up another poor Angel with a crushing blindside. A few minutes later, I blacked out two more Angels to put my tally at four.

A second or so after I laid out my final victim, two black cops began chasing me. I knew that if they caught me, the legal system was the least of my worries. As they were about to tackle me, I saw two white cops I knew. So I screamed, "Help me, officers! These guys are chasing me and are going to beat me up!" My law enforcement friends convinced the black cops to let them take me in for disorderly conduct.

About a week after my knockout fest, I got word from his people that Curtis Sliwa, the founder of the Guardian Angels and an accomplished martial artist, was coming to Boston and that he and I were going to take care of the problem one-on-one. He offered the Boston Common as the site for the fight. I suggested we fight in Columbus Park in Southie where I knew I'd have three projects full of backup. And not only would I knock him out, but I promised to pull his pants down in front of his fellow Angels and spank him. He never accepted my offer.

Maybe it made us feel good, being outlaws but still helping to maintain order on the streets. It made us feel big, helping out old people and even sometimes sticking up for the weak. We also kept the crime organized, which basically meant that Whitey was allowed to oversee everything. One of the biggest ironies is that when Whitey went on the lam in 1995, South Boston became a more dangerous place to live. I could feel and see the difference, walking around the streets, and reading newspaper accounts of Southie crimes. Without Whitey's influence, crazed bottom-feeders started shooting at each other to claim a piece of turf, kids began stumbling across hypodermic needles in the playground, the incidences of car thefts and break-ins and teen suicides rocketed, more women were attacked, and heroin and angel dust started turning young minds to tapioca. But it didn't excuse the fact that he had condoned the poisoning of many of South Boston's youth by allowing his personal battalion of soldiers to sell drugs — marijuana and cocaine — which coincidentally created more stable druggies than those hooked on angel dust and heroin. Where there had been maybe a handful of heroin users five years earlier, suddenly, in a five-month period in 1999, there were at least six fatal overdoses. No wonder residents were putting up signs begging Whitey to return.

I look back now and see a neighborhood that was a fiefdom for me and the boys. We ruled. Or at least we thought we ruled. But there was one thing we didn't understand until it was too late. We may have owned the neighborhood. But Whitey owned us.

A few months after Whitey introduced himself, I met another man who may have been the second most powerful influence on my life. A complex man whose life was destined to end tragically by the Southie mainstays: booze and a bullet.

# The Tough Guys

Johnny Pretzie, known to many as The Tiger, was a local legend. A heavyweight boxer who had fought Rocky Marciano and Jake LaMotta, he'd helped steer two generations of South Boston youth toward a life of clean living and rigorous exercise. Two of his most devoted disciples were Whitey Bulger and Stevie Flemmi, who considered him their personal trainer. Pretzie was tough to figure. Like so many of us in Southie, he was a contributor to, and role model for, kids, yet also a friend to murderers, thieves, and drug dealers. Pretzie was, I later learned, an informant for a smorgasbord of law-enforcement agencies. That Southie mentality again. Work both sides of the fence.

I watched Pretzie in awe for nearly six years before I met him. Finally in 1980 I got in tight with him after he saw me holding my own, outnumbered three-to-one in a bar brawl. He was soon instructing me in training and boxing, and helped train my students at the Academy of Martial Arts, a gym I founded in 1980 in Andrew Square in Southie. I ran my gym for more than six years in different locations in Southie, never making much money but also never turning away a kid who wanted to learn how to protect himself. Pretzie, who was in his sixties at the time, was a big help to me with these kids. Even though he could be crazy when he started to drink, the two of us soon became like father and son.

By hanging with Pretzie, I ran into Whitey more frequently. He'd long admired Pretzie, and he began to take more notice of me. Pretzie was tough and so was I. Another tough guy Whitey admired was Freddy Weichel, the guy who gave me the ass-kicking introduction to the world of judo. Weichel was not only a judo instructor, but also, during the 1970s, an occasional legman for Whitey. Whitey trusted and liked Freddy so much that he asked him if he wanted to take over the drug business in Southie. Freddy refused because he had his own thing and didn't want to be owned by anyone.

The Weichel boys may not get the big play that other criminals like

Flemmi and Weeks do, but in Southie the seventies were, in many ways, the Weichel years. Freddy and his two brothers, Stephen and David Weichel, wreaked enough havoc to make me look sweet. They wove in and out of Whitey Bulger's life, but their connections to him turned out to be some of the most critical of all his relationships.

Freddy Weichel became one of my closest friends, but Stephen, who was four years older than Freddy, died before I had the chance to get to know him, and David, two years younger than Freddy, went away to jail shortly thereafter. Freddy's path wasn't that much straighter, but for a time he was nearly as notorious as Whitey. Like so many other Southie heavyweights, however, the door to the big time slammed shut in his face and he found himself staring at prison bars instead.

Stephen was twenty-five when he was killed on the night of September 25, 1973, in a gang dispute that was rumored to involve two of Whitey's top henchmen, Stevie Barron and Jimmy Winn. Stephen was taken out in a gunfight near a Dunkin' Donuts on West Broadway in Southie by Bernie O'Reilley, who was arrested for the murder. Still, the names of Barron and Winn kept surfacing as major participants. We suspected Freddy and David held Barron and Winn responsible and would try to even the score, we just didn't know when.

It didn't take long before David Weichel emerged as the more menacing of the two remaining Weichels. He feared no one. Not even Whitey Bulger. But because the brothers were cagey and pulled off a lot of jobs, Whitey saw promise in them. They paid their share of tribute, and they might be useful in his ever-growing syndicate, of which Freddy would soon become a member. Also, by bringing them in, Whitey could monitor them to ensure they weren't becoming too powerful on their own. You see, Whitey had many ways of getting rid of his competition before he could be challenged.

In the beginning, the Weichels were good sources of money for Whitey. But David Weichel soon became too crazy even for Whitey. Take what happened at the Mullen Club on O Street in Southie. After hanging around with Whitey and some of his other friends for a few hours, just talking and relaxing, Freddy Weichel connected with a girl, and then left with her, leaving his car in front of the club. Freddy and David shared a pad, but Freddy was banging away most of the night and didn't return home, nor did he check in. The Weichel brothers were very close and always stayed in contact. David had no idea where Freddy was, but he did know that Freddy had been hanging with Whitey the previous evening.

At ten the next morning, David went over to the Mullen Club and found Freddy's car out front. No one knew where Freddy was. So, David, a semi-schizoid, decided Whitey must have done something to Freddy. He grabbed two .357s and went on the hunt, canvasing the neighborhood until someone told him that Whitey had just come into the Mullen Club and was sitting at a table in the back, having a meeting.

David sprinted for the bar entrance, guns drawn. He blew into the bar like Yosemite Sam, a .357 in each hand, a finger firmly planted on each trigger, screaming, "Where the fuck is Whitey? I'm gonna kill that motherfucker!"

Patrons hit the floor, but where was Whitey? As David was bursting in the front, King Shit was running out the back. Less than an hour later, David found out that his brother had been okay all along. David and Whitey both survived that potential disaster, but it was another notch in the scorecard Whitey kept on the Weichels; another reason to move David to a high spot on the hit list. But these hits didn't happen overnight. David wasn't strolling around Broadway with a target on his back.

He climbed even higher on the list one day when he and Freddy were walking down the street. Whitey, out driving with Flemmi and Weeks, saw the Weichel brothers and pulled his car over to talk to David about money David owed him. Whitey said, "Now, David, you owe the fucking money and you're gonna have to pay us."

Nutso David leaned into the car and said, "Hey, Jimmy, you're fucking beat. You're not getting a fucking dime from me." Then he walked away from the car like he was king of the world. Freddy followed him, but took care of the debt the next day. If Whitey hadn't liked Freddy so much it would have been too late to save David's life.

In the mid-1970s Southie was like the Wild West, with a code of frontier justice. Whitey ran the show, but not with the iron fist that he would exercise from the late 1970s up until 1995 when he went on the lam. In 1974, it was still something of a free-for-all as rival factions warred over Southie real estate. And the Weichels were in the middle of too much of it.

On the night of October 2, 1974, a neighborhood death squad, led by Barron and Winn, came looking for Freddy Weichel before he and David could avenge brother Stevie's murder. The Weichel boys were taking their time before they settled the score, but no one doubted it was coming. The brothers had no problem keeping Stevie's murderers on edge, waiting for the attack. Likewise, Barron and Winn were taking their time: hits were rarely spontaneous, and David and Freddy were elusive, keeping low profiles during the daylight hours, never stationary targets. But somebody had to get hit eventually. David Weichel had been hobbled by a drive-by shooting a few weeks earlier, when he'd been unable to run fast enough from a car spraying bullets at his back. He was, temporarily, out of commission, so the plan was to deep-six Freddy while he had no brotherly backup, then deal with David later. It was never proven, but the inside word is that two assassins showed up at the Dorchester triple-decker where Freddy lived. But there was a screw-up in the way the nameplates had been fixed to the mailboxes. So the guys with the guns rammed through the wrong door. Freddy's sixty-three-year-old step-grandmother Elizabeth Hardiman, her sister Dorothy Boughman, and Dorothy's son Glenn Boughman fell victim to the first law of the hired gun: leave no witnesses. Ironically, Freddy wasn't even home that night.

David and Freddy weren't sure who was behind the hit. And no one was ever arrested for the triple murder. But the names of Stevie Barron and Jimmy Winn kept coming up. A few months later, Freddy and David showed up at Barron and Winn's apartment, ostensibly for a talk, but packing handguns. When the chitchat ended, Winn managed to flee, but Barron took four bullets to the chest. Dead before he hit the floor. Self-defense, according to David, but, in 1975, on Winn's ID, he was convicted of second-degree murder and given a sentence of life imprisonment. He's still serving it today. Freddy was convicted of a lesser charge of assault with a dangerous weapon. Through some unbelievable back-room deal making, Freddy walked out of the courtroom on probation.

Now Freddy was on the street, and you can imagine how he felt about Winn. But Whitey Bulger and Stevie Flemmi were protecting Winn, who must have been a trusted gopher for Whitey. Whitey made his feelings clear when he called for Freddy to come to Triple O's bar and told him, "I know you're not happy with Winn, but I have to give you a little bit of advice. Stay away from him. I don't want anything to happen to him. You hear?"

"Yeah, sure, Jimmy," Freddy said. "Whatever you say."

Two days after their meeting, a fire broke out in the triple-decker where Winn lived, burning it to the ground. The day after the fire, Freddy called one of Whitey's top men, Joey Murphy, and said, "Joey, I just want you to

know I had nothing to do with burning that rat bastard's house down."
Yeah, nothing.

Years later, after we learned that Whitey had long been an informant, Freddy said he should have known that Whitey was full of shit back in 1974, when Whitey protected Winn. That it didn't add up that the high priest of the "code of honor" was sticking up for snitches like Winn. But Whitey was the best actor any of us ever knew.

Things got worse for Freddy on May 31, 1980, when he and Tommy Barrett, a second-rate thug, ran into Robert LaMonica (no relation to Rosie, who had introduced me to Al Nugent five years earlier), a Southie kid who'd already had a problem with Barrett over some girl. Barrett got out of the car and got his ass kicked by LaMonica.

The fight ended with Barrett on the ground, but early the next morning, around 12:15 A.M., he allegedly ambushed LaMonica as he entered his girlfriend's apartment building in Braintree, blowing his head off with a .38. The local cops couldn't solve it, but a break came at the end of July when a state trooper uncovered an eyewitness who placed Freddy Weichel running from the scene of LaMonica's murder.

Freddy was not unduly worried. First of all, he hadn't killed LaMonica. Second, he had what he thought was an incontrovertible alibi: an FBI special agent named Johnny Connolly, who could vouch that he was sitting at a bar in downtown Boston with Freddy when LaMonica was killed. "Really, I thought I was all set," Freddy told me later. "I was at the Exchange Bar with Connolly when LaMonica was killed. Connolly offered to buy me a beer that night. And I thought to myself, Shit, that's the first time this cheap prick ever offered to buy me a drink."

Even better, Johnny Connolly knew Freddy and was a Southie native. The two weren't friends, and Freddy was never an informant, but he knew Connolly was a long-time acquaintance of Whitey Bulger. As a teenager, Whitey, already something of a legend, had intervened in a beating Connolly was getting from a gang of local toughs. Whitey told the bullies to take a hike and then bought Connolly an ice cream. That was the start of a lifelong friendship, even though the two pursued careers on opposite sides of the law. Some said that Connolly felt something like hero worship for Whitey. Others wondered why an FBI agent was seen late at night talking with a crime lord down by the South Boston waterfront. After all, wasn't it Johnny Connolly's job to put Whitey Bulger in prison?

Then there was the way Connolly dressed on the job. Not in the dark suits and solid ties typically worn by FBI agents, but like a Don wanna-be, in Armani suits and gold jewelry.

I knew about Freddy's alibi because, after he was picked up, I was at Connolly's Thomas Park condo in Southie, having coffee with Connolly and Johnny Pretzie. Connolly liked Pretzie a lot and the two of them were very close. "I hope Freddy beats this charge," I told the FBI agent. "I like the guy. He's my judo instructor and he has always shown me respect."

"He has no worries, Ed," Connolly assured me, looking right at me and Pretzie. "He was with me at the time of the murder, having a beer at the Exchange."

As soon as Freddy learned he was going to be pinched, he asked Whitey to call Connolly. Whitey told Freddy that the cops didn't have anything on him and that the entire mess would be laughed out of court. As a matter of fact, it was such a laugher that it wasn't a good idea to bring Connolly into it. He also told Freddy to give him five thousand to ensure a low bail. Freddy did.

But a few days later when Freddy was arraigned for first-degree murder, the judge set bail at a million dollars. Freddy was pissed. Would Whitey do this to a loyal lieutenant just to score a lousy five grand? A few days later, the judge suddenly reduced bail to five thousand. There was almost no one Whitey couldn't touch.

But Whitey was wrong; Freddy was up against it after all. Freddy sent an emissary to make sure that Connolly would corroborate Freddy's alibi, and the word that came back from Connolly was this: "I can't do anything to help him, but I won't do anything to hurt him either." Translation: "Something is going on here intended to screw you over in the worst way."

By this time, Tommy Barrett, LaMonica's supposed killer, had fled the state and was living in California; Freddy had advised him to take a vacation. If I were Freddy, I would have deep-sixed the code and turned over that dirtball Barrett. But Freddy kept his mouth shut.

Freddy hired a defense attorney named Anthony Cardinale. Today, Cardinale is *the* man in terms of getting gangsters off. But, unfortunately for Freddy, this was the first murder trial Cardinale had ever tried. The fix was in. The state offered Freddy a chance to plead to second-degree murder with the possibility of parole, instead of the mandatory life for first-degree murder. Freddy said no way; he was innocent.

On the basis of one shaky eyewitness, Freddy, then twenty-nine, was convicted on August 20, 1981, of first-degree murder and sentenced to life without the possibility of parole. He went to prison for life because he refused to disgrace himself. He believed he knew why he'd been set up; he was a sacrificial lamb offered up to protect someone else. But he was missing a major part of the equation, and it would be twenty years before any of us would be able to complete the math.

As 1981 came to a close and Freddy was settling into life behind bars, I kept busy teaching students at the Andrews Square Athletic Club, as well as training for what would be the first of my three victories in the Eastern United States Kung Fu Heavyweight Division Championships. After winning three in a row, I was given the title of SiFu, which means teacher or master, and is the equivalent of a third-degree black belt in karate.

Our first kung fu tournament was held at the Dorothy Quincy Hall in the John Hancock Auditorium on October 25, 1981; athletes from all over the northeast competed for the Eastern United States championship. The hometown crowd went nuts as I faced my final opponent, a 6' 3", 230-pound, three-time New England champion from Worcester named Johnny Washington.

Washington was good. I was already dazed when, with a few seconds remaining in the second round, he hooked a thunderous punch to the side of my head. That rocked me, but I was still able to grapple with him and tie him up until the round was out.

My head was still ringing when I came out for the final round. Fifteen seconds into the round, figuring I was more hurt than I really was, Washington let his guard down. Taking advantage of that, I executed a perfect reverse spin kick to his temple that knocked him out cold. Game, match, point, championship: Eddie Mac.

When I wasn't in the ring, I was raging with Frankie, working construction, working as a bouncer, and breaking into homes. With the exception of the gym and martial arts training, to which I gave full attention, everything else was half-assed, even the B&Es. I was a classic low-level thug. But life was exciting. Hey, I was a brawler, womanizer, and thief, who almost always carried a gun. With that profile, staying off the obituary page was a dicey proposition.

Once a month, I visited Freddy Weichel in Walpole State Prison, a maximum-security facility twenty-five miles south of Boston. It wasn't long before Freddy had established himself — like his brother David, who served time with him for a while in Walpole, as well as in Leavenworth and other prisons — as one of the most respected inmates in the joint. He had all the contacts, inside and outside the walls. If Whitey, or anyone else, needed a new inmate protected, or another punished, Freddy would handle it. He even devised ways to have himself put in solitary confinement so beautiful women could visit him while the guard agreed to take a walk down the hall.

It was a miracle that I didn't end up in Walpole in a cell next to Freddy. Trouble always found me. Nearly a year after my memorable encounter with Whitey Bulger and Stevie Flemmi, I was up against some other nasty members of the Southie crime world. I was twenty-three years old; smart money in Vegas wouldn't bet I'd see twenty-four.

I owed this near disaster to my good friend Barry Wong, who owned a Chinese restaurant in Southie called the Ho Toy. On a December evening in 1981, at three in the morning, Barry phoned to tell me that someone had called him to report intruders in his restaurant. My place was a lot closer to the Ho Toy than his, so he asked if I could run over there and hold the fort until he arrived. I woke up one of my toughest students, Mike Binda, who was fifteen but looked years older, and picked him up ten minutes later. When we got to the Ho Toy, I looked through the window and saw three guys laughing and eating. They were average height but looked to weigh more than two hundred pounds each. When Mike and I stepped through the door, they looked at us without a hell of a lot of concern. "Hey, motherfucker, what the fuck do you want?" one of them asked me.

I was on my guard and did not want to cause any unnecessary problems. I said, "Hey, calm down. My friend owns this place and just got a call that someone was in here. He asked me to stop by and see what's going on."

Tough Guy Number One pulled a big double-edged knife out of a drawer and started stabbing the counter. "You want some of this, pal?" he asked. "And not only will you get some of this, but my friend here, he's got a nine millimeter, and my other buddy is packing, too." His buddies chuckled and continued digging into the food.

Well, they were messing with the wrong guy. I stepped back, reached inside my coat and pulled out a .357 magnum snub-nose pistol. I went into a police stance and pointed the barrel directly at the tough guy with the mouth. "As God is my witness," I shouted, "if any of you cocksuckers take your hands off the counter, I'm going to blow your fucking heads off!"

The guy with the big mouth put his hands on the counter. One of the other two guys yelled, "Whoa, whoa, wait a minute! Shit, he was only kidding! Everything is cool!"

I didn't let my guard down. "I said I'll kill you motherfuckers if you move."

"Wait, wait, this isn't what it looks like, pal," said Tough Guy Number Two, who seemed to have taken over as lead mouth. He had black curly hair and blue eyes. "I'm Kevin and this is Jackie." He pointed to Tough Guy Number One. "This is Chucka. We're friends of Barry's and we ordered some food but were late picking it up. When we got here, the door was open so we came in and got the food. We're not looking for any trouble and I apologize for my friend. He's had too much to drink tonight."

"Listen, I'm not looking for any trouble either," I said, maintaining my ready-to-fire stance. "Let's just stay cool and wait for Barry."

So we waited there: me, Mike, Kevin, Jackie, and Chucka. Mike, who had balls of steel, didn't flinch. I kept my gun trained on Kevin, the ringleader. No one moved. Everybody was on full alert. Ten minutes later, I heard the front door of the Ho Toy open behind me and . . . "Oh, shit, Eddie, put that gun away! These guys are my friends!" Barry had arrived.

I lowered the gun and backed up as Barry ran between me and Mike, and the three guys behind the counter. A wave of relief rolled over their faces. I felt the same way, but I still kept the gun at my side with my finger on the trigger. All of us shook hands. Kevin, with a smirk on his face, said, "Hey, it was a misunderstanding, pal. Thanks for not killing us."

"Hell, Eddie, you had me nervous back there," Mike admitted on our ride home.

"Yeah, but you did great," I told him. And I meant it. Mike would become my brother-in-law three years later when I married his sister Carolyn. He is a huge source of pride for me. After spending three years in the Navy, he joined the Marine Corps. Today, he's active in the Air Force. That night, I knew I could have counted on him if I'd needed him.

I was none too happy to learn the next day that the guy who introduced himself to me as Kevin was none other than Kevin Weeks, Whitey's number-one bodyguard. Chucka was a hard-nosed bouncer at one of Whitey's favorite hangouts, and Jackie was reputed to be a stone-cold killer. I had to do damage control and fast. I didn't want these guys on the hunt for me.

I wasted no time in explaining the story to Pretzie, who brought me down to the South Boston Liquor Mart, where I straightened things out with Whitey and Weeks. Whitey told me he was impressed, that I had "big balls." Word was reinforced on the street, and in Whitey's inner sanctum, that I was someone not to be fucked with.

# Inside and Outside the Ring

During the early eighties, as I improved as an athlete, I also enhanced my reputation as a vicious street fighter. Still, I'm glad to say that there were times when, by some strange twist of fate, I found myself righting a wrong rather than creating one.

An article in the *South Boston Tribune* titled "South Boston Man Hero" told the story: "On Monday, November 1, 1982, while visiting relatives in Jamaica Plain, Edward J. MacKenzie noticed that an elderly woman was being harassed by five men. [There were actually four; the newspaper story was incorrect here.] Mr. MacKenzie stopped his car and went to her assistance. While others just watched, Eddy [sic] asked the youths to stop tormenting the woman. Their answer was to pull out a knife; in the ensuing moments, 3 of the youths got a vacation to the Boston City Hospital while the other is still running." Yeah, that was me. Mr. Do-Gooder.

In the ring, though, I showed no mercy. My trainers nicknamed me "La Machine," because you could hit me all night long and I wouldn't quit. Sometimes my trainer would have to jump into the ring to restrain me. Frankie, on the other hand, was a pure light heavyweight pugilist, weighing between 168 and 178 pounds. He looked like Hercules and was ten times more disciplined than I was. Unlike Frankie, I could never be bothered watching what I ate. I wasn't fat — but I sure wasn't skinny.

I ran three to five miles a day, and trained in the gym for at least two hours a day, sparring, hitting the heavy bag and the speed bag, doing lots of sit-ups and jumping rope. My years in the Southie rings taught me everything I know about protecting my body. In Southie, boxing has always been huge. Every year, on St. Patrick's Day, we held the Baby Golden Gloves tournament at the Municipal Building, to which fighters brought their kids, ages five to thirteen, to box. All the politicians attended this event and cheered like crazy. Many South Boston youth fought at the Lowell Sun Auditorium in Lowell for the title of New England Golden Glove champion, which I won in 1986. But, from 1981 through 1983, when

I won the Eastern United States Heavyweight Kung Fu Championships in kickboxing, kickboxing was my ticket to ride.

Whitey knew about my fighting skills. He even sent some of his up-and-coming gangsters to the gym where I taught martial arts and conditioning. The guy was paranoid about appearing in public, but he still watched lots of my matches, sitting in the back, one eye on me in the ring, the other on the door.

I never knew, nor cared, if he was there. When I was in the ring, nothing else mattered except landing that punch or that kick. To this day, whenever I enter the boxing gym and smell the stale sweat, the wintergreen tang of liniment, and the aged leather of boxing gloves — when I hear the rappitty-rap whirring cadence of a fighter skipping rope or the shift and pivot of feet on canvas, along with the whoomp, whoomp of a glove-encased fist slamming into a heavy bag — I feel a rush of adrenaline, a chill deep inside my body like nothing else.

Kickboxing, which uses both legs and fists, seemed a natural progression from the movements of kung fu and Tiger Crane. So, I became a heavyweight kickboxer, meaning I never fought anybody weighing less than 202 pounds. Because the Professional Karate Association wouldn't let the Massachusetts Boxing Commission control kickboxing, the sport was banned in Massachusetts. As a result, I fought most of my matches in Rhode Island and New Hampshire.

The rules are simple. No hitting below the belt. Use your legs as well as your fists. If you teach a boxer how to block kicks, there is no kickboxer in the world that can beat him in the ring, in my opinion. When the boxer plants his feet, he knows how to create a more solid foundation than the kickboxer. For me, the attraction of kickboxing over boxing was the fanciness of the kickboxing. I liked jumping up and throwing kicks. I never had any aspirations to become world champ of either kickboxing or boxing. I just liked the whole fight game because it's in a class of its own. You get big respect if you win. And, deep down, I relished beating the snot out of people. I'd look at my opponent and see the face of someone who had abused me when I was a foster kid and want to hurt him the way he'd hurt me. Later, those faces weren't as clear. I fought 'cause I wanted to win.

No matter how many kickboxing matches or street fights I won, I was still afraid before every fight. Not of bodily harm or pain, but of being knocked out by a lucky punch. And of being humiliated in front of my friends. But when that bell rang, the fear evaporated, and I threw everything I had at the other guy. That's how I knocked out seventeen of my eighteen opponents.

# Losing Frankie

'll never understand why Frankie did it. Maybe he needed more money for his boxing career than he got from our B&Es. I would've helped him get more cake. God knows we were tight. I'm sure Frankie didn't want to do that heist. He was talked into it by two friends. He never told me about it and never asked me to participate. But I wouldn't have even if I'd been asked. I wasn't into armed robberies.

On the morning of July 17, 1984, a Wells Fargo truck making a delivery stopped in front of a Bay Bank in Medford. Frankie's job was to score the cash. There were so many different stories about exactly what happened that day that I was never sure which one to believe. The most believable version is that one of Frankie's two partners put a gun to the back of the Wells Fargo security guard who came around to open the back of the truck. Then Frankie jumped into the truck to grab the loot. The third partner was supposed to jump into the front seat and keep a gun on the driver. But something went wrong and the third partner never did his job. So the driver of the truck turned around and shot Frankie through the porthole in the window separating the guards from the back of the truck.

The worst part of the whole thing was that Frankie wasn't hurt that bad. But his two "partners" took off and abandoned him. Frankie was in such amazing shape that he managed to drag himself to the getaway car. Again, his partners screwed him, switching cars, taking the money with them, and leaving Frankie to bleed to death. I'll never get over the fact that they left him for dead. I would have carried him on my back.

Frankie had filled the grooves on his fingertips with glue so his fingerprints couldn't be identified. I had no idea he had done that until his death. He must have done it just before the robbery so that no one could identify his fingerprints in the truck after they got away with the money. This was the biggest heist he'd ever committed. It took a day until the police figured out who had been killed.

I wanted to kill the bastards who screwed him. And Ma MacDonald was out of her mind with grief; Frankie was her favorite. The funeral was held at O'Brien's Funeral Home on Dorchester Street in Southie. Five or six hundred mourners lined the streets outside O'Brien's. I was a pallbearer. They'd had to comb the jungles of South America for his brother Johnny, now a Lieutenant Commander in the Navy Seals, and pluck him out with a helicopter.

Frankie was laid out in his purple boxing robe, with rosaries wrapped around his hands, made enormous by boxing. When Helen tried to rip Frankie's body out of the coffin, it took three of us to pull her off him. I can still hear her screams. Then, incredibly, I glanced up and happened to notice one of Frankie's "partners" at the back of the crowd. I reached for the .357 magnum strapped to my waist, but I felt another hand touch mine and saw Johnny MacDonald staring down at me.

"I have to kill the motherfucker, Johnny," I choked out.

"He's not worth it, Eddie," he said into my ear. I pulled my hand away from the cold steel.

I found out later that there were detectives at the funeral. There was an investigation into the robbery, but, to my knowledge, no one was arrested. Like everybody else with an ear to the street, I knew who did it, but Johnny's words stayed with me. I did make sure that the MacDonald family got Frankie's equal share from the heist, about $100,000, but Johnny would have no part of the blood money and threw it into the ocean.

It's been close to twenty years without Frankie. He was twenty-four, on the verge of turning pro. If only he'd kept to the brawling and small break-ins with me. He was never meant to be a big-time hoodlum; he was meant for greatness in the ring. God, I loved him. Like no one else on the planet. I spent hours after the funeral just remembering Frankie and the fun and trouble we'd shared. One memory kept coming at me from nine years earlier, during that summer of 1975 when we'd nearly gotten killed shooting at Columbia Point. Frankie, who was sixteen then, hadn't gotten laid yet. By then, I was banging all the time, but he was basically a quiet kid who spent most of his time working out and committing B&Es with me. But I took care of that little problem. And when I did, I unleashed an animal that started fucking everything in sight.

I had done it in style for my boy, Frankie. One night, the two of us were driving around in a Fleetwood '69 Caddy, a giant of a car, on the Franklin Parkway that connects JP and Roxbury. Frankie was driving and we were having a few beers when we picked up a girl who'd been hitchhiking. She wasn't bad looking so we put her in back and said, "What do you want to do now?"

"Anything you like," she said. Ten seconds later, I was in the back seat with her, banging her like crazy. I was lifting her cheeks way up in the air, blowing my wad all over the place while Frankie was cruising around.

When I caught a glimpse of his face in the rearview mirror, I knew his time had arrived. I stopped and said, "Frankie, pull over, it's your time. Pop your cherry, Bro." He pulled over, got into the back, and I began driving around. It was pitch black, and he was naked on top of her and couldn't see where I was driving. I pulled up to Papa Gino's, a local pizza hangout, and saw thirty of our friends. They all came over to the car and began peering in while he was pounding away.

You had to see his face when he finally looked up and saw them all staring in at him. "You asshole!" he screamed at me. I sped the hell out of there as fast as I could. But, man, did I laugh.

Frankie always broke my balls over that time, but he thanked me in the long run. It was unbelievable what happened to him after that night. He was a regular Don Juan. He could never get enough. And I could never get enough of him. No one will ever understand me like Frankie. No one will care about me or make me laugh as much as Frankie. I miss him every day.

# Family Man

I don't know if I could have gotten through Frankie's death without Carolyn Binda. We'd met in my gym in Andrew Square in 1981. She was sixteen and I was twenty-three. Her older brother, Mike, was one of my best students, and the kid who stood by me during the confrontation at Ho Toy. For two years she was also a student, coming in a couple of times a week to learn kickboxing, kung fu, Tiger Crane. The gym had become a hangout for teens, so sometimes she came in to meet friends. She was outgoing, sexy and beautiful, with long dark blond hair, big blue eyes, and a great ass. I fell for her right away.

By the end of 1983, she was pregnant. I don't know exactly how it happened. I called it a "sperm of the moment" thing. I told her to have an abortion. But I was sure the kid was mine, and when she refused, I knew I'd have to do the right thing and marry her. She came from a decent family and I wasn't going to let her go through the pregnancy alone. But I also wasn't going to have her walk down the aisle pregnant, so we decided to wait until our child was born. Courtney was born just five days before we lost Frankie. On July 12, 1984, I was at the hospital watching my firstborn enter the world. She was perfect. I couldn't take my eyes off her. The next week, I was in a funeral home, staring at the body of my best friend.

I started to make a little dough working for Whitey, so I could take good care of Carolyn and my daughter. I made a pledge the day Courtney was born that she'd never have to live the life I'd led. She'd never sleep under a porch or go to school with a rotten apple or a piece of baloney for her lunch. Someone would always care whether she lived or died, whether she was happy or sad, safe or in danger. Eighteen years later, I've kept that pledge.

When Courtney was eight months old, Carolyn and I got married at St. Augustine's Church in South Boston. From the beginning, Courtney has been the joy of my life. I wouldn't let her out of my arms. I fed her and changed her and spent more time taking care of her than Carolyn did. Courtney's a big girl, built a little like me, real powerful. Today, she's continuing her hockey career as a star goalie at a prep school. I think and worry about her all the time, but mostly I just love her. She's been in private schools all her life and never wanted for anything. I've never missed one of her hockey games. I've taught her how to fight and helped her build self-confidence. I've taken her to countless movies and discussed them with her afterward, always trying, often times unsuccessfully, to find some lesson in each one. I never let a day go by without at least talking to her. When she graduated in June 2002 from Monsignor Ryan Memorial High School in Dorchester, a private Catholic school, I bought her a 2001 Mitsubishi Eclipse. There is nothing I wouldn't do for Courtney or my four other girls.

The one thing I want for my kids is that they never have to go through what I did when I was growing up. I'm always thinking of what I was like when I was their age, and do everything in my power to make their life happier and easier. I try to be a good role model for them and, in that vein, haven't forgotten the two people who, when I was a kid, were the most decent role models that I knew: Mom and Pops Cossitt.

Growing up, I had no idea what a mother was like, but Mom Cossitt was the closest thing to a mother I ever had. She paid attention to me and smiled at me. She didn't hit me. I'll always be grateful to her for that. Pops died in 1998, but Mom lives in Colorado now, near her son. I call Mom often and write her, too. Whenever she comes to Boston to visit her daughter Linda, I see her. My girls visit Mom when she's in town and call her Grandma.

Their daughter, Linda Cossitt, is eight years older than me. She used to baby-sit for the kids at the home when her parents weren't there. Today, she occasionally helps me out with Devin and Kayla. One night she complained that I spoil them rotten by letting them stay up late or sneak cookies at bedtime. Linda's right. I am too much of a softy with all my girls. But I can't help it. I can't forget what it was like growing up, having no ice cream from the ice cream truck, never getting to watch a good cartoon or the end of a movie because it was past bedtime and listening to the kids at school the next day telling me what I missed.

Linda also said, "Eddie, don't you remember how it was with Mom?"

And I said, "Yes, Linda, I do. It sucked." There wasn't an extra cent anywhere to buy any of us kids a treat. I'll always remember how hard life was then. I don't want my girls to know that kind of life.

Things were pretty good for Carolyn and me until March 1986, when Carolyn was seven months pregnant with our second daughter, Lauren. Carolyn called me at the gym and we talked for a few minutes. When the phone call ended, I turned my attention back to the cute chick I was banging on a part-time basis; time to give her a lesson in the fine art of oral sex. I took the receiver off the hook so that I could teach undisturbed.

When I put the phone back on its receiver, it rang ten seconds later. Carolyn was on the line, hysterical. She hadn't hung up after our call. "I heard everything, you piece of shit!" she yelled. "Your bags will be on the front stairs by the time you get home!" And they were. The marriage was over that night, but not my relationship with Courtney and Lauren, or even with Carolyn. She never let me down. She's the best mother imaginable and never wavered from her responsibility to our children.

When she threw me out, I was ashamed at what I'd done to Courtney and our unborn child. I knew that, like a dog, I had done my thinking with my dick. I begged her to let me stay. I promised it would never happen again, but Carolyn knew better. While I realized there was no way to make her change her mind, I also knew that she would never tear me away from our children, and that I would never abandon them. And that, even though we could never be man and wife again, I'd always love and respect her.

I'd screwed up again. I may have had a wife and two kids but I was still a street-hustling, irresponsible, angry predator without direction, moving from scam to scam, danger to danger, hanging out with all the wrong people. And getting closer to Whitey with every step.

# Connolly's Corner Café, Established 1985

In 1996, the TV show *Unsolved Mysteries* devoted a segment to the FBI's search for Whitey, which has since been repeated several times. One of the men interviewed was shown only in silhouette, his identity concealed for his own protection. That was funny to us guys from Southie, because any of us watching recognized the talking shadow almost instantly. First of all, we all knew he'd blabbed, but it was also hard to miss the similarity between the shadow and a 6'5", 260-pound guy with a head that resembled a peanut and a body that was a dead ringer for the fat-bellied, long-necked anteater in the *Pink Panther* cartoons we used to watch as kids.

His name was Timmy Connolly (no relation to FBI agent Johnny Connolly), a cowardly but very smart pussy, a real estate and financial scam artist, a small-time jeweler, a bar owner, and a king dirtball. In 1991, he turned state's evidence, ratting on Whitey and many of the boys from Southie in exchange for the feds forgiving an entire file of illegal activity. A lot of what he said was bullshit, but the government bought enough of it to score him a sweet deal. Connolly is now in the federal witness protection program. He'd better stay there. There are a lot of people in Southie who want to meet up with him — and not to discuss the good ol' days.

Timmy and I first met in 1981 when he came to my gym on Andrews Street. He was interested in working out and learning boxing and martial arts. He was a big guy, about 6' 5" and two hundred and forty pounds, maybe two years younger than me. He talked a tough game, but was a real pussy. He wanted to look like a tough guy, give the impression he was connected.

In 1984, Timmy bought a building on West Broadway in Southie that housed a jewelry store and a bar called the Broadway Casino Tavern. The bar had lots of potential, but at the time it was tough to envision. Dirty, poorly lit, it catered to a clientele of the chronically drugged out, drunk, jobless, and stupid. Most of the patrons were harmless, except for one biker gang that was causing Timmy big problems. They were mouthy and, in an attempt to claim the place as their own, started to act threatening.

Timmy knew there was no way that the bar, which he'd renamed Connolly's Corner Café, would become a winner if the bikers stayed. It didn't take him long to come to me, begging for help. I told him I'd take care of his problem. And I wasn't even going to ask him for any money in exchange. But it was understood that he was going to owe me big time.

The first thing I did was to case the bar, hang out, look inconspicuous. The bikers were what I expected: Loud-mouthed, acting tough, a bunch of dirty hippies who could have used a bath, shave, and haircut. They were into the black leather thing, with earrings and tattoos. They loved their booze, and probably drugs as well. I took note of everything, from the way they stood to who seemed the most assertive. And, of course, I took note of any weapons. No guns, but a few knives. If my plan worked, they wouldn't even have a chance to use them. I decided the best time to put my plan into motion was at seven on a Wednesday evening, when the place was loaded with bikers, but the population of inoffensive lowlifes was at a minimum.

I recruited Paul Blair, from my Tiger Crane days. He was one of the best, someone as strong and vicious as they come. Someone I didn't have to worry about baby-sitting. We went into the bar a few times during business hours to scout it out. One night after Connolly's was closed, we did a dry run. Finally, we were ready.

On the night of our mission, Paul and I walked into Connolly's. We headed toward the back where the pool tables were located, a good ninety feet from the door. We hung out there for a few minutes surveying the scene. There must have been some thirty people in the bar area, either sitting at the bar itself or standing nearby, nearly all of them bikers. As usual, they were loud and arrogant, pushing people out of their seats and spilling drinks on them, cutting in on a guy dancing with his girl, and insulting people.

No one noticed when Paul and I each pulled on a pair of sap gloves, leather gloves with lead sewn in across the knuckle area — nasty weapons that cops used to use, but which are now illegal. Whitey loved them. You didn't have to be a prizefighter to inflict damage if you wore sap gloves. Nor did you have to worry about hurting your hand. I had a hard-on to beat the world.

I looked at Paul, nodded, and we sprang toward the bar. No one had a chance. Just running and swinging, we smashed everyone, women as well as men. We went right down the bar, busting skulls, jaws, and ribs. What a rush. The bikers were getting thumped, going limp, spilling off the stools. Only a few of them really had time to understand what was happening and try to defend themselves. But those attempts were futile: a weak hands-in-front-of-the-face, and a quick pleading, "No, no, no," before one of us threw a haymaker that parted their hands and crushed their face.

I'm sure the last thing many of these dirtballs remembered before waking up — in an ambulance or the floor of the bar with a paramedic over them — was a bright flash and then darkness. We must have scored twenty knockouts in thirty seconds. The few we didn't get our hands on managed to avoid a beating by falling down and rolling into a fetal position.

We got out of there right away. But, like a good reconnaissance team, we circled back a half hour later. Ambulances and stretchers and paramedics were everywhere, and a number of people were still horizontal. And who was in the middle of the entire mess, walking around, looking concerned? None other than Timmy Connolly. If you didn't know better, you might've figured that the poor prick was upset about what happened.

Mission accomplished.

The next day, I was walking down Broadway when Whitey and Stevie Flemmi stopped their car and motioned me over. As always, Whitey was in the driver's seat. For the past few years, I'd been doing odds and ends for him, having little chats with him at Castle Island, sometimes just to shoot the breeze, other times to get assignments for punching people out and collecting money. Some of the money was from drugs, some was from loan-sharking. I never asked. I just did the job and collected $500 here and $1000 there. Sometimes he just wanted a favor, like training someone how to fight, which I gladly did. He was recruiting me slowly, breaking me in.

"That was an unbelievable piece of work — fucking beautiful," Whitey said when I got over to the car.

"What are you talking about?" I asked with a smile.

"You know what I'm talking about," he said. "I know that was you in there. I found out. That was good stuff."

Then Stevie said over Whitey's shoulder, "Yeah, we heard you were in the Marines. I was in Korea with a lot of Marines." I couldn't help but feel proud of this bond. I knew Flemmi had been a paratrooper in the Army's

82nd Airborne Division. There was no doubt about it; my star was rising ever higher in the bad-guy sky.

After the night of carnage at Connolly's, we spread the word that the bar was protected. Bikers either had to get out or be carried out. From the looks of things over the next few days, the word had been well-heeded. Timmy was impressed with the results. Understanding you don't get something for nothing, it wasn't long before he offered me a manager's job, which I accepted. It was a great way to supplement my income from the gym.

Under my administration, Connolly's started to pick up. I was the doorman, bouncer, bartender, everything. We had a DJ in there five nights a week and we started to pack 'em in — all kinds. In addition to the rough and rowdy Southie partiers, we had a bunch of freaks as well. Drug-crazed bottom-feeders and lowlifes straight out of a methadone clinic. They all looked dirty and glassy-eyed. At times it looked more like the bar in Star Wars; you know, aliens from all over the galaxy. The only ones who looked neat and together were my friends or people I invited. But I didn't care who showed up, as long as they didn't cause problems. No matter how out of it these bums looked, you could never underestimate just how dangerous they could become if provoked.

You had to love the women. They were tougher than most of the guys. They had no teeth, mattresses strapped to their backs, and, for a Budweiser, could outfight any guy in the city. With the wink of an eye to any one of them, if I wanted you bottled — that is, whacked on the side of the head with a bottle — you were bottled.

The first and the fifteenth of every month were our busiest days. Government check day: welfare, Social Security, disability, you name it. People would come in with their checks on Friday, be broke by Monday, and borrow ten bucks from us on Tuesday.

Because the docks were nearby, a lot of American and foreign sailors used to come in. They'd get their liberty and head into town to have fun, and we welcomed them. As long as the money was American, we didn't care who it came from. A lot of vets drank there and we sure didn't want to be inhospitable to anyone serving his country. But some of these guys used to get a few in them, begin to enjoy their freedom a bit too much, and start acting up. Big mistake. I hired a bunch of guys from my gym and, when sailors started to cause problems, we'd peddle some serious damage on them. More than a few got tossed into the dumpster out back. You would've figured that my reputation would save me from having to prove myself in fights. No way. I heard that when Rocky Marciano was heavyweight champion of the world, he'd still run into wise-asses who would challenge him. I believe it.

No doubt about it; Connolly's was becoming a South Boston hot spot. Its popularity wasn't lost on Whitey Bulger. During the mid-1980s, coke was in full swing across the nation, and Southie was no exception. Whitey saw possibilities in the bar — and in me. Before long he moved to take advantage of both. About the time I started working at Connolly's, I became heavily seduced by the drug trade. Until then, I'd certainly filled my rap sheet with plenty of offenses, but drug dealing wasn't one of them. I'd dabbled in drugs myself but was never happy with the loss of control I felt when I used them. They just weren't a big part of my life. Until Whitey.

I didn't want drugs in Connolly's. Too many problems, I figured. But even while I booted dealers from the bar, I saw the demand for drugs and the money that people were willing to spend. Also, a lot of the guys I knew were getting involved in the distribution game, making lots of money. It seemed like easy cake. Maybe I should be grabbing a bigger piece of this life for myself. Here I was, a wife and baby to take care of, working a couple steady, legitimate, but low-paying jobs, winning boxing and kung fu championships, but still scraping to get by. Okay, maybe I wasn't such an honest guy. But I was no big-time drug dealer. Yeah, Whitey was throwing some work at me. But I wanted much more.

I had lots of "good" reasons to enter that world. Hell, I needed more cash just to take care of the kids who came into the gym wanting to work out but unable to pay a cent. I was making a name for myself as a neighborhood mentor to these needy kids. Something about helping them got to me. I'd remember the shitty foster homes I lived in and how the kids used to make fun of the clothes Ronnie and I wore and the lunches we ate. Nothing was more satisfying to me than doing something to make those kids feel better. I worked with them in the gym, teaching them the discipline of martial arts, helping them to solve problems and keep their grades up, improving their physical skills so they could defend themselves on the street. At night, I'd take them to the movies or to Chinatown. I got a special feeling helping them, even when I was working regularly for Whitey. They listened to me. Today, if I won the lottery, there'd be a lot of kids reaping the rewards.

So I felt proud when WCVB-TV Channel 5, a local television station, awarded me the Good Sport Hall of Fame Award in 1983. They spent a day filming me in my gym, working with the boys and girls. For a week the channel ran thirty-second commercials for the station featuring me and the kids. They even invited us to the Boston premiere of *The Natural* with Robert Redford, whom I met personally.

In 1985, when Courtney was just a baby and Carolyn and I were still together, Channel 5 did a story about people giving back to the community for its nightly magazine show *The Chronicle*. They sent the *Boston Globe* columnist Mike Barnicle to our apartment on Norcross Place in Southie, and my gym, to interview me. The segment, which Barnicle narrated, ran for twenty minutes and was terrific.

But it soon became clear that, in order to look after my family, myself, and these kids, I needed a lot more money. Maybe peddling drugs *was* the answer to my financial problems. I never gave a moment's thought to whether I might be doing something bad to accomplish something good. No matter what else I did with my life, I was still a predator, and a hungry predator does what he has to do to fill his belly.

Whitey was well aware of the power that money had over me. He'd scouted me well. And he'd been prepping me to become part of his network. The visit to my apartment, the meeting after the Ho Toy scene, the small jobs he'd thrown my way, the congratulations he offered on my cleanup of Connolly's — he was slowly reeling me in. He didn't waste time shooting the shit with people. I had been fished too well not to take the bait.

Another reason to get me on board was that I was disrupting his cocaine distribution ring. Unbeknownst to me, Whitey was trying to use Connolly's as a hub for drug trafficking. But he was having a tough go of it, because I'd let it be known that drugs were a no-no at the bar and that anybody caught selling or buying or using would get booted out or banged up. I was just trying to do the right thing and keep the problems to a minimum. I didn't need any violations that would close down the club.

But this policy undermined Whitey's business operations. I finally realized this one night when I pounded out one of his distributors who was trying to make a sale in the bar. The next day Whitey showed up at Connolly's to have a talk. "Okay, Ed, I know you didn't know who he was. We aren't going to get into that," he said. "The thing is, though, that I have always shown you respect and you have always shown me respect, and this is just the way it is going to be. You've done fine every time I've asked you to do something to help me out. But now we're going to get a little something different going here. We're going to have our dealers going in here, and they're going to sell coke, pot, and do whatever the fuck they want, and you're going to get an envelope. We're going to take care of you. If this is all right with you, then everything will be fine. If you have a problem with it, then you're out of business. You're done. We'll shut the fucking place down."

If I could undo one moment in my life, that would be it.

If I'd said, "I do have a problem," and taken off instead of deciding to get involved in Whitey's drug trade, I would have saved myself years of grief. But I didn't say those words. No, I toed the line. Of course, Timmy Connolly had already been briefed and brought on board.

The bar quickly became an important cog in Whitey's drug machine, an organization that ran as effectively as his brother's political campaigns and enjoyed almost exclusive control over the cocaine and pot distribution in Southie, Dorchester, and Quincy. Whitey's operation also did a nice piece of business in Charlestown, but it was a tough area to control because the addicts on angel dust were notorious for being driven nuts by the drug.

It didn't take long for me to become blinded by the drug money. I received an envelope weekly that contained, on the average, five thousand in cash. Just for ensuring that Whitey's guys were able to do their business, and no unauthorized dealers were working the bar. I wasn't even commissioned to act if I found an outsider selling at Connolly's. I just reported it and Whitey's boys took care of it themselves. I didn't have to sell a thing. I also made sure that the trade was limited to coke and pot, and maybe some speed. Heroin, acid, and dust were banned.

It was as if everything leading up to working for Whitey — fighting, kickboxing, small-time crime, prison, Army Reserves, Marines — had prepared me for this. I had made it to the big time. And there'd be no turning back. Not unless Whitey decided I was through.

# Dealing

nce I became a drug dealer for Whitey, my life changed. Until then, all I'd been doing in Connolly's was paving the way for Whitey's drug dealers. That was bringing me a nice bit of cash, but I wanted more than just hush money. So, in 1985, after a few short months of taking the hush money, I began dealing drugs. The drug work itself was pretty routine, but excessively profitable. It didn't take long before I became a well-off thug.

When I decided to sell drugs in South Boston, I automatically became part of the Whitey Bulger crime machine. Remember, nothing illegal was done in Southie without his okay. If you ran, or were part of a racket in the neighborhood, then you worked for Whitey. This is part of the underworld system of paying tribute. The greedier or more power-hungry the mob boss, the greater his tribute demand. The more money you made, the more tribute you paid. Whitey was as greedy and as power hungry as they come. Per his order, no drugs were allowed to come into the neighborhood except through his suppliers. Smart. He controlled all the inventory. Whitey knew what was on the street and what his return should be. He was like a medieval king, sucking his subjects dry. Failure to pay tribute meant that you first received a warning. If you didn't heed the warning, then you ended up seriously hurt. No more than two warnings preceded death.

But Whitey was schizophrenic on drugs. If there was money to be made selling something, then Whitey wanted in. Still, the word in Southie has always been that Whitey kept drugs off the streets. Technically, it's true. He kept heroin and angel dust off the streets, but not because he cared about the health of the neighborhood or its future. His prohibition on heroin and dust was inspired by his concern about the health of his crime rackets. He knew from experience that a neighborhood strung out on heroin and dust becomes unmanageable. That aside, Whitey and his army of drug soldiers hooked more kids on coke and pot than we can ever know. Southie was smokin' and snortin' mounds of product all moved under the oversight of James J. "Whitey" Bulger. Whitey made more than a hundred million dollars in the drug trade. And that's a conservative estimate.

Predictably, Billy Bulger eloquently helped to craft the impression that Whitey was anti-drug. In his book, *While the Music Lasts: My Life in Politics,* Billy writes that his older brother was a "physical culturist and kept himself in prime condition. He neither smoked nor drank. He was so concerned with impurities that he would plead with our mother not to spray Flit or other insecticides in our house. He abhorred addictive drugs."

The fact is Whitey didn't do drugs because he wanted to be in top physical condition and on top of his game, which you're not when you're high or drunk. But he made sure that the drugs he "abhorred" got into the hands of those who didn't abhor them. During Whitey's reign the neighborhood was awash in violent death, particularly the violent death of young males. But most of these poor pricks called it on themselves. If I came across a crowd, cops, cruisers, and a white sheet covering a cold, still body, I figured there was a rhyme and a reason for the untimely demise. Almost always, when someone took that bullet, it could be traced back one way or another to Whitey. People got killed for doing stupid things; it was a way of life. As was the infamous Code of Silence, which protected murderers and forced others to take the rap for crimes they did not commit. Today, I prefer to call it the Code of Bullshit.

But back then I bought it. And sold drugs. With Whitey in charge, I was a capable, no-nonsense dealer. When I try to remember his instructions regarding drug distribution or even missions, I realize how little he said to me. During conversations about his philosophy of life, he could be wordy. But when it came to drugs, he was terse, one or two words at most. He was so sly. Of course, his major concern was that he was being taped, but it was more than that. He just didn't want to give you anything at all. He was careful not to have anyone answer directly to him regarding drugs. For that, he had middlemen, like Kevin Weeks, who was his major liaison to me, and my buddy Tommy Dixon.

The distribution and selling quickly became routine. Tommy and I would pick up a couple kilos of cocaine that had come straight from Miami, usually at a safe house in Quincy, called the Vault, that belonged to a relation of Stevie Flemmi. The coke always came in brick form; the shinier and rockier the brick, the better the quality. Usually, Tommy and I went to work around 11 A.M. so we wouldn't attract much attention. At that time of the morning, the cops were usually eating donuts or going to court, so we'd drive over to the Vault, either in my Lincoln or Tommy's.

I remember when Tommy bought a BMW and Whitey went nuts. Made him get rid of it. Said people get jealous and cops start to notice, especially when you aren't showing an income. Whitey drove a blue Mercury Marquis. He also had an $80,000 Mercedes that he kept at his condo in Louisburg Square (same name but rather different residents from the snooty Beacon Hill version), in the Wollaston Beach area of Quincy. But he never let anybody see him in the Benz. He never drove it in Southie. I was surprised he let Tommy and me drive our Lincolns, but he did. He set all the rules. Anything received from the Vault, Whitey knew about, and we had to pay tribute or a piece of the profits. Whitey was a master at guessing what we were making. He never set the prices, but if we paid him less than he was due, he'd send a message to raise it and to never try that again.

When executing the actual transfer of the stuff from hand to hand, I couldn't go right up to the safe house. For safety reasons, Whitey wanted only one person, Tommy, who was higher up in the hierarchy than I was, to take care of that. Tommy would drop me off a half mile away from the transfer point and pick up the drugs himself, usually two to five kilos a week, sometimes ten if demand was high. Occasionally we saw no action when things were dry or the Vault was out of stock.

Tommy always placed the coke in a gym bag, which he then stuffed into the trunk of his car. No money changed hands in this transfer. We were *cuffed* the coke, which, in street slang, means extended the drugs on credit. We were good customers and never left our source hanging for payment. We understood full well the consequences of ripping him off. Being fronted the drugs without having to pay up front was no trivial consideration. A kilo, depending on the vagaries of the market, was selling for $17,000 to $21,000, so we would leave the Vault with anywhere from thirty-four grand to over two hundred K in product. And that figure represented the wholesale price, which, of course, was significantly less than the value the coke represented to us.

After he'd stashed the stuff in his car, Tommy would drive around the corner to where I waited, then we'd head over to the condo I rented from Whitey in Louisburg Square in Quincy. Once, we got pulled over for a broken taillight in Quincy. We both shit ourselves because we had five kilos in our gym bag. We told the cop we had no idea the light was out and that we were on our way home from the gym. We looked like two clean-cut guys, not maggots, so he let us go with a warning. After we calmed down, we stopped at the local CVS pharmacy, like we always did, to pick up the necessary supplies: the disposable plastic liners that fit into baby bottles and inositol, which is vitamin B in a powdered form. We mixed the inositol with the coke to dilute the potency.

At the condo, the two of us would spend the next few hours breaking down the cocaine. Each kilo came in two one-and-a-half-inch bricks, ten inches long, usually wrapped in plastic and then duct tape. We worked pretty steadily, careful what we said in case Whitey had the place bugged, mostly talking about fighting, boxing, and pussy. We ate pizza and subs and salad while we worked. There wasn't much excitement; it had become routine. If the coke wasn't shiny, which indicated high quality, we'd put some Absolut vodka in a spray bottle, lightly spray it on the broken-up kilo, and then bake it at high heat for two minutes. The vodka gave it a nice shine that made it look like Peruvian Flake, a style of cocaine then popular among users.

Tommy and I invented a machine that made the coke rockier or chunkier so that when we broke it down it looked more natural, less doctored. The machine resembled a nine-inch square cake pan, about three inches high and made of steel. We'd fill it with cocaine, put a lid on it, place vises on it, and tighten them down as hard as we could. We'd let it sit for ten or fifteen minutes, and out would come rock-hard coke. Next, we divided the kilos, typically bagging the little rocks into roughly forty separate sandwich baggies, one ounce per bag. We'd sell an ounce, on average, for $1500 to $2000 a pop, depending upon which "dope" we were selling it to. If we could get roughly 40 to 50 ounces from each kilo, you're talking serious money. If we bought a kilo for twenty grand, our profit on one kilo was roughly sixty grand, tax-free, depending on how much inositol we cut it with. Multiply that by seven kilos, and you're looking at three hundred K. We were rolling in money, even after we paid Whitey his tribute money, which could range anywhere from five to ten thousand bucks a week, depending on what Whitey guessed it should be. Of course, we didn't always move the drugs in ounce quantities. Sometimes, we just turned the kilo around to someone else for a $4000 or $5000 profit, but that was rare.

After we finished setting up the coke, we waited for our calls. Again, the first and the fifteenth — welfare-check and food-stamp days — were my busiest. Some of my customers traded food stamps for drugs: $160 worth of food stamps could get you one-sixteenth-ounce of coke or three halves — three $50 bags. We met them in their houses, bars, street corners, wherever.

Timmy Connolly was one of our best customers. He had parties for the wealthy friends he supplied with phony mortgages, and always needed a big supply to keep them happy. A typical customer would page me and say, "Hey, Eddie, want to go for a run tonight? Maybe three miles." Three miles, three ounces. And I'd say, "Yeah, meet you at the park at five." Another would call and ask, "How 'bout a couple of beers tonight, Eddie?" Two ounces, which we'd exchange at Connolly's.

The feds got all that, and more, on tape, and broke down our codes through their wiretapping. They once audiotaped a mailbox where the kids in the neighborhood used to meet to wait for their stuff. One of the feds dressed up as a mailman to keep an eye on the tapes and pick them up and replace them as needed. That wasn't how they got me in 1990. I didn't hang out like that. They got me by taping a couple of my telephone conversations with customers: "Use of a communication facility to further a drug transaction," to be exact. One guy swept up in the 1990 sting had a million and a half dollars stacked up like clothes in the bottom drawer of his dresser. Another guy probably had five to six million stashed away, waiting for him when he got out of prison.

As for me, let's just say that the drug sales financed an extremely comfortable lifestyle, providing me with the cash to buy whatever I wanted. On one trip to Disney World, Tommy, me, and another buddy showed up at the nicest hotel down there with five shopping bags of cash, each containing thousands of dollars. At the time of my arrest in 1990, I had more than $175,000 in cash stashed underneath the fireplace in Whitey's Louisburg Square condo in Quincy, and another couple hundred grand buried in the woods in Winchester, Massachusetts, where I used to run while in training for the Golden Gloves. Every cent of the money in Quincy disappeared around the same time the feds raided the condo. Where did that money go? I'll tell you one thing: when the feds smashed into my house, they broke down the front door and just left it open. Anybody could have come in and grabbed the cash. As for the money buried in the woods, I dug it up when I got out of jail and used most of it to pay my legal bills.

—

Christmastime. I was nine years old.

Kids from the foster home on a trip to Damariscotta, Maine, with Mom and Pops. I'm on the far left; Ronnie is on the right in the striped shirt.

Mom and Pops visit me at the Louisburg Square condo.

U.S. Army soldier Edward J. MacKenzie Jr.

To my
superdad
I'll Respect you Forever
And try to Follow in your Footsteps
Love your #1 adopted son
Edward J. McEskerye Ji

Michael McGoff

With Johnny Pretzie as we get ready for the national kick-boxing championships. Pretzie was 70. Not bad shape for his age.

All New England Golden Glove champs. From left to right: Jimmy Brennick, Dennis Le'Clair, Joey De'Grandis, myself, and Scott Phiney.

Practice. I'm in the middle with an HK 91 assault rifle; Ronnie is on my left with a shotgun.

Whitey Bulger.

John Connolly.

Visiting with Freddy Weichel at Walpole State Prison.

Kevin Weeks and Freddy Weichel on the grounds of Walpole State Prison.

Stevie "The Rifleman" Flemmi.

Johnny Martorano.

Ron MacKenzie

One of the proudest days of my life — graduation from UMass.
Note Whitey's brother Billy, president of UMass, signed my diploma.

We spent our drug money on clothes, cars, jewelry, and girls — the usual expenditures of crooks, especially young and inexperienced crooks. Rolex watches and stylish threads were big statements among the Southie drug-dealing fraternity. Tommy and I used to go to a store called Belarian of Paris in the fancy Copley Place shopping mall in Boston's Back Bay. The manager, Marianne, took care of us. We'd walk in with five grand apiece and say, "Dress us." Man, she outfitted us in the best stuff. Armani suits, the works. Then she'd walk us over to Bally's to help us pick out shoes. I still have a pair of $550 lizard-skin shoes in my closet that I bought on one of our shopping trips. They're the ugliest things I've ever seen.

Tommy and I were tight, but not so tight that I could ever trust him completely. His first loyalty was to Whitey. I felt that Tommy would bad-mouth me, if necessary, to curry favor with him. I also heard that he complained about me on occasion to Tom Spenser, his boxing instructor. He'd tell him I was making too much money or stealing from the pot or punching out the wrong guy. None of this bothered me terribly. Hell, I complained about Tommy enough myself. But it did keep me alert.

You're always nervous when dealing. You worry most about getting set up by the cops. No one else would put their life in jeopardy just to be a good doo-bee. What was the sense in ratting on a dealer, if it meant that you, or somebody you loved, would be targeted for a hit? If someone wanted to rat us out, he had to be prepared to go into witness protection. Not a reasonable price to pay — unless, of course, you were a criminal buying escape from a lengthy prison sentence.

Personally, I never sold drugs to anyone under the age of twenty. With the exception of the beautiful teenage girls. Not only did they have the bodies of twenty-one-year olds, they had the mileage of a '65 Chevy. Sure, someone I sold drugs to might have sold them to underage kids, but I didn't. Still, there were problems with customers of all ages.

This one kid, nicknamed Bush, owed me about three thousand bucks. Bush was new to the drug trade when he started buying from me. It didn't take long before he was screwed up and dependent on drugs, and ran into a cash problem. He didn't have the money to pay me and was so terrified that he bolted the area and hid. If I really wanted to hunt him down I could have, but he was a friend of my brother Ronnie, so I didn't expend too much effort tracking him down. He was the only guy who ever beat me and got away with it.

A few years after that, I was at Canobie Lake Park in New Hampshire with Courtney and Lauren, and I saw him with his family. Quite a hiding place, huh? When Bush saw me, he started backing away from me with this look of sheer terror on his face. I'm convinced he would have left his wife and kids right there. But I waved to him and shouted, "Don't worry about it — it's over. I don't have any problems." I didn't do anything. It wasn't worth it.

But did Bush take advantage of the break I gave him? Nah, he came back to Southie and, to make matters worse, was suspected of doing some serious ratting on the Southie boys. The penalty for treason was death. No New Hampshire this time.

One night me and two buddies kidnapped Bush from his apartment in Southie. We duct-taped his arms and legs, threw him into the trunk of a black Ford LTD and headed out to the Blue Hills in Canton, Massachusetts, where we'd put two bullets in the back of his head and bury him. It was the first time I'd had to kill anybody, but I wasn't thinking much about what that meant. All I knew was that if a kid has to go, he has to go. It's business. Nothing personal. Everything was going according to plan. We only had a couple turns to make before we were on 93 South, when we saw the blue lights of a cop car flashing behind us. Turned out the car had a broken taillight. Well, the two cops looked in the car and recognized its occupants. One of them, smartly, asked us if we minded if he looked in the trunk. We said, "Yeah, we kind of do."

That answer guaranteed ten cruisers surrounding our car within about ninety seconds. While they were running the plates on the car, I conveyed a very important message from the backseat, where I was sitting, to the trunk, where Bush was still hidden. I told Bush that he was going to tell our friends in blue that we were playing war games, that he was our prisoner, and that we were just driving around doing a mock interrogation. As a reward for being such a good sport, he'd get ten grand and a chance to leave the area with his family. If, on the other hand, he was a poor sport and ratted us out, his mother, father, sister, nieces, and nephew would all be big-time losers. Like dead, big-time losers. I had no difficulty hearing Bush say, "I'll play."

The trunk was popped and the condemned was discovered. Me and my cohorts were arrested on kidnapping charges, even though Bush kept insisting it was just a game. They dragged us all into court and the DA and cops kept drilling Bush, trying to get him to turn. But he stuck to his story. Finally, they had no choice but to release us. On our way out of court, one police sergeant grabbed us and said, "You're all dirty, you maggots. And when you slip up, just once, you little pricks are going away for a long, long time!"

As always, we never got fresh to cops. We just listened and said, "Yes, sir, officer."

Within forty-eight hours, Bush and his family, along with ten grand, were headed to Florida. This time he was smart and didn't return. I never saw him again.

When you're a drug dealer, there will always be problems with underlings. There were always different prices for different people, dealers or underlings or the street customer, depending on their intelligence or their relationship with me. The stupider the person, the higher the price of cocaine. But if I was selling to someone I knew from the gym, I might cut him a break. Even though we had to buy from Whitey's source, every once in a while we'd come across some on our own. It was risky, but we did it. Me and Tommy also had some great flimflams we worked on our own. One scam we liked was selling rabbit food as pot. Go to a pet store sometime and ask to take a look at the rabbit food. You'll see immediately that it looks just like pot. We must have sold nearly thirty pounds of rabbit food at seven hundred bucks a pound.

Once our customers had the real coke in their hands, they'd break it down some more with inositol, step on it a few more times, and sell it for between $2600 and $3200 an ounce. If they were late in paying, or were snorting it themselves and not paying us, I'd handle it. Whitey taught me how to do that well. Sometimes, I'd push the kid around a bit and then cuff him another ounce. But they all knew nothing was free. I followed Whitey's instructions clearly in dealing with those punks who tried to stiff us. I usually simply reminded them they had a family and I knew exactly who and where they were. It would be a much healthier decision for them and their families if they paid what they owed. "If you play, you pay," I told them, and they nearly always got the message. I was becoming feared on the streets — and feared in the gym as well.

# Golden Gloves

My Southie gym had no frills, just good competition and instruction. We attracted some tough and talented fighters, many of whom went on to win a New England Golden Gloves championship, some multiple times. There was Johnny "Speedy" Donovan, twice New England Golden Gloves welterweight champion, and once lightweight champion; the year that he won the New England lightweight title, he went on to finish second in the national Golden Gloves. We also claimed Paul "Polecat" Moore, a New England Golden Glove light-heavyweight champion, as well as my best pal Frankie MacDonald, who won at light heavyweight three times. Kevin "Andre the Giant" MacDonald and Frankie's brother Johnny MacDonald both won New England Golden Gloves heavyweight titles. Whitey's lieutenant Kevin Weeks even worked out in the gym. Although Weeks was great with his fists, he was mostly a gym fighter and never won any major tournaments.

None of us ever fought each other in the Golden Gloves, although we frequently sparred in the gym. And we did not hold back. We went at each other as fiercely as two animals in the woods, just like me and Frankie used to. There was no better training. After we were done sparring, we'd laugh and go out and have a beer.

Almost all of these top fighters ran drugs for Whitey. We were among his most prized dealers because we didn't do drugs or drink heavily. We kept in shape and stayed sharp. If you take a look at the indictment sheet from the drug sweep in August 1990, you have one hell of a list of guys who could handle themselves with their fists. We thought of ourselves as pugilists first, drug dealers second.

I did my best to keep the worlds separate. I was still doing community work at the gym. It seemed as if a new kid needing help ended up there every day. Talk about putting your best face forward! Here I was getting publicity as a major asset to the community, even while I stocked that community with drugs. Let that be a lesson. It's always good to check under the hood.

In the summer of 1985, I finally decided to take a shot at the 1986 New England Golden Gloves super-heavyweight (220 pounds and up) title. It seemed like the perfect test. I was a bull — strong, coordinated, with decent quickness — but I didn't think I had what it takes to be a success in the pro ranks. I did know that I would face top competitors and that it would be a tremendous test of mind and body. I couldn't pass it up.

My trainer, Johnny Pretzie, was at my side during the tournament, which was held in Lowell. My second trainer was Al Kivlin, whom I'd met when we were doing time together in Billerica ten years earlier. I won both my quarterfinal and semifinal bouts with second-round knockouts. In the final, I faced a 6' 4", 240-pound black firefighter from Lynn, Massachusetts, named Harvey Moore. Like me, he'd won both his preliminary fights by knockout. I saw his semifinal, and it made me more than a bit nervous. A righty, he slugged hard to the body, then finished up even harder to the head. And talk about pressure. Not only were my two trainers, Pretzie and Kivlin, in my corner, the crowd was packed with my students from the gym and thirty other Southie residents.

When the bell rang for the first round, Moore rushed me and took the offensive. I was backing up and he scored easily for the first minute and a half. About midway through the round, I caught him with a hook to the jaw. That wobbled him, and I attacked, hoping to end it. But a wounded animal is a dangerous animal. No sooner was I on him, trying to drive home a winner, than Moore, in pain and desperate, threw a shot to my solar plexus that knocked the wind out of me. Fortunately for me, Moore was hurt himself. For the final forty-five seconds of the first round, we clinched and did a dance, me trying to get my wind back, him trying to clear his head. We were both happy as hell when the bell rang.

Between rounds, my two trainers shouted something at me, but I couldn't hear much. I just knew I had to be careful with Moore. When the bell rang for the second round, I was cautious, looking for my shot. I'd learned my lesson. Thirty seconds into the round, as we both were feinting in the middle of the ring, Moore made the mistake of reaching out with a weak left jab delivered too low. I countered hard to the side of his head with a left haymaker that rocked him. He shuffled away, then sat down to collect his thoughts and get the ringing out of his head. I ran to a neutral corner as the crowd screeched and hollered for me to finish him off.

The referee took the count to five before Moore got up. After making sure that Moore wanted to go on and was able to defend himself, the ref waved us back together. I knew Moore was done. I delivered a right, a left, both to the head. Moore backpedaled and lost his balance. I was getting ready to slam another punch home when the ref grabbed me in a bear hug from behind. The fight was over.

Pretzie and Kivlin were hugging me and slapping my back. I spotted Johnny Donovan and Polecat and Andre on the ring apron, shouting and whooping it up for all it was worth. It was one of the best nights of my life.

Two weeks after the fight, Whitey showed up at the gym with his own trophy: a solid-gold ring with three clover leaves, each surrounded by three fifteen-point diamond chips, adding up to a karat, and, in the center of the setting, an almost flawless, twenty-five-point emerald. I found out later that it was one of a kind, from a mold created especially for Whitey by a Southie jeweler; Whitey commissioned ten similar rings for other gangsters who'd pleased him. Whitey always had a rich way of letting you know that you had made him proud.

# A Different Breed

So much has been written about Whitey's intelligence and psychology. He continues to intrigue and perplex people. Then again, Whitey was a gangster, and America has long been fascinated by organized crime and figures like Al Capone, Dutch Schultz, Myer Lansky, Lucky Luciano, and John Gotti. Whitey Bulger was like all those guys, and like none of them. He intimidated, controlled, killed, and made lots of money from the rackets. But he had his own way of doing things and a cunning pathology that separated him from the rest. As proof, I submit that while almost all of America's major organized mob bosses have died either by violence or in prison, including John Gotti, Whitey is still out there, somewhere.

It wasn't difficult to see how Whitey became a leader of street thugs like myself. In the mean streets of Southie, you not only had to be smart and disciplined, you also had to be ruthless, willing to kill when necessary. Whitey Bulger was the total package, and every one of us loved him for it. We wanted to be like him and be near him, because we saw the way he was treated. People not only respected him, they feared him. We saw the way he manipulated people and created an organization that served him perfectly. We saw his money, his girls, his connections, his power. We saw the way he did his time in prison and got out. We saw the way he beat the authorities year after year, running his rackets and staying out of handcuffs. We knew he wasn't fearless, that he didn't have the physical courage to go one-on-one like many of us, but that was okay. He had us to take care of that part of the business. He was still a ferocious bastard and he could send the fear of the devil through all of Southie.

Whitey taught us that smart criminals didn't call attention to themselves. Even in what he wore, he led by example. He didn't wear, or drive, big money, but we still knew the big money was his. Most of us had no clue how to make a successful living in the legitimate world. We knew nothing about college and suits and ties and offices in big buildings downtown. We knew about the successes of the "other" people and their beautiful homes, cars, and kids, but that was never going to be us. If we were going to make serious loot, we were going to have to earn it differently. Whitey Bulger showed us the way.

He mocked polite society, telling us that only suckers played it straight and fought in the thankless trenches of a nine-to-five world. He told us that in the world of supposedly legitimate business, the major winners and richest executives were thieves in white collars. He told us that they screwed as many people, if not more, than he and his mob associates. The only difference was that society had determined that when they screwed people, it was legal. In the jungle, you can't play by the rules of a civilized and law-abiding society, so you ignore them. You steal and intimidate and brutalize. You do it to the other guy before he has a chance to do it to you. Preaching his sermon, Whitey recruited an army of outlaw zealots. We couldn't thank him enough.

Whitey was part genius, part madman, part businessman, part killer, part sex maniac, part community caretaker. He was always telling me to improve my mind and read more books, like *The Rise and Fall of the Roman Empire, The Odyssey, I, Claudius, Caligula,* and *Desert Fox,* a biography of the brilliant German General Erwin Rommel. I read and loved every one. Homer's language was a little over my head but I was fascinated by Odysseus, and reading about Caesar and the military might of the Roman Republic was just as compelling. Whitey was complex. There were so many sides to him that sometimes I didn't know which Whitey I was dealing with.

Take the day in early 1983 when five of us were hanging around near the South Boston Library in Flood Square. This old lady walks by and nudges my buddy. "Well, excuse me, ma'am," he says in response, real fresh-mouthed.

"There's no excuse for you, you cocksucker," she answers him, walking on. We're all staring at her, our mouths wide open. She looked like such a sweet little thing, in a long dark skirt, black gloves, thick black boots, long black coat, gray hair under a black hat tied under her chin, thick glasses perched high up on her nose, hugging this big, dark brown pocketbook to her chest like her life savings were inside. She hadn't gone more than ten feet when she turns around and says, her voice no longer an old woman's, but Whitey Bulger's, "I could've whacked every one of you motherfuckers if I'd wanted to."

Our mouths open even wider, she turns back around, and this time she's gone for good. It took a few minutes for us to catch our breath, but when we did, we all understood what had just happened. In the first place, we were lucky we were alive. Whitey could easily have taken out a modified Mac Ten with a silencer and quietly offed one or two or all five of us. And, in the second place, his disguise wasn't meant just to shock us. He was on a mission. Some poor prick's number was up, and the last person he'd see before his lights went out permanently would be a sweet little old lady, probably with an ice pick in her black-gloved hands.

Not only could my boss turn effortlessly into a woman, but sometimes he acted like Robin Hood. That was one image people in Southie loved to toss around. And it did exist. Like the time Whitey bought a truckload of sneakers someone else had stolen from the Reebok factory so that we could pass them out to the kids in the projects. Another time, I happened to be there when he received a complaint from one of the mothers in the neighborhood. She had balls. She came right into his headquarters at the South Boston Liquor Mart on Old Colony Avenue and asked loudly, "Is Whitey here?"

Someone said, "You mean Jimmy B?" and she shrugged her shoulders impatiently.

Whitey came out and said, real sweetly, "Can I help you, dear?"

"Yes, you can," she answered him. "Mr. Bulger, my children were playing in the field right next door to my house and they brought home a hypodermic needle they found under the window of the house next door. I called the police, and they said they have no proof it belongs to the people in the house, so they can't do a thing about it. Can you please help me, sir?"

Whitey put his hand on her shoulder. "Now don't you worry about a thing, hon," he told her. "I'll look into this for you." When she left, he turned to me, red with anger. "Eddie, go find out who the fuck lives there. Don't do anything. I just want to know."

I came back about a half hour later and gave him the report. "Jimmy, that's Al's house," I told him. "He's a dealer and they're all fucking junkies in there."

A few days later, Whitey went to the house with me and his two top lieutenants, Kevin Weeks and Stevie Flemmi. Whitey warned us to do nothing and let him do all the talking. The front door was open, and Al was sitting on a chair in his living room, watching TV with another junkie. Al looked like he was in a heroin stupor, but his eyes lit up when he saw who'd just walked in. Whitey went over to him, pulled out a .357 magnum, and jammed it so hard into Al's mouth that Al's lip split open. "You have till this weekend to pack up and get the fuck out of my town," he told him. He pointed to me and Kevin and Stevie. "Or they will bury you here." Then he calmly walked out, with the three of us in tow. Al moved out the next day. No more needles were ever found in the field. Yeah, that was Whitey. Always worried about pins bothering the gentle residents of his town.

Whitey did what he had to do to get rid of the people he termed undesirable. I'm certain that he was personally responsible for at least thirty executions. How did he kill them? Shooting them in the head or hog-tying them so they strangled themselves were two of his preferred methods. He had no problem using guns, but his expertise was with knives. He loved knives. All kinds of knives, although he was partial to one six-inch hunting knife. He could hang out with you all night, and then kill you while you were sitting beside him. However he did it, he did it with great pleasure. He was a sociopath. Everyone knew that.

One night, I was standing in the corner of Triple O's bar on West Broadway. I saw Whitey, standing with Kevin Weeks, but before I could say hello, Whitey walked over and punched this low-level punk right in the chest without saying a word. Kevin gave a wave that said, "Everybody mind your own business and stay put." Whitey stared at the punk, who looked pretty white in the face. Then he smiled this sick, scary smile, and strolled leisurely out of the bar, followed by Weeks.

The punk walked a few steps, real slowly, sat down on a barstool, and passed out two minutes later. After they took him away in an ambulance, we found out he'd been stabbed with an ice pick. Ice picks leave very little blood, but they can cause hemorrhaging, and if you don't get to the hospital quickly, you'll bleed to death. The guy lived, but never looked healthy again. We saw his scar a few weeks later when he came back to the bar and lifted his shirt. They'd had to open his whole chest as if he were undergoing coronary bypass surgery. I later learned he'd been disrespectful to one of Whitey's little girls from Cardinal Cushing High School.

There were some instances when Whitey didn't handle situations as smoothly as he'd intended. Sometimes he made a mess. Sometimes other people, besides his legbreakers and hitmen, had to come in and clean up that mess. Like with Trooper Johnson.

On September 8, 1987, Whitey was en route to Canada, according to word on the street, for the wedding of the daughter of his mistress, Theresa Stanley, to Montreal Canadiens forward Chris Nilan. Whitey was carrying a present for the couple, plus extra cash to store away for a rainy day. He was like a squirrel, storing his nuts in the States, Canada, Europe, and the Caribbean, stashing large amounts of cash in safe-deposit boxes all over the world, in case he had to make a quick getaway. But before Whitey could get to Montreal, he was stopped at Logan Airport. Officials at a security checkpoint detected one hundred thousand in cash, in crisp hundred-dollar bills, concealed in Whitey's black leather garment bag as it passed through an X-ray machine. Seems any time you take more than $10,000 out of the country, you need to declare it. But Whitey being Whitey, he wouldn't submit to any further investigation and deftly lateraled the garment bag to his sidekick, Kevin Weeks, waiting nearby. Kevin sprinted for an exit with Whitey trailing close behind. Weeks made it through an exit door onto the sidewalk while Whitey blocked the exit so a guard couldn't follow.

Holding another bag with "only" ten thousand dollars in cash, Whitey was apprehended by a state trooper named William A. Johnson Jr., who made the mistake of pinning Whitey to a wall. But Kevin and the big money, thought to be at least $100,000, got away. Obviously, Whitey had been prepared for such an emergency; he'd had the smarts to travel with a dummy bag containing $9,923. The dummy bag was confiscated at the airport, but Whitey and Teresa Stanley ended up flying to Montreal anyway.

Funny thing, but nothing ended up happening to Whitey. Could it have been that Billy Bulger interfered with the investigation? Could the senate president have made the problem go away? That's an interesting question.

As for Trooper Johnson, a highly respected member of the state police and a former Green Beret, things were never quite the same again. For some strange reason, his promising career was derailed and he was demoted from narcotics to patrolling the parking lot at Logan. In 1993, Johnson was named Trooper of the Year for stopping a guy with a knife who was threatening to kill some airport workers. But a year later he was handed a court-martial transfer to state police barracks in Andover because he showed the lieutenant governor around the airport without permission. It was like they were waiting for him to make a mistake and he did. Johnson suffered emotional problems after the incident, went through a bitter divorce, and never seemed to regain his stride, finally retiring in 1997. In September of

1998, he walked into a field in New Hampshire, took out a gun, and blew his brains out. He was fifty years old. He left a suicide note that specified, "I do not want a Massachusetts state trooper in uniform within 100 miles of my funeral — I mean it." Moral of the story? Don't mess with the Bulgers.

And God help those who did. Whitey liked to combine physical and mental torture with killing. He got off on violence and suffering and agony. He had trick after trick to satiate his pleasure. With him, killing was more than just business. It seemed to provide him a twisted form of recreation. I don't know if this sickness was always in him or if it developed over time. Maybe his experience as an LSD guinea pig in prison in the 1960s also disconnected some of his circuitry. His savagery frightened us and yet, in a perverse way, it cemented our allegiance to him.

Naturally, Whitey's methods bothered some more than others. Like this one buddy of mine, who had been working mostly as a bagman for Whitey. Larry was a player, and had seen at least one guy get clipped. But, for some reason, Whitey had spared him from witnessing his unique "medieval" type of torture. When Larry got his first taste of it, it almost sent him over the edge.

Around eleven on a cold and rainy night, a bunch of us guys were at the gym, just hanging around. Suddenly, the front door flew open, and Larry came stumbling in, drenched, looking like a drowned rat, his eyes wide with terror. It took us a while but we finally got him to divulge what he'd seen an hour earlier inside one of the warehouses on the waterfront where Whitey liked to take care of "business."

Whitey had been there with some other members of his front office. Also present was some poor prick — we'll call him "Joey," — tied to a chair. Joey had made the mistake of scoring a nice pile of cash on Whitey's home turf without informing Whitey. He'd obviously forgotten Southie's eleventh commandment: "Thou shalt not attempt to beat Whitey." One way or another, Whitey was going to make Joey pay tribute.

"They had Joey tied up tight and Whitey was slapping him hard," Larry said. "Joey took some shots, but was still holding out. You should've seen his face — all puffed up, swollen, cuts all over it. I'm telling you guys, I wanted to tell him to stop being a hero and just give it up. But he hung in there and that only made Whitey angrier."

By now, I was fairly confident I knew how the story was going to end.

Larry kept talking. "Whitey is telling this guy, 'Hey, Joey, we know you have the money. All we want is a cut. This is my backyard, and what's fair is fair. You tell us where to pick it up, and we'll grab our percentage. I'm a fair and reasonable man. After I get what's mine, I'll let you go on your way.'"

Yeah, right, "on his way." On his way to a hole in the ground. And Joey must have been in a hurry to get there because he told Whitey, "What do you think I am, a fucking idiot? Go fuck yourself." With that comment, Joey had answered his own question.

"Whitey pulled a pair of pliers out of his back pocket," Larry told us, "and waved them six inches in front of Joey's face. I'm thinking to myself, Ah, shit, I don't want to watch this. Just kill him. Just blow his head off. And Joey is brain dead because he is giving Whitey a 'go-fuck-yourself' look."

"Whitey told Davey to hold him still," Larry continued. "I was thinking that Whitey knew this was getting a bit heavy for me. Davey walks around behind Joey, and this bastard is still just looking right at Whitey, not even blinking. Davey gets Joey in a half nelson and grabs a hold of his hair and pulls his head back and holds it steady. Joey is struggling like hell. He's trying to topple over in the chair, but Davey had his head in a vise."

Larry stopped and just shook his head. "I don't know how he did it, but Whitey just straddled this guy's lap and got the pliers in his mouth. And I just want to get the fuck out of there. And, Joey is half gacking and screaming, but I still don't think he believes Whitey is going to do it, because he's yelling, but still holding out.

"And then, he did it quick. You should have heard it. Crunching and grinding sounds all mixed together, like Whitey was digging around with those pliers inside the guy's mouth. Joey is trying to get some words out, but Whitey isn't listening. He's just grinning, and he has that sick look in his eyes. Joey is shaking, and his eyes are bulging out. I think Davey was enjoying it too, 'cause, man, he was laughing. It must have taken only two or three seconds. Whitey just yanks his arm back, and you should have seen the blood splatter. Shit, Whitey got some on his shirt and face. Fucking Joey shuddered for a second and then passed out. And Whitey steps off this guy, and right there in the pliers he's holding, blood dripping off it, is Joey's motherfucking tooth. Edzo! Whitey ripped that poor prick's tooth out of his head!"

Larry was looking at all of us, trying to get it to register. I wasn't the least bit surprised by what we'd just heard. "You had to see this," he went on.

"Whitey's just standing there with blood on him, which he's not even bothering to wipe off. He has a grin on his face. You know that sick grin — half Satan and half Big Cat. He has his arms at his side, and he's still holding onto those pliers with the bloody tooth in it. Davey has let go of this guy, 'cause he's out cold from pain. And I'm almost wetting myself. Whitey's grinning, taking it all in for about half a minute or so. Then he steps forward and slaps the guy back into consciousness. You should've seen Joey. I swear, he was more dead than alive. His face looked like a slab of raw meat. He had blood dribbling out of his mouth. And he's blinking through all the blood and mumbling, 'All right, all right, I'll tell you where the money is. Just no more. No fucking more.' I was happy as hell. Fuck Joey, I couldn't take it anymore."

"Well, did he tell you where the money was?" one of my buddies asked.

"Yeah, yeah, it was in some basement in some triple-decker down by the water. He blurted out the address. And Whitey says, 'Good, good, now you're acting reasonable.' Whitey got on his cell phone and called Timmy and gave him directions to the place, and then told Joey, 'Okay, this is all going to come out all right. As soon as I get the call that the money is in hand, you take a walk. You and I are all set. 'Cause I'm in a good mood.'

"That poor prick just nods his head lightly and slips off into la-la land. I was getting sicker and sicker every time I looked at that bloody pair of pliers. All I wanted was to get the hell out of there, but I couldn't. Whitey and Davey stood off to the side, shooting the shit. I was walking around, trying not to lose it. It must've been a half hour or so, and Whitey gets the call. Timmy had the money. Joey is in and out of consciousness, but he was able to pick his head up when Whitey walked over and stood in front of him and says, 'Joey, you're all set. We have the money. You get to go.'

"Joey mumbled something. I think it was, 'Thanks, Jimmy.' Whitey just keeps smiling, and walks behind Joey's chair. He looks back over his shoulder, where I'm standing, and tells me to untie the poor prick. I took about three steps toward Joey. . . ." My friend stopped talking and just started shaking his head.

"What the fuck happened?" I asked.

"What the fuck happened, Edzo, is that I started puking so bad Whitey told Davey to throw me the fuck out the door. I have no idea what happened to Joey after I left."

There was silence in the room as we all tried to imagine what had happened to Joey once Larry got booted out. I imagined Whitey standing there holding the gun, arm still outstretched, the nose of the barrel about two feet from what was left of Joey's head, blood and brains splattered everywhere. And, calmly, he'd say, while looking into that crater he had just made, "Davey, I told you I was in a good mood, didn't I?"

Whitey had the sickest sense of humor of any of us, and, believe me, we were all demented when it came to what we thought was funny. One time I went on a boat ride with him. Whitey was so paranoid about being overheard that he used to take these "fishing" trips in order to discuss business; he figured that being way out on the Atlantic prevented audio and video surveillance. He was right, of course. But a trip out into the great blue with Captain Jimmy wasn't about deep-sea fishing and coming back with a bucketful of flounder, and sometimes it wasn't about coming back at all.

On a late summer afternoon, Whitey and four of his local "crew" pulled away from the South Boston Yacht Club in a thirty-foot white Sea Ray. Whitey was at the helm, classically outfitted with a Red Sox hat, mirror shades, and a tan barracuda jacket. We'd just lost sight of land when Whitey put the throttle in neutral and said, "Eddie, take over the controls for a minute."

I wasn't that comfortable at the helm, but the boat didn't seem to be going anywhere in neutral, so that made me feel more at ease. I stood there, occasionally throttling the engine to keep us away from stray lobster buoys. It was a warm afternoon. The skies were clear, and once we got beyond the stink of fetid Boston Harbor, it was refreshing. Even as I let the boat drift, I was still on high alert — the only way to act around my boss, no matter where you were. It was calm out on the water, peaceful. Everyone on board seemed relaxed. But not for long.

Minutes later I heard a loud *whoomp* behind me. I spun around to see one of Whitey's guests, a big guy named Danny Bryant, pitching sideways and crashing to the deck, out cold. Whitey stood directly over him, holding a blackjack in his right hand. (Whitey had a special affection for anything with lead in it, whether a blackjack or a pair of sap gloves.)

He stood there looking at Danny, oblivious to everyone around him. I remained at the wheel, not saying a word, alternately looking ahead at the ocean and behind at my shipmates. Danny lay there, head split open nicely, blood oozing onto the white deck. "Hey, Jimmy, do you think he's dead?" said this fat tub named Vincent, who bent over the body, hands on his knees, looking at Danny like he was some weird starfish he'd just found in the sand.

Whitey snapped out of it. "Nah, he's not fucking dead, just in deep sleep," he said. At this point I was paying almost no attention to my steering. Whitey crouched down next to a wraparound sofa and pulled out a white canvas bag, from which he removed a long loop of heavy chain. "Hey, Kevin, Vinny, bind Danny up nice and tight."

Kevin and Vincent went to work on Danny, who still wasn't moving. Maybe he *was* dead. I was impressed with how quickly they cinched the poor prick in an iron straitjacket, with his arms crossed and his legs tied together. The chain was fastened with a couple rusty Yale locks that Whitey thoughtfully provided. They left Danny lying on his back.

Soon Danny came to: groggy and moaning and moving his eyelids, blood still oozing out of a cut on his face that would require a dozen stitches, if he ever made it to an emergency room. Which seemed unlikely. A few minutes later, he was very much awake, obviously suffering a murderous headache, and terrified. Although Danny had to keep blinking in order to see through the blood trickling into his eyes, he recognized Whitey, sitting next to him in a deck chair, sipping from a bottle of ice-cold Poland Spring water. "Jimmy, what's going on?" Danny pleaded. "Please tell me what's happening."

I put the boat back in gear and throttled the engine to avoid an approaching blue-and-white striped buoy, glancing back and forth between the water and the poor prick about to sleep with the fishes behind me. Whitey calmly answered Danny's questions. "We have a bit of a problem, Danny. It seems you were shooting off your mouth the other night. You'd had one too many, which was your first mistake. But you made matters worse by telling the crowd in the bar that you were thinking of becoming an informant. You said you had a ton of information that could make the FBI very happy. That wasn't smart, was it?"

"I was only joking," Danny blubbered, trying desperately to move his arms, unable to wipe the blood from his eyes. "I was drunk. I didn't know what I was saying. I'd never say a word to no one. You know that, Jimmy."

"Yeah, Danny, I do know that," Whitey said. "But I don't appreciate your joking about those things. I'm thinking this time I'm going to let it go by, and you can be sure this is the only time I'll be so generous. But I'm just thinking about it."

Hollywood could never realistically portray the fear on Danny's face. Because Danny was not at all certain he wasn't going overboard. And what consumed him was not so much the fear of dying, as the fear of an awful death. Drowning, especially with chains around your body and no chance to escape, has to be second only to burning as the nastiest way to check out. Danny began blubbering. "God, no, Jimmy. I would never, never. I swear on my mother and father's life. Oh, God, Jimmy, please, please —"

"Shut the fuck up!" Whitey snapped, leaning forward and putting his face close to Danny's. Then, just as quickly, the sudden rage passed. His voice was soft as he sat in the deck chair, a satisfied smile on his face, those icy eyes hidden beneath the lenses of his Foster Grants. "This is your lucky day," he told Danny. "Untie him, boys. We'll use him as bait another day."

"Nice job, Eddie," Whitey said as he again assumed control of the wheel. "But I think it's time to head home." Truth be told, I was getting seasick. He advanced the throttle, as the bloodied mass on the floor was thanking him, Vincent, Kevin, me, the Pope, any saint he could think of, and some he made up. Whitey didn't even look back. He just gunned the boat for home.

That night, I ran into Whitey at Castle Island. Kevin was, of course, beside him. "So, Eddie," he said as soon as he saw me, "did you learn anything from our little boat trip this afternoon?"

"Yeah," I said. "I learned not to fuck with Jimmy B."

He gave me a little slap on my shoulder, grabbed the corner of my shirt and drew me closer. "No, that's not the point I'm trying to make," he said. "I want you to get the whole picture of what happened out there. You know how I'm always talking to you about fear?"

"Sure, Jimmy," I answered. "You're always saying how the thought of pain is so much more severe than the actual thing itself."

"That's right," he said, smiling slightly. "What I did today was an example of that. Danny didn't suffer that much pain. Well, a little, but he didn't die, did he?" I shook my head. "No, Danny's still alive. Alive enough to tell four or five of his friends what happened to him. How he woke up and saw two heavyweights about to give him a saloon throw overboard for one final swim. How he now knows what happens to someone who even thinks of becoming an informant. Those four or five guys will repeat that story to at least four or five others. It's a trickle-down effect and, before you know it, the story's all over the city. And I'm saved a lot of work with future informants. Haven't I told you that before, Eddie?"

"Yeah," I agreed. "You told me one good fight can save me a hundred others. If someone comes into the bar and says, 'Eddie Mac bit off Joe's ear and beat him within an inch of his life,' I'm home free for a good long while. Like a fish that starts as a minnow and turns into a tuna, the story just keeps growing, keeps feeding."

Whitey smiled again. "That's it, my boy. I could've dumped that load off the boat like nothing this afternoon. But I didn't for a couple of reasons. First of all, Danny's worth a lot of money to me if he's alive. He's made me a lot of drug money over the years. But, even more important, if we whacked him, who could he have told? None of us could talk if we hit him. But he's back. And the fear of death is going to stay with him for a long, long time."

Whitey, as always, was right. Danny was a different man when he got off that boat. He'd seen the look of death in Whitey's eyes and learned his lesson well. I hardly ever saw him again. He was through hanging around in local bars and even went to AA and quit drinking for good. He was still a top money earner for Whitey, but he was humbled after that trip.

That was far from the only time that my stomach got a little queasy after a "ride" with my boss. A month after that fishing trip, I was standing outside a bar in Southie late one Saturday night with a few of my buddies, when Whitey's car slowed down beside me. Kevin Weeks was driving and another player I'd heard of, but never met, was in the passenger seat. Whitey was in the back seat. He opened his window and called out to me. "Hey, Edzo, come join us for a little ride." For a second I thought about how those might be the last words some poor prick would ever hear, but I felt no more fear than usual. I'd convinced myself early in the game that I was lucky to be one of Whitey's boys and I was not going to let fear rule me. "Fuck Fear" was my motto.

I got into the car and glanced at the clock. 2 A.M. Everything seemed cool and easy in the car. We drove around South Boston for a half hour or so, shooting the breeze and making jokes, having a fine old time. Suddenly, with no warning, Whitey reached over and shot the guy in the passenger seat in the back of the head. What the fuck, I said to myself. There goes another one. Better him than me. You see, by then I'd seen it many times before and didn't have any feelings one way or the other.

"Pull over," he ordered Kevin, who looked a little shaken himself, as if he hadn't expected this. But he followed his instructions immediately. As soon as the car hit the curb, Whitey said to me, "Dump the prick out." I did exactly as I was told, leaving the guy on the sidewalk to die, and then Kevin hightailed it outta there.

The next day I read in the *Herald* that someone with a gunshot to the back of the head was found on First Street in South Boston and listed in critical condition at Boston City Hospital. The guy survived and told the police he was hit in a drive-by shooting and that the shooters were black. He never so much as hinted that Whitey did it. Probably out of fear that Whitey would whack his entire family. Smart guy.

If one thing got me thinking that this guy might have the power of God, it was the series of murders that went down in 1981, just before Freddy Weichel went away for good, all of them orchestrated by Jimmy B.

It all started on May 27, 1981, when Roger Wheeler, a millionaire businessman from Tulsa, and the new owner of the World Jai Alai Company in Bridgeport, Connecticut, was shot to death outside a country club in Tulsa. Johnny Martorano, Whitey's top hitman, did the job at the request of Whitey, Stevie Flemmi, and a guy named John Callahan, a major money man for World Jai Alai. Callahan was a CPA and consultant to Boston banks by day, a mobster player by night, and he'd involved Whitey and Flemmi in the heavy-betting scene at World Jai Alai in Bridgeport, as well as its other outlets in Connecticut and Florida.

Whitey doubtless had the final say on who did the hit, and Martorano was a natural selection. Always thorough, he was as good as they get.

Supposedly, Wheeler was killed because he suspected that the Winter Hill Gang, a group of Irish and Italian gangsters led by Howie Winter, to which both Bulger and Flemmi were tied, was skimming funds from the World Jai Alai Company. Eight months after the Wheeler hit, Brian Halloran, a wise-guy wanna-be from Boston who never elevated himself above the status of two-bit punk, was set to go to trial for killing a drug dealer. But Halloran had also been a reject for the Wheeler hit squad. Attempting to get leniency on his upcoming case, Halloran told the FBI that Martorano had done the hit and that Whitey and Flemmi were in the getaway car. One way or another, word got around that Halloran wanted to cooperate. Needless to say, this leak was not good for Halloran's health.

On the night of May 11, 1982, just two weeks short of the year anniversary of Wheeler's dirt nap, Halloran and a buddy, Michael J. Donahue, were leaving a bar on Northern Avenue in Southie. Whitey and an accomplice jumped out of a car about twenty feet away and opened fire with machine guns. Who was the accomplice? I don't know for sure, but it's been whispered that the second gunman was Joey Murphy, a deeply feared man high up in Whitey's organization. (Murphy got out of prison in late 2000, and we all thought if he could stay out of prison — a big if — he would be running the Southie rackets. But he surprised a lot of us by remaining conspicuously off the radar screen and noticeably absent from any of the witness lists from recent trials. All this led us to wonder if he's cooperating with the feds.)

When the two gunmen spent their chambers, they jumped back in the car and tore out, leaving behind a pair of badly riddled corpses who posed very little risk of becoming informants. A few months after Halloran got his, Martorano also took care of Callahan, who'd become a liability as a potential witness, killing him near the World Jai Alai outlet in Miami.

Two or three months after the murders, I ran into Whitey at Castle Island. I had just finished reading yet another newspaper article hinting at Whitey's involvement in the Halloran-Donahue murders. "Hell, Jimmy," I said to him, pointing to the *Boston Herald* story. "They just keep breaking your balls on that one, don't they?"

He smiled faintly and said, talking as softly as always, "Big Brother was looking over my shoulder on that one, Eddie."

"What do you mean?"

"Johnny Connolly of our beloved FBI, who do you think?" he said, as I strained to hear his every word. "He was out there with binoculars. Positioned a half mile away on the Northern Avenue Bridge. Staking out the ambush site. Two clicks on the walkie-talkie meant it was a go. One click, don't do it. Covering my shoulder the whole night. It doesn't get any sweeter than that."

I kept walking, saying nothing, but I was thinking, Jesus Christ, this is the man. What a king. Fucking incredible. We knew that Whitey was tight with Connolly. And we heard rumors we never dared ask the top brass about — like Whitey had helped the FBI with information that gutted the local Italian Mob. Now, getting rid of the competition helped all of us out, but to be so tight with an FBI agent that you could enlist his help for a hit? That confirmed that Whitey had more power than we could comprehend.

# Street Soldier

**W**orking for Whitey gave me a feeling of ultimate power. With my background as a fighter, selling drugs for Whitey made it inevitable that I would do other things for him as well. I'll say it again: Whitey ruled through intimidation and fear. Anyone who assisted Whitey in creating a climate of intimidation and fear became, as the *Boston Globe* said of me, a "Bulger favorite."

All I wanted was for Whitey to be pleased with the work I did. My job description was simple: from 1985 to 1990, I worked for him as a street soldier, an enforcer, a leg-breaker, a drug runner. I was the hired muscle who distributed drugs for my boss and broke the limbs of those who disrespected him. I was often sent on missions that made me feel I was pushing up against the icy shoulder of death, made me feel closer to Frankie. I couldn't explain it, but after Frankie's death, I felt even looser than before. There was little I wouldn't do.

Whitey was thirty years older than me and it didn't take long for him to become my leader. I wanted to believe that he could give me back some of what I had lost. My innocence had died early. I'm not trying to place all the blame for what I became on the shoulders of the Department of Social Services or the biological parents who never gave a shit. Thousands who grew up like me did not embrace lives of crime. They don't have blood on their hands. I am who I am. For better or worse, this is the man I became. Whitey was as evil as Lucifer, but he liked me enough to educate me in the ways of the South Boston streets that, despite my smarts, I hadn't yet learned. And I was a grateful student.

When I first started working for Whitey, my life was filled with more than enough connections to keep me occupied twenty-four/seven. But, as the years passed and my involvement grew deeper, there were profound changes in my life. The pain of losing Frankie seemed to deepen rather than lessen with time, making me less grounded and more dangerous. My marriage to Carolyn had shattered. My brother Ronnie was in and out of jail and still hooked on drugs. But I also had two daughters to care for and adored both of them, determined to be a better parent than any I'd ever known.

The more work I did for Whitey, the better I liked it. If I received a rare smile from the man, an extra bonus for a job well done, that could keep me going for days. I loved to listen to his theories about the great military strategists of the world — like Alexander the Great, Caesar, Maximus, Patton, and MacArthur — and how they moved deliberately, evaluating every possible outcome before acting. Nothing could match the high of standing beside the king of South Boston. I did everything I could to win his praise and respect.

The work created a sense of order out of the surrounding chaos. I had no idea what a real family was like. No mother who smiled at me. No father who disciplined or loved me. No plan for my life, except to survive the tough streets on which I had raised myself. I was violent and pathetic. Someone to fear. Someone to weep over. But Whitey made some of the pain and confusion disappear. It was so simple with him in charge. He made the rules and we followed them. If someone disobeyed, he would be punished. No one entered our world without understanding the consequences of his actions. That was, I imagined, how fathers handled sons: teaching them the consequences of their actions.

And since I was, above all else, a good son, I handed out the punishments. Unlike Whitey's hit men who fired their shots from a distance and went home with a clean shirt, I did the dirty work. I wasn't a hit man. I left that to Johnny Martorano and other Bulger assassins. I learned early on that leg-breaking and beatings required more discipline, more balls, than killing someone. Any dope can pull a trigger.

Sometimes the beating wasn't for money, but for disrespect. Like mouthing off to one of Whitey's employees at the South Boston Liquor Mart. Or flirting with a fourteen-year-old girl who Whitey was fucking. It didn't matter what the reason was. I simply inflicted the damage. And enjoyed every second of it. As I've said, my boss didn't like his employees to sample the goods, so I didn't drink or snort or smoke; the best high was the sound of a leg breaking beneath my two hands.

After I started working for Whitey in 1985, no more than a few days would elapse between jobs; I'd be asked to take care of a situation, to collect some money, or to send someone a message. Most of the time, Kevin Weeks would call to give me my assignment. When Whitey dealt with me directly, he didn't say much. Sometimes, he wouldn't talk at all. He'd just sit in his car and show me a piece of paper with a name and instructions on it. I'd look at the paper, and then Whitey would fold it up and put it away.

Most of my missions did not require "permanent" solutions. Some did not even require violence. Sometimes, all I had to do was explain a situation to someone. My trademark line was, "I don't want this to get ugly." That line was often sufficient to take care of the matter. But when I had to get tough, I did so willingly.

Some missions were so easy I almost felt guilty getting paid. Like the one I did for a guy who knew Whitey. All Whitey told me was that the guy owned a pool-cleaning business and didn't like the way his only daughter was being treated by her boyfriend. I located the boyfriend — a tall, red-headed guy in his twenties with muscles and an attitude — in front of a Southie bar early one Friday evening. "Listen," I told him, "there's a lot of pussy in South Boston. The girl that you're banging – well, her father is a very, very fucking good friend of mine. You need to see someone else if you want to keep our friendship. You'd be smart to take this advice, because, you know, I don't want this to get ugly."

The guy looked at me for a long minute, sizing me up. He came to the right conclusion. He shrugged, said, "Fucking bitch. Who needs her?" Truthfully, I would have liked to have smashed in his face before he took off. He was a prick who abused women, I was certain, and I wouldn't have minded busting his ass. But I didn't. Whitey wanted the guy to leave his friend's daughter alone, nothing more. Mission accomplished.

If a beating was necessary, then I would give the guy a pounding and finish by telling him what he had to do to avoid an even worse fate. Leaving a guy no out means that sooner or later, probably when he's drunk or tripping, he's going to get a gun and shoot you dead. Or at least try. Bullies don't last long. I don't care if you live in the South Bronx or in Greenwich, Connecticut; justice has a way of visiting the bully.

Tom Nee was a habitual bully, a tough street fighter who managed a bar called On Broadway in Southie. He was vicious and showed no mercy when he banged people up. One day at the Penn Tavern, a few doors down from his bar, he made the mistake of smashing a beer bottle across the face of the brother of one of Whitey's people. He paid for it. About a week later, on the street outside his bar, Nee got two in the head in front of about fifty people. Dead. Needless to say, no one saw a thing.

Funny thing is, I remember seeing Nee step out of a car a few months earlier onto the same spot, tightly holding the hands of his two little daughters. The girls were dressed beautifully in their First Communion dresses, and he was making like the perfect daddy, as proud as could be as he led them into the party he had arranged for them in his bar. Reminds me now of me and my little girls. But he and I were nothing alike. I did what I did because it was my job. Never simply to take away someone's self-respect. He was a bully. He got what he deserved.

Tim Brown was another merciless bully. One night, Brown was beating the crap out of this kid in front of Triple O's, the hard-nosed roadhouse bar that was one of Whitey's hangouts. The kid was begging Brown to stop. But Brown, a mean prick, wouldn't let up. He was shouting at the kid, "Every time I see you on the streets, motherfucker, I'm going to beat the shit out of you!"

Brown left the kid with not much choice, especially in our part of the neighborhood. The kid went home, got a gun, came back and blew Brown's head off. Brown received his payback, sitting in the front seat of his car on Broadway, in front of a hundred people. And you know what? Big surprise. The cops couldn't locate a single witness.

Some people are given a second chance to give up on their bullying ways. Take Kevin Watts, the younger brother of my good friend Ronny Watts. Kevin was a real wise-ass when he was in his teens. That was a problem for me, because when Ronny went away for five and a half years, it was my job to look after Kevin. Kevin's attitude didn't make this chore easy. Even worse, it almost cost him his life.

Kevin was having problems with his girlfriend, the niece of a guy named Richie Denn. Kevin couldn't seem to get it through his head that no meant no. Richie was a bit of a punk with something of a mean streak, which made him normal for the regulars who hung around Connolly's bar. After hearing about the abuse, Richie approached Kevin and told him to keep his hands off her. In response, Kevin kicked the shit out of Richie. Richie took his lumps but didn't let it die. A few days later, he approached Kevin again and tried to be a diplomat. "Listen, bro," Richie said, "if you want to beat the fuck out of me, fine. I can take it. But I'm telling you to keep your hands off my niece."

Kevin Watts was not moved in the least. "Listen, I'll do whatever the fuck I want, and the next time you get in my face, I'm going to beat the fuck out of you all over again."

Some people know only one language. And Richie Denn was about to speak it. "Okay, you're real fucking tough. Let's see how tough you are when you're dead." Then, right in the middle of Broadway, and in full daylight, Richie took out a .25 Baretta, a real favorite among Southie thugs, and shot Kevin in the stomach. Kevin collapsed on the ground, and Richie bolted down the street. Kevin was rushed to the hospital and survived, eventually making a full recovery.

This time, someone squealed. Richie was arrested, charged, and convicted of attempted murder. Unfortunately, he got sent away to Massachusetts Correctional Institute, in Norfolk, where Kevin's big brother Ronny was also doing time. You don't have to be a rocket scientist to know this wasn't good for Richie's health. Richie had only been there a few months when a couple inmates threw him off a tier twenty feet off the ground. Richie was all messed up, but he lived. After a stay in the infirmary, he was transferred to another prison. From my point of view, Richie got off easy.

But Kevin Watts learned his lesson. He's no longer a bully. Maybe it has as much to do with the fact that he's now a successful pro boxer, with a healthy respect and appreciation for the damage fists can do, as it does with his brush with death.

I got a particular charge out of banging out this one dickhead one summer. It was pure enjoyment and adrenaline rush. Whitey told me that this maggot needed a big lesson, that he should be handled with "extreme prejudice." I knew the club where the maggot was drinking, but didn't want to create a big scene. And it wasn't necessary. I knew where he lived, by the beach in Southie. It was a summer night, pouring rain. I prepared by breaking a toothpick off in his front-door lock so he couldn't give me the slip by quickly disappearing inside. I hid in the bushes in front of the house, wearing a military-issue rain poncho and armed with a baseball bat. I was all fired up. That's why Whitey and his gang loved me: I treated missions like I was a Marine on recon. Sometimes I wanted to put shoe polish on my face, throw on my cammies, and go to work.

The dickhead was out drinking late and he kept me waiting in the rain. This really pissed me off. Eventually he showed up at three-thirty in the morning, stumbling shit-faced out of a cab in drenching rain. I watched him walk up the walkway and try to get into the house.

After fifteen seconds of struggling to get the key in the lock, it finally dawned on him that he'd been set up. When he turned around, I made my move. The look of terror in his eyes was a turn-on. I was on him in a second. *Whack!... Bam!... Whack!*

He never even screamed, just opened his mouth and whimpered as I beat him with the bat. To make sure I didn't kill him, but simply inflicted enduring agony, I aimed at his arms and legs. You should have heard the cracks, the pitiful whimpers. After he crumbled on the front step, rolling around in a fetal position, I delivered my trademark punt to the ribs. *Whoomp!* That prick was in a world of hurt. But he lived. I left, thinking, What a great night. Even with the pouring rain. I didn't think it could get any better.

But one was better. This one was nasty. In some ways, it was worse than clipping someone. A pal of Whitey's was on the outs with his wife. And there was this other guy, an asshole I'll call Paul, who figured that, with the marriage on the rocks, he might be able to gain a bit of the wife's affection. One afternoon, Paul arrived at the woman's house. She was the only one home. Paul came on to her but when he was rebuffed, he gave her a hard time. Turned out he was whacked out on Percodans. He must have been really whacked, because he ended up slapping the woman in the face. The woman started screaming at Paul, telling him that her husband was a friend of Whitey's and that he was playing with all sorts of trouble. He shouted right back at her, "I don't give a fuck who your husband knows!" Real stupid.

It wasn't long before Whitey got a call, filling him in. And it might've been on the same day that Whitey pulled his car over to where I was standing on the corner of E Street and Broadway. "Hey, Ed, have you seen Paul around?" Whitey asked.

"Nah, Jimmy, haven't seen him. Is everything all right?"

Whitey told me what had happened, adding that, from what he'd heard, Paul had made a point of saying that Whitey's name didn't intimidate him. That was all I needed to know. I gave Whitey a wink. He gave me a wave and drove away.

Now I was on the hunt. Man, did I love this. I went right to his house and he wasn't home. But in a little field next to his house was a small camper with the door open. I looked inside and there he was, out cold on the floor, sleeping with one leg resting on a built-in couch. Sleeping like a baby, probably drugged out or drunk. Before going inside, I stood at the door and checked outside to make sure no one was looking. All was clear. I noticed a cinder block on the ground, which I scooped up, and then I entered the camper. Numb-nuts was still lying on the floor with one leg resting on the couch, sleeping peacefully.

I raised the cinder block over my head, as if it were one of those amusement park mallets that shoot a ball to the bell at the top of a tower, and looked down at his leg to make sure I had it lined up right. Then I came down full force, driving the cinder block right above the knee.

What an unbelievable sound of bone splintering, cracking, breaking. There's nothing like it. Then the scream of absolute terror and agony. "Aagggghhh! My god! . . . Don't kill me! Please don't kill me!"

You should've seen Paul's face. He was in so much shock that the pain hadn't set in yet. His eyes were wide open and his mouth was open even wider. Pure horror. He had his arms up, trying to shield himself. I reached down, grabbed him by the throat and backhanded him. With my hand on his throat, I kneeled next to him and brought my face to within six inches of his. "Listen, you fucking piece of shit," I said. "If you even look at my friend's wife again, you will be fucking gone. You hear me, you maggot?"

"Yeah, yeah, yeah," he whimpered. "I understand. Please . . . please . . . just don't kill me." I gave him an open-handed bitch-slap and walked out the door. As I was walking away from the camper, I looked at my crotch and noticed I had a semi. It was better than sex, especially when I heard that bone crack.

A week later, Paul wobbled into Connolly's on a pair of crutches and begged me to drop things. His leg was like an erector set, held together with pins. The bone had snapped in two. I told him we were all set as long as he heeded my advice.

To me, that was a perfect mission: Whitey was pleased, my victim was grateful he was still alive, the story of my vicious beating added to my clout, and a wife's reputation had been restored. And I'd inflicted great pain upon a loser sorrier than me.

# A Member of the Family

No question, I was making inroads into Whitey's crew. I began to feel more confident of my position as someone who mattered. In 1986, not long after I won the New England Golden Gloves title, I got a pretty good idea of the regard in which Whitey held me when my brother Ronnie, strung out on drugs, just about committed suicide by robbing and pistol-whipping Whitey's personal florist, the owner of Stapleton Flowers in Southie. This guy had been serving Whitey for decades.

"Are you out of your fucking mind?" I said. "Messing with Whitey's man?! You couldn't have ripped off someone else or come to me? Guys have been killed for far less than what you just did." But Ronnie was too stoned to hear one word I said.

The minute I left him, I went straight to Whitey. "My brother's got a bad drug problem, Jimmy," I told him. "My lawyer and I have been shopping around for judges who'll sentence him to a jail program that'll help him. I know what he did to your man and I'm here to rectify it any way I can."

"It's a good thing you came here today," Whitey told me. "Because we were about to make a move on him. Out of respect for you, I'll let you handle it."

I was grateful for his consideration, and aware that he was doing me a favor. But if he had tried to wipe out Ronnie, I would have killed him. When it comes to my brother, I never waver. This time, all three of us were lucky. Whitey let me replace the $1500 my brother had stolen and already used on drugs. I tried to give the florist more money, but the old man wouldn't take a cent more. If I hadn't spoken to Whitey, my brother would have been buried over by Florian Hall in Dorchester, the function hall and meeting place for off-duty firefighters that doubled as the dumping ground for all the guys who'd pissed off Whitey.

As one of my boss's most trusted enforcers, I was called in to resolve a "territory" issue: a kid named Richard was dealing angel dust in South

Boston, a severe no-no with Whitey. When he first heard what Richard was doing, he dispatched one of his "community relations" liaisons to communicate both his displeasure and a cease-and-desist order. Whitey was nice about it, though. He suggested that Richard might find more fertile ground for business in nearby Charlestown. Weakening another criminal organization's infrastructure always made Whitey happy.

But Richard didn't get the message. Not long after Whitey's outreach effort, word came back that Richard was peddling junk again. Around the same time, I got a call on my cell phone from Kevin Weeks. "Hey, Edzo, what are you up to?" he asked.

"On my way out to the gym, bro." I said.

"Why don't you stop on over to Castle Island before you work out? Jimmy needs to talk with you."

"Everything all right?"

"Yeah, no biggie. Jimmy just needs a piece of business taken care of. He needs a message delivered." When I heard that, I felt a delicious jolt of adrenaline. I jumped in my truck and blew over to Castle Island. To hell with the speed limit.

Whitey was waiting for me near the main entrance to the fort with Weeks and the usual hangers-on: younger wanna-bes and older, ruddy-faced Southie natives with flat, narrow-rimmed, beretlike scally caps covering their heads, who played life straight but knew Bulger long before he was "Whitey." Whitey usually enjoyed the company, but when he needed to discuss business, he'd make a point of grabbing Kevin or another insider and bid everyone else adieu. Sometimes, guys didn't get the message and tried trailing him, but Whitey always had a signal in that case. One of his favorite signals was twisting the claddagh ring on his finger, indicating that Kevin was to divert the clueless prick. This was almost always done nicely, with no harsh words. After all, Whitey had a public image to maintain.

As I approached, Kevin waved. Whitey, as usual, didn't react. But behind his mirrored shades, he did what he always did: studied the grass, the ocean, the seagulls, mothers with their strollers, some teenager walking by, the hangers-on, a plane flying overhead, Kevin, and, oh yeah, me. He didn't miss a thing. He was always on the alert, taking it all in. It was the Whitey M.O.: cool, noncommittal, power held in reserve. When I got up to the castle entrance, I said hello to everyone, but just nodded at Whitey.

"Eddie Mac, my boy," Whitey said and smiled lightly.

"Hey, Jimmy," I said.

To his groupies, Whitey said, "Hey, boys, Kevin and Eddie Mac and I have some things to talk over. We're going to take a walk, so if you'll excuse us."

Everyone grumbled their respectful assent. Whitey then turned and started walking down a twisted path that ran along the castle perimeter. Kevin followed a step behind Whitey and I was a step behind Kevin. Whitey had his hands in the front pockets of his pants, his head turned toward the water. We walked for fifty yards in silence, then Whitey stopped and turned around. He didn't say anything, just looked out at the ocean, his hands still in his pockets. Kevin and I stood there, quiet. This was a situation in which we didn't speak unless spoken to. After a few seconds of silence, Whitey fixed his gaze on me.

"Eddie, a situation has developed," he said calmly. "There is this fuck-up. Well, you know the kid. Richard. He's been selling the dust and smack. I had Bobby go over and talk to him about closing up shop and moving on, but, for some reason, Eddie, Richard didn't get the message. I don't know if it's his hearing or what. But the situation has deeply disturbed me and a lot of other people here in town. You know what I'm saying, Eddie, right?"

"Absolutely, Jimmy," I replied.

"Yes, yes, that's good, Eddie. Here's what I'd like to see happen. You have an excellent track record in being able to resolve issues like this. And, well, what I'd really like, Eddie, is for you to go pay him a visit and. . . ." Whitey suddenly stopped talking. With his flair for the dramatic, he casually reached up with his right hand and pulled his Foster Grants away from his face, revealing those unsettling and beautiful ice-blue eyes. He fixed them on me and, with the most chilling emphasis, said calmly, "Eddie, what Richard needs to know is that if he doesn't immediately leave this neighborhood, then he will never leave this neighborhood. You understand what I'm saying?"

"Of course, Jimmy."

"Good, Eddie. Like I always say, I can count on Eddie Mac."

"Jimmy, I'm on it."

I had my marching orders. I gave Whitey and Kevin the Southie wave and headed toward my truck. (The Southie Wave, which was invented by Johnnie Pretzie, is a version of the University of Texas "hook 'em horns," in which your thumb, index finger, and pinky point upward and your two middle fingers are clenched down, and you give your wrist a little pivot.) I hadn't taken more than a few steps when I heard Whitey say, "And Eddie Mac . . . "

I turned around immediately. "Yeah, Jimmy?"

"Eddie, I just wanted to make sure that you understood that this is an issue that needs to be handled with extreme prejudice."

"Absolutely," I said. Whitey gave me a nod, and turned back to talk with Kevin.

This particular mission was no easy payday. Richard was not only stupid and fearless, always a dangerous combination, but young, about twenty-five, and solid, about 6' 4", 230 pounds, with a reputation as a brawler. He had no problem pulling a trigger or wielding a knife or the nearest heavy object at hand. (In another life, I might have enjoyed hanging around with ol' Richard). But whatever I did had to leave a lasting impression, the type of message that would not only persuade him to leave Southie, but disabuse him of any idea of retaliation. I liked to give my victims something to remember me by. Sometimes, that something to remember was a permanent limp or even a scar, kind of a hoodlum's scarlet letter. No matter what it was, Richard would forever remember Whitey Bulger and Eddie Mac.

Richard was a typical dealer, a nocturnal animal; he didn't start roaming the streets until ten or eleven at night. He was smart about one thing; he didn't use the junk himself. Or if he did, he kept it to a minimum.

No one knew where he lived, but, like most drug dealers, Richard had a pattern. I knew that the Old Colony Projects in Southie were one of his favorite haunts. I planned to run him down there that night. I know this doesn't sound like sophisticated detective work, but then again, locating my game wasn't what endeared me to Whitey. It was what I did *after* I'd located my game that made me a franchise player.

I was on my own, because if I had to kill anyone, I didn't want any witnesses. It was close to midnight, the witching hour, when I finally found our boy, a mere ten hours after Whitey put me on the job. He was on a corner on the outskirts of the projects, just as I'd suspected. I'd been driving around for two hours looking for the prick, which only added to my ill humor. I pulled my truck over to the curb, a hundred yards from where Richard was shooting the shit with some walking-skeleton junkies. They were nicely illuminated under a street light. Did I tell you how stupid this guy was?

Richard didn't even notice me. If he'd had better street sense, he would have picked me up while he still had time to run. He would have wondered why, on a warm spring evening, a guy wearing a full-length leather coat had just stepped out of a truck. If he'd had any brains, any instinct, he would have seen the trench coat and thought Concealed Weapon, and disappeared. No dice. He remained blissfully clueless. Meanwhile, bedecked in my stylish, and, of course, stolen maxi coat, I slipped into the shadows of a nearby apartment building. The folds of my coat concealed my Mossberg pump-action shotgun, custom outfitted with a handle rather than a stock end, which made it less like a rifle and more like a juiced-up handgun. One shell in the chamber of that Mossberg had Richard's name on it.

I hugged the side of the building. It took just minutes until I was twenty-five yards away and parallel to my prey. His back to me, he couldn't see a thing. The addicts he was talking with were facing me, but I was still hidden in shadow.

I felt inside my coat to make sure the Mossberg was hanging properly, and then stepped out of the shadows. I didn't run, but tiptoed quickly forward. I'd taken only a few strides when the junkies picked me up. I held my finger to my lips, to no use, because Richard could tell, from the expression in their eyes, that someone was coming. He turned and froze. With less than fifteen yards remaining between us, he knew he was toast. The druggies were already backing up. Richard pretended to be cool, but, in reality, he was about to shit himself. I was five yards from him, and he realized I was all business.

"Hey, hey, Eddie Mac, whaatttt . . . whaattt's . . . goin' on?" he stammered. By this point, the junkies were hauling ass.

I pulled out the Mossberg and pointed the barrel directly at his head. "Awwwwww, shiittttt, Edddieeeee Mac!" He was crying out the words while he gripped his head with his hands. "Please!!!! Please!!! Don't kill me! Don't kill me!"

I balanced the shotgun, keeping the business end about a foot from his face. Richard was now whimpering incoherently. "Weren't you fucking told not to sell dust and smack in this neighborhood?" I said, gazing over the barrel.

"Ah, Eddie Mac, Eddie Mac, please, please, I'll never do it again. I learned my lesson," he whimpered. He reached out and tried to grab my coat in a plea for mercy. I slapped his hand away with my free arm.

"You're fucking right you'll never do it again," I said. Then I smacked him on the side of the head with the gun. As he stumbled sideways, I aimed at his calf and pulled the trigger. There was an almost instantaneous report and a scream of agony. I was so close to Richard that the force of the blast tore open his calf to the bone.

Richard collapsed. He rolled on the ground and then recoiled into a fetal position, making God-awful animal noises. I kneeled next to him. "There better not be a next time, Richard," I said evenly. "Because if there is, I am going to take this rifle," and I tapped the Mossberg against his cheek, "and blow your head off while you're eating supper with your mother. Now, you have a good night." I stood up and walked away.

We never saw Richard again in South Boston. We did hear, sad to say, that he was crippled for life. But, then again, at least he got a chance to leave town. Others weren't so lucky. Whitey was so pleased with my handling of the situation that he gave me a "performance bonus" of $5000 and told me to go shopping. I bought a couple of suits and some sneakers and sweaters, but the clothes weren't the important thing. I had made my leader very happy.

# The Dog Room

Whitey forbade his runners to use drugs and stayed away from the junk himself, but sex was an acceptable avenue of pleasure. As in everything Whitey did, he exhibited his own unique brand of deviance here as well. Like a good soldier, I helped him every way I could.

My main contribution to this pastime was through MacKenzie's Gym, which was also known as the South Boston Academy of Martial Arts, as well as the Andrews Square Athletic Club. From 1979 to 1987, I ran MacKenzie's as a wholesome place where everybody got his money's worth and was given lots of personal attention. The kids I took in used the time to skip rope and box, take classes with me, or just hang out. They got in shape and learned kung fu and boxing, but it was the discipline and self-respect introduced to their lives that paid the biggest dividends.

Yet MacKenzie's had another side to it. Most of it took place after the gym was closed at night, but not all of it. Day or night, MacKenzie's Gym was a veritable animal farm of sucking, fucking, and voyeurism.

In addition to the main shower area, we had another shower area, actually a large stall with a single shower head, that was part of a room that measured about twenty feet by twenty feet and in which we had a four-seater Jacuzzi. The layout catered to our flesh obsession. Behind one of the walls was a big open space, which the public knew as a "utility room." We replaced part of that wall with a two-way mirror that gave us a full view of the shower and hot tub. You could fit four people comfortably into that space, but we often crammed in as many as ten.

In addition, there was a storage area on top of an eight-foot wall. You got up there by climbing a ladder. We turned that space into a small lounge, complete with two couches and a coffee table. The area also had a view, courtesy of another two-way mirror, of the shower and Jacuzzi. But spying from the lounge was tougher. You had to climb onto a ledge that could hold two people. On many occasions, we defied physics and stuffed four bodies up there.

It didn't take long for us insiders — the trainers and top fighters — to give that area another name: the Dog Room. That's where privileged spectators would assemble for the "dog shows" — sex shows, usually involving women we'd picked up that night at Connolly's, three hundred yards down the street. Other unwitting participants in our theater of flesh were the Cardinal Cushing High School girls who trained at the gym, or whom we'd lured into our den with promises of a free and private Jacuzzi. Nice guys, huh?

Most of the Cardinal Cushing girls would have nothing to do with our roughhouse gang of fighters and street punks. We were in top physical condition, didn't do drugs, and hardly took a drink, but that didn't mean that these good Catholic schoolgirls weren't scared off by our violent streaks and drug-dealing tendencies. So, if we couldn't have 'em physically, we were gonna get our rocks off anyway.

And it wasn't that difficult. When the Cushing girls took a look around the gym because they were thinking of joining, we told them they should feel free to stop in anytime they wanted to use the hot tub. When they got there, I informed the girls that for health-code reasons they had to shower before jumping in the tub. They understood. After all, we were talking about cleanliness and their own protection.

As soon as the girls walked into the shower and Jacuzzi area and locked the door, I'd circle through the main area of the gym and into the back entrance of the Dog Room. By the time I got there, the tiny room was already packed with my friends, many of whom were panting and grabbing their crotches.

You had to see these girls, sixteen and seventeen years old, most of the time wearing nothing but their birthday suits, soaping up and giggling. Sometimes, a couple would jump in the shower together. They'd be slapping suds on and bending over, driving us bonkers. And if four girls were going to use the Jacuzzi, two or three might stand around naked, waiting for the shower to free up. The heat and tension in the Dog Room were nearly unbearable. The toughest thing to do was to keep quiet. What exquisite torture.

Then the girls would scurry over to the hot tub and jump in. As the guys in the Dog Room jockeyed for position, fighting for a turn to peer in from the ledge next door, the girls relaxed in that hot, bubbling water, a nice sweaty glow spreading all over their faces and shoulders and tits. After a few minutes, they'd get all reflective; the suds seemed to soak away their inhibitions. They'd talk about all sorts of things: sex and guys and guys' cocks and who they wanted to fuck. Man, this wasn't the stuff I thought got tossed around at slumber parties.

Guess who was one of the most enthusiastic voyeurs? Yeah, Whitey. He loved it. If he wasn't fucking the young adoring girls of Southie, he was spying on them. Of course, there was no way he was going to sit with us. When he wanted the Dog Room, he got private shows, at eleven or twelve at night, often with high school girls from the projects whose parents had no idea or interest in where the hell they were.

We were not allowed in the gym when he was there. He usually arranged for this guy named John to perform with women because he had a huge stick. John worshipped Whitey and would do anything to impress him. Other times, Whitey and Kevin would bang two girls together in the Dog Room. But no one ever got to watch Whitey. He never allowed me to see him come into the Dog Room. No surprise. He trusted no one. But he was there. Often.

The rest of us guys had plenty of great moments there ourselves. Like the day one of my buddies showed up at the gym to show off his foxy new girlfriend. As soon as he'd introduced her, he pulled a few of us aside to explain that she wasn't from the neighborhood and didn't have the same "edge" or experience as our Southie ladies. She was innocent and pure, he explained, and we should watch our mouths and actions around her. He was acting like a girl. Ridiculous. Anyway, he asked for it.

A few days later, he stopped by without her. "Hey, bro," I told him, "if you and your new lady are free tonight, why don't you come over here and use the Jacuzzi? I'll even leave a bottle of Dom here for you. Here's an extra key. We'll be out of here by seven." He didn't hesitate, thanked me, and grabbed the key.

Of course, that night, we had the place staked out. Our boy and his little honey showed up at about eight and headed inside for a little fun. Seven of us followed right behind. By the time we made our way into the Dog Room for our private screening, the little couple were already out of their clothes and in the water. As usual, all the Dog Room boys were jockeying for position and fighting over ledge space.

And what a show. Man, this girl may not have been from the neighborhood, and she may have been pure and innocent, but she could suck cock like a champion. And as she was doing it, she was purring just loud enough for us to hear: "Please tell me, baby, when you're going to come. I just love it."

Ah, the perfect time to announce our appearance. I took out a cigarette lighter and flicked it with one hand, and tapped on the mirror with my other hand. If you placed a bright light against the mirror, the people on the blind side could see something of the area on the see-through side. Romeo spotted us first. What a horrifying specter we must have been: our four mugs plastered up against the window, licking our lips, and giving him the finger. He went quickly from shocked to pissed, and started pointing and yelling. Then the girl saw us; she screamed and reached for her clothes. Time to bolt. We were laughing like hell and tripping over each other as we beat a retreat out to Broadway.

When Mike Barnicle interviewed me in 1985 for the television show *Chronicle,* he brought the television cameras to the gym. He saw the door to the Dog Room and asked me what it was. "Just a dressing room," I told him. "No big deal." That could have made an interesting addition to the segment if the cameras had shown what was really behind that door.

Sadly, all good things come to an end. So it was with the Dog Room. Predictably, something mundane led to its downfall. The Dog Room had a window to the outside, which was always covered by a curtain for two reasons. First, so no one on the outside could look in and see what was going on. More important, if the curtain wasn't closed, sunlight could stream through the window and hit the two-way mirror, exposing us Peeping Toms to the girls.

One cloudy, dark afternoon in the spring of '87, a couple of hot high-school seniors who were skipping school stopped into the gym to ask if they could use the Jacuzzi. "Sure," I said. "But, remember, you have to take a shower first." The girls headed for the shower, and I headed for the Dog Room. But I was so fired up that I didn't realize someone had left the window curtain open. Because it was so dark and overcast, I didn't even notice. The girls started doing their best rub-a-dub-dub. Standing directly behind the mirror, I dropped my drawers and started spanking my cock for all it was worth, stroking away, and then . . . disaster.

The clouds parted. A brilliant beam of sunshine slanted through the window of the Dog Room leaving me exposed in a most compromising position. There I was, in full masturbating glory, pants at my ankles, mouth uttering a silent, frozen scream. It took only a second for the girls to ID me. "Eddie MacKenzie! . . . We see you!" the girls screamed in unison. "You fucking sicko!"

The girls were screaming as I yanked up my pants. I pulled open the door and stumbled into the hallway that led to the main area of the gym. I collected myself as best I could, then headed for the front door. I tried to play it cool as I walked stiff-legged across the main part of the gym. Out on the street, I broke into a run until I made it to Connolly's. I hid out for ten minutes at the bar before going back to the scene of the crime. Then I ripped down the two-way mirrors, smashed them, and had them carted away. I bought regular mirrors and had them installed by evening. For a long time after, I denied everything.

But the end of the Dog Room didn't really affect Whitey. He loved young pussy and scored the best of the best when it came to girls from the projects: gorgeous, innocent, and plain stupid. He also had a healthy appetite for the Cardinal Cushing High School teenyboppers in their school uniforms: short, navy-blue skirts, white shirts, and knee-high white socks. He liked them young, around fourteen or fifteen. I couldn't believe the way he handled them. If a group of girls walked by the South Boston Liquor Mart, which was a good two miles from Cardinal Cushing, he'd leave his favorite spot by the door to say hi. He was more than thirty years older than these girls, but he flirted with them as if he were sixteen again. Whitey might have been middle-aged, but he was a star, like Sting, and these girls wanted to be his groupies. The girls he liked looked more sophisticated and more experienced than other girls their age. Whitey took them to the malls and offered them nice clothes, sneakers, gold jewelry, anything at all.

One night, I was trying to get into this beautiful girl's pants myself. She wouldn't let me, and after I'd asked, over and over, "What's wrong?" she suddenly broke down crying.

"Whitey raped me," she told me through her tears. "He made me blow him."

I consoled her, but I didn't really care because all I wanted was to get laid myself; she had gorgeous blond hair and an incredible body. What an asshole I was. The truth is I was never sure exactly what this girl meant by rape. I suspected it wasn't rape by physical force, but rape through sheer intimidation. (For someone like Steve Flemmi, who'd rip off a girl's clothes and sodomize her, it was rape by force.)

Whitey had beaten a rape charge many years before in Montana, and no one in Southie ever dared to file one against him. But I'd bet a month's drug wages that he raped a number of Southie girls. He never had to worry about the parents. Most of them were completely clueless or too busy spending their welfare checks in my bar to notice that their daughters weren't home very often — and looked pale and worried when they were. Just because the girls went to a Catholic school didn't mean anybody in their house was living by the Holy Book.

I heard young girls, thirteen and fourteen, complain about how Whitey liked anal sex. How he paid them extra for it, but they still didn't think it was worth it. Whitey and Stevie would take a girl to Disney World or Ireland, just the three of them for a week or two. Once he even bought a three-decker for the family of a thirteen-year-old named Tammy who looked like a young Playboy Bunny. Talk about a house of prostitution. The parents of yet another of his teenage concubines were awarded a vacation in Hawaii.

I worked uncomplainingly. One time I got a message from Whitey telling me to take care of the delivery of a brand-new living-room set to a house in the projects. "It's coming from Levitz's in Dedham," he told me in the same calm voice with which he'd tell me to break some prick's legs. "Make sure the delivery goes smoothly."

"No problem, Jimmy," I assured him. I knew he was violating somebody's beautiful daughter and this was his way of buying off her parents. To some of these people, a living room set was like hitting the lottery. On a rainy day in early March, 1987, I walked into the girl's home and said to her mother, "I have a special delivery for you, Ma'am. This is from a friend of your daughter, who wants you to have this gift."

The daughter was in school that afternoon — middle school. Her mother said, "Oh, thank you, thank you."

The Levitz delivery men walked in behind me, carrying a beautiful leather couch, a suede loveseat, a glass and brass coffee table, two top-quality end tables, and two lamps. I'd called the family the day before to schedule delivery, so their crappy furniture was gone and the large room was empty and waiting for its new contents. The mother looked adoringly at the furniture, unable to resist touching each piece as the delivery men settled it in its proper place. It was that look of entitlement, of pure pleasure, on that mother's face that got to me. Once everything was settled, I tipped the delivery men and, ever the polite Whitey boy, said good-bye to the mother.

Today, just thinking about that part of my job makes me feel filthy and refuels my desire to be honest about my past. Two rape charges are printed boldly on my criminal record, although in one case the verdict was not guilty, and, in the second case, the charges were dropped. You've got to understand that in my world, there's nothing lower than a rapist. Except for a child molester.

I was seventeen when I was first charged with rape. A buddy and me had picked up a hitchhiker, gone to a dance club with her, and partied till closing. Then the three of us went to my friend's house, where my buddy and I had consensual sex with her. We dropped her off at her home after eating pancakes at IHOP. We didn't know that a jealous boyfriend was stalking her and happened to be waiting nearby when we dropped her off. He then proceeded to beat the piss out of her, and she cried rape. The next day, my buddy and I were arrested. On the first court appearance, she recanted and explained that she'd filed the charge to avoid trouble with her boyfriend. The judge found us not guilty.

The second rape charge was filed in early 1995, when I was going to the University of Massachusetts in Boston, living on Morrissey Boulevard in Dorchester, and sharing a downstairs apartment in a house with a seventeen-year-old named Andy, whose grandmother owned the place. One night, Andy brought home a sixteen-year-old girl and got her drunk. When she puked all over herself and passed out, Andy took off her clothes and washed them while she slept. Then he laid the clothes on the edge of the bed in his room, which was next to mine, and took off. I came home a few hours later. She was still drunk, but had her clothes on and was walking around the apartment. When I asked her where Andy was, she gave me a dirty look. But when I asked her if she wanted a ride home, she said, "Sure."

A few months later, I got a summons in the mail to appear in court for rape of a minor. I was shocked, because I had no memory of ever doing anything like that. Apparently, when Andy's friend got home, she had decided that both me and Andy had raped her. I told Al Nugent, my lawyer, that I got a sense she had done that sort of thing before. When you have a background like mine, people convict you without asking questions, but fortunately the prosecution decided there was no credible evidence against me and dropped all the charges. That's it. No more rapes on my record. Funny thing is, I was watching the *Jerry Springer Show* a few years later, and that same girl bolted from the audience and started wailing on her boyfriend for cheating on her. I called Al and told him to turn on the show right away. Seeing her so wacko on Springer helped remove any doubt from Al's mind that I had been innocent all along.

While I thank God for the wonderful gift of my five daughters, I also wonder if He was punishing me for being a swordsman by giving me girls. And now that two of them are teenagers, growing up in the same city where I, among others, took advantage of so many girls, I'm even more scared. Every day, I face the reality of having to look at my daughters and protect them from predators like the one I used to be. If I could change one thing about my past, it would be that. When I look at their innocence, I apologize for all that I have done to others. If I found out an older guy was trying to go out with one of my daughters, I would make him an offer that he could never refuse: move on or DIE!

My little girls — Devin, ten, Kayla, nine, and Brittany, four — are too young for lectures, but I have talked to their older sisters — Courtney, eighteen, and Lauren, sixteen. I've told them that if they ever have a boyfriend and are in love with him and are thinking about having sex, to talk to Daddy first. They asked me why, and I said I'd make sure they were using contraceptives first. I went on to say that if one or both ever got pregnant, I'd kill the boyfriend. So if they really cared for him, get protection. I went on to say that I didn't expect them to have boyfriends until they were both twenty-one anyway. That part, I said jokingly. But not the part about killing their boyfriends.

The truth is, today I don't find anything having to do with my daughters and sex very funny. If you're not from my world, you can never understand what happens in the inner city today. It's not that different from when I was growing up. These girls are getting laid at the ages of twelve and thirteen. It's impossible to live a sheltered life in the city. There's just too much going on, especially in the projects.

Besides, with Hollywood producing such sexually provocative movies, what's a kid to think? Not too long ago, I took my kids to see *Scary Movie*, a spoof of recent teen movies like *Scream* and *I Know What You Did Last Summer*. In it, the teenaged actors simulated blow jobs; and, in one scene, the filmmakers actually showed a picture of some guy's dick. I was outraged, but my older daughters laughed like it meant nothing to them. The sad part is, if I didn't take them, they'd be pissed because they'd be the only ones among their friends who hadn't seen it. The shoe's on the other foot now.

Today, I think back on the things Whitey used to do with horror. Whitey had no scruples about playing games with somebody else's little girl that aren't described in any textbook on sex education. I remember a cold night in the late winter of '87. I was at Connolly's and, around midnight, realized I'd left something at the gym. I walked out the back door of the bar and started to head up Silver Street to the gym. It was midnight, so I wasn't expecting anyone to be there. I let myself in and started toward my office. When I heard noises in the Dog Room, I thought maybe one of my buddies was getting laid, and headed to the two-way mirror for a private viewing.

What I saw shocked even me. Jimmy Blue Eyes himself. I wanted to get out of there quickly, but curiosity killed the cat; I stayed. A naked girl lay face-down on a plastic tarp on the floor. Whitey, equally naked, kneeled over her. He was spreading different colors of paint all over her body; she looked like a tie-dye T-shirt. She was no older than fifteen or sixteen.

I knew it would mean imminent death if Whitey found out he had an audience, but I couldn't look away. He didn't say a word, just silently did his Picasso routine on her body. The girl, who had long blond hair, looked scared to death, and barely moved as the painter worked on his canvas. I could see her face, and realized I'd seen her hanging around the South Boston Liquor Mart. She was one of Whitey's Cardinal Cushing groupies. When he was finished, he turned her over and began having sex with her. What a wacko.

But Whitey being Whitey, he also had a "normal" relationship that made you wonder if what you'd see in the Dog Room was a mirage. Like the one he shared with Teresa Stanley. To our knowledge, he never married her. But here she was, a drop-dead knockout on his arm for close to twenty-five years. She had a bunch of kids, and lived up on Fourth and H Streets in Southie, right next door to the mother of Kevin Weeks. Whitey was like a father to Teresa's kids, although he disowned her junkie son when his efforts to help the kid failed. Guess he couldn't handle a kid strung out on the drugs he peddled. We all would have bet a nice chunk of the bank that he was more than just "like" a father to two of her beautiful daughters. The blond hair and blue eyes sure looked familiar.

It wasn't like we saw Whitey and Teresa dining out every night. If he took her out, it wasn't in his familiar blue Marquis, but in the rarely seen Mercedes. It was part of the Whitey mystique that we never knew what he was doing or with whom. Even when he went away for a few weeks, you had no clue he'd gone, any more than you knew when he was around. I knew he went to Ft. Lauderdale a lot when he and Stevie Flemmi were trying to open a restaurant there. But, most of the time, he was like a fog, something you couldn't quite touch and couldn't quite penetrate, a fog that enveloped you and stripped you of your bearings. But when you felt its icy chill, you sure as hell knew it was there.

If Teresa Stanley was his one "normal" relationship, there were far more examples of his "abnormal" sexual activity. His years in Alcatraz fueled the opinion, held by some of us, that Whitey played both sides of the coin. Even Boston cops and reporters repeated that rumor. Which bring us to the Choctaw Kid, Whitey's closest buddy at Alcatraz. The Choctaw Kid was Clarence Carnes, a full-blooded Choctaw Indian born to poor parents on the Choctaw Reservation in Atoka, Oklahoma. He committed his first crime at eight, when he stole candy bars at school.

At sixteen, the Choctaw Kid was sentenced to life in prison at Granite Reformatory in Oklahoma for the murder of a service-station attendant during a holdup. But he didn't stay there long. A year later, he and two other men escaped from the reformatory and hijacked a truck driven by an elderly couple. He was convicted on federal kidnapping charges and sentenced to ninety-nine years in Leavenworth. But he acted up and was transferred to Alcatraz in 1945, when he was eighteen, one of the youngest inmates to be locked up there.

A year later, the Choctaw Kid and five other inmates took part in an escape attempt that went bad. After a three-day siege, two guards and three inmates were dead. The Choctaw Kid survived and, unlike the other two inmates, was spared the death penalty because he had refused to murder the guards he had been assigned to kill.

When they closed Alcatraz in 1963, Carnes was transferred to Springfield, Missouri, and then to Leavenworth, from which he was released in 1973. But he spent his last fifteen years in and out of prison on parole violations, mostly because of a drinking problem. He died at age sixty-one in 1988 at the Medical Center for Federal Prisoners in Springfield, Missouri, having spent most of his adult life in prisons. Now, here's where my boss enters the picture. It wasn't widely publicized, but, after Whitey went on the lam, FBI agents searching for him discovered that, in early 1989, he paid to have Carnes's body pulled out of a pauper's grave outside the Missouri prison hospital and moved to Daisy, Oklahoma, for a proper Choctaw Indian burial that included a $4,000 bronze casket and Choctaw preacher and singers.

The funeral director in Atoka, Robert Embry, told the *Boston Herald* that he'd gotten a call from a "James" in Boston who wanted to bury his friend in Billy Cemetery on Indian land. According to the *Herald*, James told the director that Carnes had taken care of him in Alcatraz and even saved his life. James explained that he ran a liquor store in Boston and might buy a boat and take a cruise around the world.

According to Carnes's nephew James Erkin, Whitey pulled up in a Lincoln Continental, wearing a sweatsuit, tennis shoes, and a pile of gold jewelry, and accompanied by a blond woman who was, in all likelihood, Catherine Greig, the broad he took off with when he went on the lam six years later.

Before the funeral, Whitey even drove 240 miles to Tulsa, to bail the Choctaw Kid's grandnephew out of jail. He couldn't have been nicer at the funeral itself, chatting away with the thirty-five people there, paying $500 for a headstone that still stands at Carnes's grave, and handing out $50 and $100 bills to anyone else involved in the funeral service. According to the funeral director, Whitey spent around $10,000 to give the Choctaw Kid a proper Indian good-bye.

I have trouble picturing the Choctaw Kid with my boss. Even though they were less than three years apart in age, the two of them must have been one odd pair when they met at Alcatraz in the late 1950s. Bulger was this tough Irish kid raised in Southie, while Carnes was an Indian raised on farmland in the middle of nowhere. Whitey was new to the prison system, while Carnes had received a life sentence for murder when he was sixteen. Whitey might have told Carnes's relatives at the funeral that he viewed the Choctaw Kid as his prison protector and owed him his life. From what I've heard many times, the only thing that Whitey owed him was his virginity.

A pal of mine told me a story that he swears is true. He said Catherine Greig, whose picture is next to Whitey's on the FBI's Most Wanted List and who is allegedly on the run with him today, had a younger brother,

David, who lived on the Cape. A mighty handsome boy in his twenties, David did some accounting for Whitey. When David committed suicide in 1978, the word on the street was that he'd killed himself because he was Whitey's boy toy. Freddy Weichel, who was good friends with the Greig family, said the kid just couldn't take it anymore. He says Whitey started off by raping the kid. Then he bought him a car and showered him with gifts, all for the privilege of fucking him. At first, people said Greig died of an accidental drug overdose, but those who knew him well said it was because of Whitey's constant advances. And it was no overdose. The kid shot himself in the bathroom.

Of all the stories I've ever heard about Whitey, the one that most upset me came from my friend Mike Regan. Mikey, the stepson of one of Whitey's major partners in the Southie drug scene, is eleven years younger than me, and he has been a friend for fifteen years. He's always looked up to me and I've tried to teach him how to get along in the world. I've gotten him jobs and stayed with him, even when he was behind bars. I wasn't the least bit surprised when he finally told me the story he'd been hiding for twenty-two years. I'd always known that years earlier he'd been molested and raped. But when he finally told me that it was Whitey, it all made sense. Sick, disgusting, pathetic Whitey Bulger sense.

Mikey's life might actually be weirder than mine. A brilliant, athletically gifted, movie-star-handsome kid, he had lots of chips lined up in his favor. Except for two big problems: his stepfather and Whitey. In 1986, Mikey was a senior at the Florida Air Academy in Melbourne, a competitive prep school and military academy for future pilots. He was distinguishing himself as a top student and cross-country runner when he laid into his stepfather for beating his mother. He fled Florida and headed back to Southie, where nothing but trouble lay waiting. He ended up in jail on a manslaughter charge in connection with a fatal hit-and-run; he'd stolen a car, but wasn't the driver at the time of the accident. Mikey had learned the lesson well at the knee of his stepfather and Uncle Jimmy: Thou Shalt Not Rat. So he spent the next five and a half years in jails throughout Massachusetts. He's been out for seven and a half years now. He's never looked better, is in love with a great woman who loves his six-year-old son from his first marriage, and is hoping to get a college degree. But he'll probably never get over the rage that still burns deep inside.

It isn't difficult to imagine how adorable Mikey was back then. With his curly black hair and deep dimples, he was natural fodder for a pedophile like Whitey, who spent countless hours in Mikey's home in the D Street Project, always bearing presents like U.S. savings bonds and gift certificates. Mikey was only nine years old when Whitey molested him.

It started innocently enough. One day when Mikey had gathered up his ice skates to go to the Donovan Rink in South Boston, Whitey offered to drive him to the MDC (Metropolitan District Commission) rink instead. Whitey, wearing his trademark dark glasses and baseball cap, was in one of his talkative moods that day. He went on and on, lecturing him about sports and politics and people and any subject that came to his mind. Mikey never bothered to try and join in these one-way conversations. He just sat there in Whitey's big blue Marquis, hugging his skates, looking out the window.

Whitey did terrible things to him en route to the skating rink, things Mikey refused to think about for twenty-two years. But when I finally told Mikey what my tutor had done to me, he had the guts to tell me what had happened to him.

Whitey took Mikey to a secluded spot where he pulled over his car, took off his sunglasses, and unzipped his zipper. He took out his dick and expertly placed his hand on the back of young Mikey's head, gently pulling him toward his erect penis. He told Mikey to open his mouth, and the rest, I know only too well, is history. Mikey remembers Whitey staring at him the entire time. "Don't worry about it," Whitey told him when he was finished and had put his sunglasses back on. "You're not going to get into trouble because of this. Don't tell your stepfather. You know what he's like." Mikey did know. He knew how badly his stepfather could, and did, beat him for little things. How could he ever tell him about this?

This scene repeated itself. Whitey went to the rink with Mikey and stayed there while he skated, or tried to skate, his mind so full of what had happened that he could barely move around the rink. Whitey stayed there the whole time, talking to people, waving to others, and watching Mikey. Afterward, he'd take him out for ice cream before bringing him back home. I don't know what it is about ice cream that makes child molesters think the kids want a cone. Maybe, in a warped way, they think they're giving the powerless kids back their innocence with this gift. God knows no kid who was ever molested could swallow one lick of any ice cream. "Tell your stepdad I'll call him later," he'd say before he drove off, leaving Mikey to go in the house alone, dragging his skates toward his front door, his head down, his body hurting.

One day, Whitey came into the variety store that Mikey's mother and stepfather ran and, while Mikey's grandmother was at the front of the store, Whitey led Mikey to the back where he made Mikey blow him again. After five more assaults, in Whitey's car and in the store, Mikey knew he couldn't take any more. He tried to talk to his mother about it, but she had too many problems of her own with his stepfather to pay much attention to him. He was a quiet kid and didn't say much, so it was real easy for his parents to ignore him. After that, Mikey managed to avoid Whitey, leaving the house the minute he walked in, making sure he never ended up in that blue Marquis again. Whitey wasn't stupid. He knew when the kid had had enough, so he packed up his games and found other toys to play with.

As for Mikey, he's deeply ashamed by what happened to him when he was too innocent to protect himself. He knows that if anyone ever touched his son the way Whitey touched him, he'd mutilate that person with his bare hands. His only regret is that he believes Whitey is dead, because he had always planned, somehow, someday, to do it himself.

And imagine how the Southie crowd, which gets its underwear in knots over the gays marching in the St. Patty's Day Parade, would react to the thought that their Robin Hood hero swings both ways, a cross-dressing, bisexual killer and pedophile.

# Family Problems

In 1989 I was thirty, making big dough and doing my best to make Whitey's world a happier place. Yet, I wasn't able to do a damn thing to help the guy who was the closest thing to a father I'd ever have, Johnny Pretzie. We'd even had adoption papers drawn up in probate court making our father-son relationship legal, but we kept procrastinating and they never got signed.

Late in 1986, after we won the New England Golden Gloves championship, things began to unravel for Pretzie. The booze was destroying his mind. His big problems had actually begun in '83 when, at sixty-seven, lonely, sober, and a sucker for companionship, he met Laura, a Roslindale skank in her mid-twenties. She was the lethal poison that would eventually kill him. He started to drink more heavily whenever they were together. He started out sipping milk and coffee liqueur cocktails at bars, and within a year or so was driving his Trans Am at top speeds while swilling from a bottle of Yukon Jack. Pretzie always had a mean streak, but he was usually able to keep it under wraps — until the booze took hold. As things got worse and worse with Laura, he'd drink more and more. She'd torture him with stories of her infidelity. He'd slap her around and she'd call the cops and they'd throw him in jail. But the next day, Laura would decide not to press charges and the two of them would leave the jail all lovey-dovey. They even had a kid together.

Yet, from 1984 through 1986, Pretzie was able to hold it together well enough to teach in the gym and give me hands-on instruction. Almost all the New England champions MacKenzie's Gym produced in the eighties owe Johnny Pretzie a major debt of gratitude. I know I'd have never won the super heavyweight title in '86 without him.

But late that year, his exercise regimen began to slip and his temper became more volatile. He was frequently in scuffles and the two of us couldn't even talk without getting into an argument. One night he had to be restrained by four cops before he was thrown in protective custody for the evening. What was most dangerous about Pretzie's behavior was that he continued to carry a gun. On more than one occasion, he took it out while in a drunken rant and waved it around, shouting and swearing at the top of his lungs.

One night at a party in the spring of 1988, the two of us got into a pissing match about something stupid. People were watching and we really embarrassed ourselves. After that we hardly talked. That fall, Laura died of alcohol poisoning. Pretzie retreated further into himself. The following summer, after midnight on July fifth, Pretzie was drinking heavily at O'Leary's Pub. He got into an argument with an off-duty Boston Housing Authority cop named Richard Geary. Words led to fists and, though Pretzie was sixty-nine and Geary thirty-three, the younger man got the worst of it. The fight was broken up and Geary bolted. But he wasn't done. He went to get his gun. Around two that morning, as Pretzie was leaning in a stupor against a car in front of the pub, Geary approached and pumped a single bullet into Pretzie's eye. He was rushed to the hospital but pronounced dead a half hour later. Geary was caught and later found guilty of second-degree murder.

Johnny Pretzie was buried in Fairview Cemetery in Hyde Park, Massachusetts. I paid $1200 for his headstone, which bears an engraving and a quote that I ordered. The engraving is of a recumbent tiger and the inscription reads: "The Tiger Finally Sleeps." I should have done more for the man I considered my father, but I could never figure out how to help him.

No wonder I gravitated toward Whitey. The list of people still there for me kept shrinking. I was terrified that my brother Ronnie's name would be struck from that list. He came too close too many times. On May 15, 1988, messed up on coke, booze, and Valium, Ronnie left his house on Silver Street, went around the corner to West Broadway, walked into a mini-mart, Store 24, and said to the clerk, "Gimme a pack of smokes." When he did, Ronnie pulled out a gun and said, "Now give me all your money." The clerk handed over the money. Ronnie pocketed the cash, grabbed a couple packs of cigarettes, and staggered out the front door. With the gun at his side, he proceeded up the street a hundred yards to Brigham's Ice Cream. At Brigham's, semi-conscious, barely aware of what he was doing, Ronnie pushed opened the door and began to wave horrified customers out of the way with the gun. He somehow made it to the counter and stammered, "Gimme a hot fudge sundae."

The clerk behind the counter, a guy from the neighborhood, replied, "Ronnie, what the fuck are you doing?"

"Don't you fucking give a fucking shit what I'm fucking doing," said Ronnie. "Just give me a fucking sundae . . . and all your money."

I don't know if the sundae had nuts or what, but Ronnie got his ice cream and about seventy bucks. He walked out of Brigham's just as the cops were running into Store 24. Then, digging into his sundae and clutching wads of cash, Ronnie walked two hundred yards to a liquor store. There he grabbed a six pack, pointed the gun at the guy behind the counter, and asked for all the money in the register, scoring about three hundred dollars. Ronnie left the liquor store just as the cops were running into Brigham's. He was totally oblivious to them. Now, juggling the cash, the cigarettes, the sundae, the six pack, and, oh yeah, the gun, Ronnie walked a quarter-mile to the triple-decker where he lived. He parked his ass on the front stoop, gobbled a few Valiums, popped open a beer, and began to shovel the ice cream in his mouth. He was sitting there all of thirty seconds when the cops pulled up. They were crying with laughter. "Hey, Ronnie, why don't you get in?" said one of the cops, holding open the rear door of the cruiser. Ronnie was so messed up that he just nodded and stood. Ice cream dripped down his face and the front of his shirt. Leaving the gun and the money and everything else on the stoop, he walked toward the cruiser and got into the backseat without a word.

Ronnie was charged with three armed robberies. The bail was ten grand, which I posted. This was no hardship for me because I was making that much a week. I called Al Nugent, who said the only way to get him help was to get him sentenced right away. Ronnie's girlfriend Maria, now his wife, was pregnant at the time with his second kid. Al got Ronnie a court date and the judge finally agreed to ten years at Massachusetts Correctional Institute Concord, a maximum-security facility, which meant Ronnie would be eligible for parole in eighteen months. Plenty of time to clean up. And when he was on parole, he'd be subjected to a urine test weekly. Getting Ronnie to court was the tough part. Al kept him at his office with a bottle of Sambuca until it was finally time to go. Ronnie ended up serving three months at Concord, and was then shipped to the medium-security facility at MCI Bridgewater for fourteen months. Due to overcrowding, he was housed in a mobile home rather than a cell. I took Maria and their two babies, Ronnie and Sherry, up there to visit him weekly. Since he didn't have access to drugs there, he managed to get clean.

I also brought food and money to Maria and the babies in their Quincy apartment. I made sure they were safe and well taken care of. Nine months into Ronnie's sentence, I dropped in unannounced and found a guy visiting Maria. I couldn't blame the woman. She knew Ronnie was doing drugs and probably figured he would be away for awhile. The kids were there, so I acted real cool. I could see that both she and the guy were scared shitless when I walked in. He was a working stiff, maybe a janitor or mechanic, judging by the dark blue uniform he was wearing. It was obvious that he had no idea Maria was connected to one of Whitey's boys.

Before I left, I spoke to Maria in the kitchen. "Don't worry about it," I told her. "Just don't tell my brother. And I wish you'd get rid of this guy." Then I left. But I didn't go home. I waited around the corner for the guy to leave. Two hours later, he came out. I walked up to him, pulled out an ice pick, and said, "If I ever see you near my brother's wife, I'll stick this ice pick in your ear. And if you ever tell her about this conversation, I'll stick it in your chest." It took every bit of control he had not to shit on the sidewalk. He managed a weak nod, and I patted him on the back and said, "Have a nice night, pal."

A week later, I brought some groceries over to Maria and asked if she was still going out with him. "Oh, no," she told me, "I broke up with him." Yeah.

Ronnie held his own in jail. Everyone knew he was a stand-up guy. He worked in the kitchen and took care of the right people. It hurt me so much every time he went away. I felt like his protector, even though he had balls of steel and could take care of himself most of the time.

But Ronnie wasn't the only brother who occasionally needed my help. I'm not as tight with my brother Bobby as I am with Ronnie. That's not surprising, when you consider that Ronnie and I were wards of the state until we were in our early teens, while Bobby was separated from us when he was still a toddler. Ronnie keeps in closer and more frequent contact with Bobby than I do. But just because I don't stay in close contact with Bobby doesn't mean that I've forgotten he's my brother. Blood is blood. There isn't anything I wouldn't do for him. And he knows this. But Joe Pryer didn't.

Pryer was a big kid, six feet and 240 pounds. He was a bouncer in a few of the local bars in Southie, with a reputation for bullying and brawling, especially when he'd been drinking. One night at Triple O's, Pryer was sloshed and in a nasty mood. Bobby was in there having a few beers. As proof that booze makes people do stupid things, Pryer started picking on Bobby and then punched him in the face. Bobby is no fighter and was smart enough to know that things would go badly for him if he tried to settle things on Pryer's home turf. So he did the reasonable thing and headed for the door. But Pryer wasn't done.

Pryer had already put himself in serious jeopardy. But not content to be merely stupid, he had to be suicidal. As Bobby was shaking off the punch and getting ready to leave, Pryer shouted, "Go get your brother Eddie. He's supposed to be so tough."

When I got wind of what had happened, I let things settle, to give Pryer time to start feeling complacent. Two weeks later, I headed over to O'Leary's Tavern, where I knew Pryer was drinking.

I did a quick inventory of who was there and where they were. Pryer saw me and immediately headed my way. He extended his hand and said, "Hey, Eddie, man, I just want to say I'm real fucking sorry about your brother and the stupid way I acted. I was drunk, bro. I didn't mean any disrespect."

I calmly listened to his apology and then said, "It's too late for that, motherfucker." A left hook to his jaw dropped him like a rag doll. Pryer was out cold. But I wasn't done.

Pryer had really disrespected me. I picked up one of his arms and sent a few nice rib-breaking kicks into his side. Old Pryer was going to need a flak jacket. Then, just to make sure he remembered me, I gave him a decent punt to the head. It just wouldn't have felt right if I hadn't finished up this way. After I figured he'd had enough, I thanked the bartender and left.

Joe Pryer was very unhappy about the beating. He put the word out on the street that he was going to kill me. But he never got around to it. On a cold December night, a month after I pummeled him, I heard from the cops that someone took care of Pryer: two in the back of his head. The cops didn't have to do too much investigating before my name came up as a suspect, and they didn't waste any time in paying me a visit.

I was on the back porch of Carolyn's house on Norcross Place with Courtney, then three, listening to the song "I Saw Mommy Kissing Santa Claus." I heard my Doberman, Attila, barking up a storm, and some guy yelling, "Search warrant! Put the fucking dog in the bathroom or we'll shoot it!"

Carolyn was terrified and screaming. I opened the front door to find about thirty cops, armored with shields and helmets and riot gear. The Boston Police Department had brought in its special entry unit. I was flattered. They looked like they were getting ready to storm a hostile beachhead. I said, "Hey, fellas, what's up?" One of the lead blue knights told me to step aside, they had a search warrant. Then they told me that Joe Pryer had been found dead the night before.

The murder weapon was a .25 Baretta pistol. The cops found nothing even close to that in my house. But when one of them searched my bedroom closet, he discovered an HK 91 assault rifle dangling from a coat hanger. The cop gave me a look and then grabbed the rifle. I started laughing and said, "You didn't think I was going to point that out to you, did you?" That HK 91 was fully loaded with a twenty-round .308-caliber clip. All you had to do was slap the side of that bad boy and you were ready to do some serious damage.

The cop started feeling good about the find, figuring he had me on illegal possession, which would be enough to send me away for at least a little while. Not quite. I owned that weapon legally and had the Firearms Identification card to prove it. I'd bought that rifle legitimately at a sporting goods store. The cop asked me how in the world an ex-con like me was able to get an FID card. I told him that the question on the application asked whether the applicant had been convicted of a felony within the past five years. I hadn't. Even so, because of my association with Whitey, my rifle was confiscated and my FID card revoked.

So, it wasn't a complete waste of time for the police that night. My gun-carrying rights were terminated, and my assault rifle probably ended up on the gun rack in some cop's house. But they found nothing connecting me to Joe Pryer's murder.

Officially, that killing remains unsolved. I didn't kill Joe Pryer. I would have if he'd come after me. And it wouldn't have bothered me a bit. But what happened, according to reliable word on the street, is that on the night Joe got clipped, he was at the wheel of his car, tooling around Southie with one of his friends in the passenger seat and another in the backseat. Everyone was boozed and coked out. On Whitey's stuff, of course.

Pryer pulled over into a parking lot so the trio could better focus on the job of putting powder up their noses. Word is, Pryer was trying to muscle in on a few too many lines of toot, and the guy in the backseat — let's call him Jerry — took all sorts of exception to having his precious coke snorted up by Pryer. So Jerry took out the Southie special, a .25 Baretta, put the end of the barrel against the back of Pryer's head, and squeezed the trigger. Pryer must have had a thick skull because when the bullet entered, he lurched forward, grabbed the back of his noggin and shouted, "What the fuck are you punching me in the back of the head for?"

Obviously surprised, Jerry raised the Baretta again and leveled the end of the barrel — higher this time. *Bang!* Second time was the charm. Joe slumped forward against the steering wheel, very dead. The boys immediately bolted on foot, leaving Joe in the driver's seat, and taking the coke with them.

# Plea Bargain

I first met Alejandro "Alex" Bustamante in the spring of 1990. He was a good-looking guy, around six feet, in his late-twenties. He worked out at the Boston Athletic Club at the same time I did, starting at 8:30 in the morning.

It took eight months until we got to know each other on a first-name basis. I found out he was originally from Venezuela. We talked only casually, never about what each of us did for a living. Maybe we both understood this was off limits. I did know, though, that he visited Venezuela frequently, every four to six weeks. I admit this got me wondering. Here's a young guy from Latin America who doesn't seem to be wanting for money and can hang around until ten or ten-thirty in the morning at the BAC, and who's jetting to South America frequently. Hmmm.

One day I was joking with Alex and said, "Hey, what are you doing going to Venezuela all the time? Grabbing keys? What's going on down there? C'mon." He just laughed and said something about visiting friends and family. But it must have got him thinking enough to have me checked out. He was probably both worried and intrigued by my questions. And when the information came back, he must have been more than pleased. Because he'd been looking for a guy just like me. Alex was connected to a Medellin drug cartel that was prepared to start moving a major amount of cocaine through Boston. He'd been scouting the lay of the land, doing research on how the locals did business. Now, he had an in with one of Whitey's boys. Jackpot.

Alex reached out to me. "Hey, were you serious when you asked me about Venezuela?" he asked one morning while we were having coffee after our workouts.

"Absolutely," I replied. "Why? You got a good connection down there?"

Yeah, he had a good connection down there. And down there was actually Colombia. He'd been saying Venezuela so as not to raise suspicion. The ice was broken and soon we were talking business. It didn't take either of us long to realize this could be a very profitable partnership. Alex was looking for a way to move his product while still cooperating with the local underworld. I'd been buying my supply from Tommy Dixon, who had a tie to South America in a Colombian named Jesus Nodarse. I'd been looking for my own South American contact. Now I had one. Eventually, I'd have to tell Whitey, but that was a long way off. The last thing I wanted to do was share. Only after I'd made enough money to retire would I reveal my contact's name to my soon-to-be-former boss.

Alex told me he was capable of moving big quantities. He said that, as soon as we could get the clearance and were sure of security, he could move two to three thousand kilos a week into Boston alone. His cartel had a ship waiting off shore, loaded with twenty thousand kilos of coke. *Twenty thousand kilos.* I played it cool, but I was thinking that since I intended to keep my source secret, a secret I would defend to the death, I was going to have to start small and build from there. But if I could make it work with a contact this big, and this connected, the sky might be the limit.

I agreed to buy twenty kilos a week from him, to start with, at a price of $18,000 a kilo. I wasn't concerned that Whitey would find out. As long as I was paying him tribute from any illegal racket I was involved with on the streets of South Boston, he didn't care what I did. All he wanted from me was a fat envelope and I'd make sure he got it. But I'd be on my own with Alex. I planned to break up the kilos and sell off various quantities, so I'd be ringing up sales of $23,000 a kilo, for a profit of $5000 a key. I was figuring on profits of about $100,000 a week. All mine! If I could make the distribution work smoothly, I'd stay in the business, paying Whitey the necessary percentage of my profits. The more I made, the more I paid, and the happier he was. Then, a year or eighteen months later, I'd sit Alex down with Whitey and say, "Alex, meet Whitey. Whitey, meet Alex. You two can make a lot of money together. I am now retired."

But before Alex and I could finalize our business plans, I was hit with my August 1990 indictment on charges of drug trafficking, along with fifty other Southie drug dealers. Not only was there an excellent chance that I'd be going away for a long time, but my connection to Whitey Bulger was permanently severed.

Alex was on one of his trips to Colombia when all this went down. You don't have to be an underboss to know it isn't a great idea to do an illegal drug deal with someone who's under indictment. Because anyone in trouble with the law has all sorts of incentive to help the criminal justice system nab other bad guys. Common sense would dictate that, after August 9, 1990, a guy like Alex Bustamante would not be doing business with a guy like Eddie MacKenzie. But Alex didn't find out until it was too late. Here's a guy entrusted by a Medellin drug cartel to lay the groundwork for the launch of a massive drug-distribution ring, and he doesn't do his homework. Alex let his guard down and it cost him — big time.

By the time Alex got back from Colombia in mid-September, 1990, Al Nugent had gotten me out of Danbury on bail with the condition that I wear an ankle monitor, or LoJack. The LoJack, worn around my right ankle and covered by my pants, was a hell of a lot better than sitting in Danbury for up to two years awaiting trial, but it was still confining. I stayed in my ex-wife Carolyn's basement and could leave only to see my lawyer or a doctor. The worst part of the whole mess was that Alex went from being my ticket to massive wealth to being my get-out-of-jail-free card. Although Al originally thought we could fight the charges against me, he decided they had me dead to rights on tape. In two telephone conversations taped by the feds, I was heard making plans to have a couple of drinks with a customer, code words that indicated an imminent cocaine sale. Uncle Sam also had equally damaging surveillance tapes of me and the other ringleaders. I was looking at fifteen years away.

While I was staying at Carolyn's, one of my most frequent visitors was Timmy Connolly, who had his own problems. He hadn't been picked up with the rest of us, but his problems were bigger. During the 1980s, he'd been orchestrating real estate scams from his own mortgage company. He'd tell the bank you bought a house for $270,000, rather than the $240 grand you actually paid, keep the other $30,000, and produce a fake certificate for a lower mortgage. But the feds were closing in on him and even though he'd never actually worked for Whitey, he was desperate enough to use him as a tool to save himself. Every time he'd visit, he'd try to convince me to be a corroborating witness for his lies about Whitey and the Southie gang.

"Just do it, bro," Timmy would urge me. "I've got good connections with the U.S. Attorney's office. Reilly, the Middlesex County DA, is a cousin of mine and he's real interested in my story. He'll take this to Wayne Budd [who was the U.S. Attorney for Massachusetts]. Just stand by me, brosky, and I'll cut you in on the Witness Protection Program. I've got a few million stashed. We'll end up living the good life on a ranch in Butte, Montana."

The more he talked, the more I began to think about cutting my own deal with the feds to avoid the fifteen years I was looking at. But I knew that if I cut a deal with anyone, it would be with the FBI and Middlesex District Attorney Thomas Reily, not the DEA or the Boston Police. I knew that the FBI was sleeping with Whitey. Unlike Timmy Connolly, I wasn't about to rat on my Southie boys. Even though Whitey had ratted on me, I wouldn't give up a word on Whitey. I sure as hell didn't know that Whitey was an FBI informant, and wouldn't learn that until 1995, when he went on the lam. All I knew from my stay in Danbury was that he had ratted on me and the other dealers to save himself. I did know that he was tight with Johnny Connolly in the FBI Boston field office — who would pass the word to Whitey about who I was, and wasn't, giving up. My plan wasn't completely formed yet. But I knew it would involve ratting on Alex and his plan to unload the cocaine, not on Whitey or any of his boys.

When Alex finally returned and called to check in, he simply asked whether I was one of the people indicted in the big sweep and I told him no. He never even tried to find out if I was telling the truth. All he had to do was pick up some back copies of the *Herald* or *Globe* and read my name. But he bought my story. I also told him that since I was close to a lot of those guys, it would be smart if we gave our discussions a six-month siesta, just to let things calm down a bit. With that bracelet on my ankle, I didn't have any other options. Alex agreed we should lay low until late winter or early spring. What an idiot.

We talked on the phone for a few minutes every three to four weeks. I was still nervous that Alex would find out I had been indicted. He only had to read a follow-up story in a Boston paper and our deal would be off, along with my potential bargaining chip with the feds.

I was also worried that my trial would come up sooner than expected, resulting in publicity that Alex would surely hear about. And there was no guarantee that the agency would be interested in working with me, no matter what I could bring to the table. But I thought that if I could deliver anything to the FBI in the ballpark of what Alex and I were capable of putting together, the agency would have to be crazy not to play ball with me.

Initially, Al was against my making any deal that would involve Whitey's Southie mob. But once he was convinced I could deliver a

Colombian drug connection without ratting on Whitey, he agreed to help me. And he'd done a thorough review of the government case against me. It was a good one. Al never advised anyone to deal unless it was a last resort. He had a track record of blowing holes in cases that the cops and the feds thought were airtight. But, in this case, he thought we should at least discuss a deal, but only with the FBI because of both the Bulger connection and my Colombian association. He felt the FBI would have the most influence with the federal judge, who had the power to reduce my sentence.

We decided that using Timmy Connolly, who was in the process of making his own deal with the feds, looked better and better. Timmy kept telling me that the DA Reilly could be trusted and how close Reilly was to U.S. Attorney Wayne Budd. We would exploit Timmy's relationship with Reilly's office to present our case. We knew we needed a connection to the U.S. Attorney's office, but I wasn't about to take Connolly's word on anything.

Meanwhile, Connolly was still after me to corroborate the bullshit information he was trying to sell the government in exchange for getting his file full of crimes forgiven. Of course, he couldn't give this up without going into the Witness Protection Program, since much of his information and misinformation involved Whitey and the Southie mob. No way he could stay out of the Program after playing that game. His life expectancy would be shorter than a fruit fly's.

I listened to everything Connolly said and told him it sounded like a great idea to cooperate. We'd enter the Witness Protection Program together and live large in Montana on the millions he'd stashed away. I even told him I was going to back him on one of his particularly creative lies, in which he would allege he was kidnapped by Kevin Weeks and dragged down to the South Boston Liquor Mart where Whitey, Weeks, and Flemmi threatened his life and extorted fifty thousand dollars from him.

As it turned out, Al knew Reilly and said that he was an honest and stand-up guy who could be trusted: the perfect guy to contact in our attempt to sell the information on the Colombian connection. Al advised me to go to a meeting with Reilly that Connolly and his attorney had already arranged. Important players would be there. Al would attend the meeting with me. I told Connolly that I would go along and work with him to cut a deal with the feds. This fired Connolly up. Just the news he needed to hear.

The meeting went down on a weekday afternoon in February 1991 at the Ramada Inn in Cambridge. On the day of the meeting, I was in the lobby, still on the ankle bracelet, when Connolly came in by himself. He looked nervous as hell, hurried over to me, and immediately started questioning me, trying to get reassurance that I was going to toe the party line. I was noncommittal, saying, "Timmy, don't fucking worry. Everything will work out. We're all set."

This sent Connolly into a fit. "What the fuck do you mean we're all set?" he asked. "You're still with me on this, right?"

I raised my hands, giving him the "calm down" sign. "Don't worry. We're all set," I repeated. But Connolly was worried. Still, he knew it was no use to keep badgering me, so he walked away, trying to get a hold of himself.

Connolly was so arrogant that he didn't even have an attorney present. When Al arrived, the three of us entered the hotel room. After formal introductions, Reilly outlined his understanding of the purpose of our meeting — something about preliminary statements, fact-finding, assistance to the government. Didn't mean much to me, but he must have been right on, because Al didn't object.

Connolly was the first to speak. He was tense and it showed. He kept nervously looking down and then up at everyone around the table, trying to gauge what the hell we were thinking. Reilly hardly ever raised his head because he was writing furiously on a notepad, trying to get everything down.

I can only imagine what went through Connolly's head as he looked at me and elaborated on his story. If he'd been attached to a polygraph, that needle would have been a roller coaster.

I was plenty nervous over what was at stake, but with every word Timmy spoke I began to feel more confident. My story was better; it was true and involved millions of dollars in drug transactions. I knew it would be a stretch for them to believe how much money I was talking about, but I'd make sure they were convinced.

Al and I hadn't let on that we had serious doubts about the idiocy Connolly was peddling. Connolly finally got to the bullshit about Kevin Weeks kidnapping him and bringing him to Whitey for the $50,000 in tribute. Then Connolly turned to me, saying, "You remember this, don't you, Ed?"

I hoped Connolly read in my face just what I thought of him as I said,

"Hey, listen and listen carefully. I'm not going to lie for anybody, Mr. Reilly. I don't know what Tim is talking about, but I do have this Colombian friend that I can give the government for my freedom. It would be worth millions in cocaine."

Connolly looked sick. Reilly looked up and said, "Edward, what you're saying is that you know nothing about this extortion?"

I said, "That's correct, sir. I'm not lying for Tim or anyone. And I'm not here to give any information that will be used against anyone indicted with me, or anyone else I know from Southie, including Whitey Bulger. What Timmy just said is his own story, not mine."

Needless to say, I wasn't Tim's best bud anymore. I continued. "What I do have which may be of interest to you is that a major Colombian drug connection is preparing to start moving five hundred kilos or more of cocaine a week through Boston." Reilly had stopped writing and was looking at me. I couldn't tell if he thought I was full of shit or not.

I didn't mention that Alex had discussed the possibility of moving thousands of kilos of cocaine a week because I didn't want to get carried away and destroy my credibility before I had a chance to establish it. When you are a convicted felon, you don't exactly start out with a strong bargaining position. I was confident that Alex was on the level when he was talking about moving the five hundred kilos a week, so that's what I offered.

The meeting ended with a statement by Reilly that he was interested in what he had been told, and that he was going to review the information and then decide on the next course of action. He told me and Al and Connolly that he would be in touch. We all shook hands, and Al and I managed to bolt the place without having to talk to Connolly.

Reilly seemed noncommittal, but I felt strongly that he would have to at least relay the information to the right people and give them an opportunity to check the story out. From that point on, the government's relationships with me and with Connolly were separate affairs and went separate ways. That day at the Ramada Inn in Cambridge was the last time I saw Timmy. Even without my corroboration, he was able to sell the government on his story in exchange for a deal and placement in the Witness Protection Program.

Within a week of the meeting, Al got a call from John Pappalardo, then second-in-command to U.S. Attorney Wayne Budd. Pappalardo told Al that the FBI wanted to meet with us at the Parker House, near Boston's

financial district, in the first week of March 1991. I showed up with Al and
met two FBI agents, John Siragusa and John Gamel, who is now head of
the FBI's Organized Crime Task Force for New England. This would be the
first of four meetings at the Parker House over the next six weeks. It was
evident early on that Siragusa and Gamel also wanted information on
Whitey and the local drug network. They weren't confident I could deliver the major Colombian prize I was offering, but they were sure I could
deliver the goods on Whitey. If the agency was going to commit a lot of
effort to a sting, they wanted to play with the best odds possible.

We got the proffer agreement straightened out, but I made it clear that
I would never say anything to hurt Whitey or my Southie pals. Siragusa
and Gamel pushed me on the issue, but I didn't budge. Eventually, they
agreed to work with me on nailing the Colombian connection. From then
on, Whitey's name was never mentioned. Both men were professional and
treated me with courtesy and respect. They understood that even though
I was working with them for a reduction in my sentence, I was putting
myself in a very dangerous situation.

Once the agreement was in place, the agents wanted to know what I
knew about Alex Bustamante and his network. I told Siragusa and Gamel
everything I remembered, from the first meeting to the most recent. I even
took my chances and brought up what Alex had said about moving thousands of kilos a week through Boston. I didn't mention the boat that was
supposedly offshore loaded with 20,000 kilos. Too risky. I could tell they had
doubts about my story, and I didn't blame them. My own lawyer wasn't
entirely convinced I wasn't full of shit.

The FBI soon had its chance to find out if my story was going to wash.
We agreed during the third meeting that all my future meetings with Alex
would be monitored by an FBI surveillance team. I would need some sort
of audio surveillance. I told the agents that I couldn't wear a body wire,
because either Alex would check me for one or a team member in the area
might be equipped with an anti-bugging or bugging detection device. So,
the agents suggested a mini-tape — a beautiful piece of equipment, taking up less space than a silver dollar — that could clearly record a whisper
twenty feet away. Since it didn't transmit anything, it couldn't be picked
up or jammed by an anti-bugging or detection device.

I had the perfect place to conceal the device: in my hairpiece, over which I
would wear a baseball cap. And if Alex found the recorder, well, he wouldn't

live to talk about it. Nothing personal, but if it came down to me or him, it was an easy choice. To let him go if he found out I was an informant would have been suicide. I couldn't give Alex the chance to deliver Colombian neckties to my family and friends. (The Colombian necktie is a method of execution and intimidation popular among some South American drug cartels, in which the victim's throat is slit and the tongue pulled down through that opening, giving it a resemblance to a tie.)

Oh, and another small issue. No way could I gather incriminating information with that LoJack clamped on my ankle. Al Nugent was brilliant at convincing Magistrate Judge Marianne B. Bowler to both remove it and keep me out of Danbury until my trial came up. No small feat, considering that my drug-running partner, Tommy Dixon, was being held on a million dollars bail until trial.

My first order of business was to head to Walpole State Prison to talk with my old friend Freddy Weichel. I needed Freddy to reach out to Whitey and Stevie and Kevin, to let the front office know that I wasn't going to roll on any Southie guys. After the August 1990 indictment, Whitey sent word to all of us who had been named that we were not allowed to initiate direct contact with him or any of his boys who had not been indicted. But even in jail, Freddy had a direct line to the top. Whitey respected Freddy; he knew the weight he carried inside.

When I told Freddy I was cooperating with the government, I could see the shock and disgust in his eyes. I felt like shit. But I kept right on talking, telling him that in no way would I ever give anything up that would hurt anyone from the neighborhood. I told him about Alex and the Colombian cartel. I told him that the deal I'd cut protected me from having to rat on my codefendants or Whitey or Stevie. I told him what Patriarca had told me about Whitey, but he shook his head and said the feds were spreading that rumor around Danbury to scare us into co-operating.

"I need you to reach out to Jimmy and explain what I'm doing," I said. "I don't know if he's hearing the entire story." Freddy agreed to help. An added value in his contacting Whitey was that it would be understood that things were cool with me and Freddy. You couldn't put a value on that.

I met with Freddy not a moment too soon. Johnny MacDonald, Frankie's older brother, was helping me out at Connolly's while I was on the LoJack. Although he had never been connected to Whitey and was super straight, he knew what was going on. He told me later that Whitey had found out about my discussions with the FBI and knew something about a Colombian connection. This had Whitey worried. He knew I was capable of hurting him in a major way and decided he couldn't take the chance. One day, when Johnny was over at the house of Joey Murphy, one of Whitey's top lieutenants, Whitey and Stevie Flemmi showed up. They started talking about my deal with the government. They were planning to kidnap me, cut me into little pieces and bury me where no one would ever find the parts. Johnny jumped in and swore that I wasn't saying anything about them. Whitey listened and said, "I have a connection in the Feds that I'm going to reach out to. If he tells me what you're saying is true, John, then MacKenzie lives." The connection, of course, was his handler, FBI agent Johnny Connolly.

While Whitey was doing his checking, which eventually corroborated what Johnny had told him, Freddy got through to Whitey, and persuaded him to call off the hit. Behind bars for a murder he didn't commit, it was Freddy Weichel, along with Johnny, who saved my life. Lucky for me, because in early 2001 Kevin Weeks, under indictment and cooperating with the feds, led a team of crime-scene specialists to some mutilated victims of Whitey's in a culvert next to the Southeast Expressway in Dorchester. At least one of them had been murdered in Joey Murphy's house, the same place where they'd planned to kill me.

About three weeks after my visit with Freddy, Whitey surprised me. He walked into my apartment and handed me a case of Moretti beer, my favorite. I was too shocked to be nervous. This visit was very different from the one eleven years earlier. This time, he was smiling and warm. "This is for you, Eddie," he said. Before I could finish thanking him, he said, "It was a brilliant maneuver you did. But we can never talk again. You understand, right?"

"Sure, I do," I said. We shook hands and he was gone. I thought about how he'd given me up a few months earlier, but somehow I couldn't hold on to any of the anger. The respect I'd always felt for his genius was still there. The guy had been able to manipulate the government to save himself. And now he understood that I, too, had had to make a deal, but, out of loyalty to him, I hadn't given him up.

I drank a cold beer and thought about nothing for a long while. Then I reflected on what Whitey had meant to me. He was like Caesar, like a god.

He could commit any crime he wanted to, even murder, and get away with it. But now we were through. I felt genuine relief that I was alive and out of jail and Whitey was out of my life for good. I loved the money and power he had brought me, but it was time for that to end. Our farewell was long overdue.

# The Colombian Cartel

For the next eight months, I put my life in a different, but no less deadly, danger. I traveled to Texas, California, and New York, meeting with Alex and his partners, so that Alex's associates could determine if I was legit. I was wired by the FBI through all of it. My first big moment with the cartel happened in May 1991, at the Boston University Burger King, of all places.

As I drove over to BU that afternoon, I knew that while I'd made the decision to work with the government, my involvement was about to become more dangerous and unpredictable. Once I started taping my talks with Alex and turned incriminating evidence over to the feds, there was no turning back. It was like being in the locker room just before a big fight. This was SHOWTIME.

I spotted Alex on Commonwealth Avenue, standing in front of the Burger King, wearing dark shades, jeans, and a sweatshirt. Student wear. He was on the lookout, unsmiling, arms crossed, facing east, the direction from which he knew I was coming. As I drove past, I looked in my side-view mirror. He was watching me with that bad-ass, stoney face, arms still crossed. Before getting out of my car, I glanced again at the sideview mirror to check out my baseball cap. No bulges or suspicious bumps. Shit, relax, he won't suspect a thing, I told myself. I got out of my truck and walked over to him. He smiled slightly and we shook hands. He wasn't looking at my hat. Or was he?

"Hey, bro, how have you been?" I asked.

"Doing great, bro," he said. He looked around, then turned back to face me. "We got a lot of shit moving real fast now."

"Are we all set for the two-oh (two ounces)?"

"Everything is going to be fine. But my boy needs to come up here and meet with you before we establish any definite transfer."

I had no problem with that. Benjamin, one of the main players in his network, wanted to meet with me in two weeks. If he felt comfortable with me, then we could get into more specifics and put into place the movement of product and money. "Benjamin," Alex told me, "is one mean, nasty, and dangerous motherfucker." And it was Benjamin who signed off on major business.

We'd talked for only five minutes when Alex went to make a call at one of the pay phones about twenty feet away. I told him to take his time. As he walked away, I thought about that little gadget concealed in my hairpiece. I imagined I could feel the tiny tape spindles turning. I wondered if everybody around me had been tipped off about the teeny-weeny tape recorder. Hey, world, I'm Eddie MacKenzie, government informant, secretly taping my conversation with a Colombian coke dealer. This wasn't fun.

When Alex returned, he told me we needed to talk in person in the next two to three days; he would then tell me when I'd meet Benjamin. A location wouldn't be established until the day of the meet. Alex would call me within twenty-four hours. We shook hands and started walking west along the sidewalk on Commonwealth Avenue. I walked back to my truck. Alex disappeared into the crowd.

Next on the schedule was a meeting with the FBI at the Embassy Suites Hotel in Cambridge, just across the Charles River from BU. Normally it would take me ten minutes to get there, but I took a good forty-five, making lots of turns, giving myself enough time to determine if I was being tailed. I wasn't. It was only when I was within a block of the hotel that I took off my cap and retrieved the recorder.

I drove up to the third level of the parking garage attached to the hotel. The garage was poorly lit, and there were only a few other cars on this level, all of them empty. In a corner of the garage, sitting behind the wheel of a Grand Marquis, was John Gamel; John Siragusa was next to him. I pulled up next to Gamel and got out. I kneeled by the open window, handed the tape cassette to Gamel and told both agents about my meeting with Alex. They listened carefully. When I told them that Alex had used one of the pay phones in front of the Burger King, Siragusa wrote something down in a small notebook.

When I finished, Gamel looked at me. "Listen, Eddie, you did good," he said. " I know this is kind of weird for you right now. But you're doing the right thing."

"Let's hope so," I said.

"You are. Now, get out of here. We're going to take this tape and listen to it. You call us as soon as you hear from Alex. You got it?"

Gamel called me at eight the next morning. He needed to speak to me right away at a small motel along Route 2. As I drove, My mind furiously worked the possibilities, trying to figure whether it was good or bad that they wanted to meet with me on such short notice. Gamel, Siragusa, and Assistant U.S. Attorney John Pappalardo were waiting for me in the motel room. There were no smiles or pleasant greetings, and the shades were down. Something was up. Siragusa got to it right away. "Eddie, do you know who Alex called during that phone call yesterday?"

"No idea," I said.

"We had the phone records pulled from the bank of pay phones at the Burger King," he told me. "At precisely the time you were meeting with Alex there yesterday, a phone call was made to a very high-powered and, let me tell you, very well-known-to-us Medellin drug organization run by Pablo Escobar. These guys are big."

Even I didn't know that Alex's network was connected to Escobar. Now the government knew I wasn't talking shit. I have to admit, though, that the name Escobar sent a quiver of anxiety through me. I knew this cartel was the most powerful crime family in the city of Medellin. Its members would kill anybody who crossed them. Their ruthlessness was legendary.

"Eddie, we're on a new playing field now," Pappalardo said. This guy was all business. "If you can provide information that will help in the apprehension of any of these dealers or will disrupt its pipeline, the government is going to consider it of the highest value."

Man, I thought to myself, this is sounding good. But could it keep my ass out of jail? The job was up to me.

For the next six to seven months, Alex worked to consummate the deal and keep me informed how things were going. He seemed to need to talk to me in person, to keep feeling me out to make sure I was still interested and ready to roll as soon as he gave me the word. We were negotiating a ten-million-dollar purchase of cocaine, which could be turned around for three times that amount on the street. Every time we met, we were under FBI surveillance; agents on the street and in cars, taking pictures, watching, listening. Sometimes they seemed painfully obvious as they drove by or walked past us, but I guess it was just me. Alex never seemed to notice.

One day, John Gamel complained that I had used the word "nigger" when talking to Alex about a black guy jogging by us. "What if a black FBI agent has to listen to those tapes?" he asked me.

"You think Alex would think it was normal for a guy like me to say, 'Hey, look at that African American jogging by. Isn't he big?' He'd pat me down in two seconds." They kept saying they wanted to write a script for me, but I told them they couldn't. I had to act normal and write my own script. I should have won an Academy Award for my performance during that operation.

The turning point came when Benjamin flew up from Medellin. He wanted to meet me and read my face, so the three of us met at Harvard Yard, right next to the statue of John Harvard. I chose Harvard because it's the best place for two dark-skinned guys to meet a light-skinned American on a sunny autumn afternoon without attracting attention. It would have been crazy for Alex and Benjamin to be seen anywhere near Southie with me. The best and the brightest kids from around the world walked right by us, oblivious. South Boston was only across the river and a few miles away, but it might as well have been the moon.

Alex introduced Benjamin. He was bigger than Alex, but not as good looking, and certainly not as outgoing. He was all business. Pretty much the mean, nasty, dangerous motherfucker Alex had described. At Benjamin's request, the three of us went into a nearby brick building, and Alex directed us to an empty side hall. It was pretty busy outside, with kids milling around, so I suspected he'd checked it out before I arrived. We walked together down the hall, not stopping until we were sixty or seventy feet away from the entrance. Alex looked around, not doing a good job of playing it cool. He said, "Hey, Eddie, man, I'm sorry I have to do this, but. . . ." He began to pat me down, stealing glances down the hall in both directions. I didn't object and raised my hands in a surrender pose to make it easier for him to check me. After ten seconds of so, Alex was satisfied I wasn't wired, and I was satisfied that the baby bug under my baseball cap was merrily recording our entire conversation for the benefit of the FBI.

After we came out of the building, Benjamin seemed more relaxed. We headed to a Pizzeria Uno, where he asked me a few questions, mostly about sports, trying to get to know me better. I told him I was into football and he said he preferred hockey. I called my ticket agent and got him and Alex great seats on center ice for a Bruins game the next evening. He asked me how much I could handle and I told him twenty kilos a week.

Then he said, "We're talking about a lot of stuff and a lot of money. I can't be too careful. If this fucks up, we are all going to get buried with the devil." Oh, how I knew.

After that, Alex and I saw each other at least three times a week at the gym. I fixed him up with some women and we went out together a few times. When it came to the final deal, Alex asked me to show him the buy money. I said I couldn't take him to it, but I would make a video of it and give him the video, along with a copy of that day's *Globe*, so he'd know everything was on the up-and-up. I went to the Federal Reserve Bank in Boston where the FBI had laid out ten million dollars on a table. Man, what a sight. That pile of money had to be two feet high and three feet wide. Alex loved the video and asked me for a money-counting machine like banks use, which I borrowed from the FBI. He invited me to Texas to meet his connection and to pick up a sample of the cocaine we'd be buying.

So, in September 1991 I went to Houston, along with my two traveling buddies, Gamel and Siragusa. The three of us traveled on the same plane, but we never spoke to one another in public and we took separate cabs to the hotel. There was a great men's club there, a real strip joint, so, after the FBI agents went to bed, I took the flash money they'd given me to make me look like a rich drug dealer and headed over there. I partied all night, got laid right there, and brought the girl back to my hotel room. I was putting government-issued five-dollar bills in G-strings all night long.

But Houston didn't go well. There was something too weird about the Texas FBI agent we met there. I knew the minute I saw him that I wouldn't feel comfortable with him. He looked too much like a cop going under-cover: scruffy looking, bearded, out of shape. All of us drug runners were athletes and clean cut, but this guy was trying too hard not to look legiti-mate. I was sure he would never fool Alex's people. The next day I headed back to Boston, preparing for a second trip to Houston. But Alex called me and told me that things were being switched to L.A., where, he prom-ised, I would get to try some samples.

A week later, Gamel, Siragusa, and I flew to L.A. This time I sat in first class while they sat in coach. Alex had explained there would be three kilos waiting for me in L.A., each kilo individually wrapped in a different Colombian newspaper, indicating it was from a certain factory. My job was to sample each one and choose the one I liked best. That would decide the factory from which we'd get our kilos.

For three days, Gamel, Siragusa, and I stayed in a hotel in Anaheim across from Anaheim Stadium. I talked the local FBI guy into getting us tickets for the San Francisco 49ers game against the Rams. Our seats were on the fifty-yard line and Joe Montana was on the sidelines. I fooled around with the FBI guys, calling out to Montana like I knew him. When Montana turned around and gave me a wave, the FBI guys wanted to know if I really knew him. "Sure," I told them. "Who do you think he parties with when he comes to Boston?"

I also went to Laguna Beach with a few agents for some pickup basketball games. One of the agents wanted me on his team because I was strong under the boards. I was a bull and had no problem elbowing someone in the face if he took the ball away from me. We played against some tough locals and had a great workout. And we always won.

Although I was nervous, I was having a great time. I took a long run outside the hotel every day, wearing shorts and a T-shirt, my recording device always under my hairpiece, enjoying the perfect October California weather. I kept singing the lyrics to "Secret Agent Man" to myself, feeling like I was part of an exciting game.

Finally I got a call from Alex directing me to a Donut King a half hour from my hotel, where he said a white Malibu would be waiting with the samples in the trunk. An FBI agent in a Mercedes, posing as one of my connections, dropped me off there early that afternoon. When I got into the white, four-door, Malibu shitbox, I took the key out of the ashtray and followed the Mercedes in a roundabout route for over an hour to make sure we weren't followed. Finally, we ended up at a secluded warehouse. There the FBI's narcotics expert, posing as one of my men, tested the samples. He was delighted with the excellent quality of each one.

I left the Malibu there, like I'd been told, and headed to the airport. On the flight back to Boston, one of the FBI agents brought up Whitey Bulger. "We know he's killed thirty people," he told me. Then why was Whitey still a free man? I wondered. Although at the time I had no idea Whitey was an informant, I did start to question who was protecting who.

A few weeks later, we went back to L.A. so that I could finally pick up the drugs from Alex's associate and prepare them for shipment back to Boston. But the run was aborted when Alex called to tell me that he was very sorry but the product wasn't ready. The truth was he was testing me to make sure I had my connections in place and could round up the money to fly first class at a moment's notice. I headed back to Boston on the next available flight.

A week later, Gamel, Siragusa, and I were back for a second dry run. This time I stayed for three days while Alex again checked me out. He made sure that wherever I went, on my runs, to the nightclubs, into the stores, I wasn't being followed by anybody except his people.

"Do you think I'm made of money for these last-minute flights?" I complained to Alex when I got back to Boston. "Plus you're tying up ten million dollars for two or three months here." He shrugged his shoulders and said nothing.

Two days before Thanksgiving, I was back in L.A. for the third and final dry run, again being watched carefully for two days. I took the red-eye back to Boston in time for Thanksgiving dinner with my family. I traveled first class and carried a gym bag full of Dom Perignon I'd ordered from the hotel room service. I'd spent more than a thousand dollars in hotel room charges over a few days, but no one in the FBI complained.

After those trips, we were finally ready to accept delivery of $25 to $40 million worth of stash earmarked for the street. On Tuesday, December 3, 1991, as soon as I arrived in L.A., I called Alex in Boston. He told me to look for a white Dodge Ram Charger, with keys in the ashtray, in the parking lot of a Taco Bell in Marina del Rey, near the motel where I was staying. When I hung up from Alex, I wasn't the least bit nervous or scared. I was excited, running on pure adrenaline, like the bell was ringing at a championship fight. I was ready to throw my punches. I had two hours leeway to pick up the van, which would be loaded with five hundred kilos of cocaine, and take it to a warehouse where my people would inspect it. As soon as I confirmed that the coke was all there and safe in my possession, I'd use my cell phone to call Boston and authorize the official release of the money from my guy in Boston to Alex's guys, who would then get busy counting it. Alex's guys in Boston would take off and that was that. Man, how I wished my original deal with Alex had gone through, and this was my cocaine to sell on the streets.

An FBI agent, driving an $80,000 white Mercedes that made him look like one of my drug contacts, picked me up at the hotel and dropped me off at the Taco Bell. When I got into the Dodge van, I realized it was a stick shift, which I had no idea how to drive. I also realized the van was completely empty, except for two black canvas suitcases. No way was there five hundred kilos in this shitbox. I didn't know what Alex was doing; I couldn't believe he thought he was fooling me. I had no idea how the FBI would handle it, but I figured I had no choice but to follow it through.

So I drove the miserable thing ten miles to a warehouse that the FBI had set up as a checkpoint. Even though I'd never driven a car with a stick shift, thanks to my motorcycle experience, I picked it up pretty quickly. I was following my guy in the white Mercedes, and there were between twenty and thirty FBI cars following me. In addition, an undercover team of eight cars, including local law enforcement, was in place to detect anyone following me. All the undercover cops were dressed like tourists so as not to arouse suspicion. Finally, two cars with Colombians in them, all armed to the teeth, were also following me, but we gave them the slip after a few miles. When we got to the warehouse, the techies raced into the van and started tearing out panels and foam rubber. They found 318 kilos of cocaine stuffed in the roof, in the seats, everywhere. Man, was that a huge relief to me. I couldn't even imagine what would have happened if it hadn't been there.

As soon as they gave me the go-ahead, I called Alex on my cell phone and said, "Everything's clear. Tell your boy to start counting the money." The ten million his guy was to count was not the same ten million Alex had seen in the video months earlier. This time it was a mere two hundred thousand, just enough to keep him busy until the FBI got to him. Incredibly, Alex had rented an office in downtown Boston on the second floor of Two Center Plaza — the same building that housed FBI headquarters! Talk about stupid.

Alex's guy, Alfredo Kolster, from Charlestown, was in the office Alex had rented, counting the money with the machine I'd given Alex months earlier. With him was an agent posing as one of my associates. I'd told Alex about "my associate" earlier and there had been no problem getting Alex to accept him as my legitimate partner. Alfredo and another guy who was waiting in a car outside were busted. Even though I wasn't there and have no idea how the actual scene was played out in the Boston office, I could well imagine how Alfredo must have felt. One minute he's counting the money, imagining a life of enormous wealth, and a few minutes later, he's being cuffed by the FBI. Alex was in his car on a cell phone calling his men, but he must have smelled a rat because he never went back to his place, and the FBI lost him.

I couldn't believe the way the sting played in the Los Angeles papers. An article in the December 5, 1991, *Los Angeles Times* reported "An FBI agent infiltrated the ring, posing as a drug buyer. The agent initially negotiated for 500 kilos of cocaine, to be shipped from Colombia." Not unless they deputized me or made me an FBI agent when I wasn't looking. Because I, alone, negotiated for the drugs. Which, by the way, the paper mistakenly reported was 118 kilos of cocaine, not the 318 kilos the FBI hauled in.

"Tuesday night," the article continued, "undercover agents were told to pick up the drug in a Dodge van, parked at a Holiday Inn near the Artesia Freeway and Beach Boulevard. As agents picked up the car, other officers were tailing the four suspects elsewhere." Yeah, right. They were trying to take credit for the whole thing.

Everybody they picked up cooperated, including the four in L.A. and the two in Boston, and some received lesser sentences. As for Alex, who knows? Maybe he's still on the run. Or he's doing business elsewhere. Or, as he and Benjamin had predicted would happen if things went wrong, they are sleeping with the devil.

Freddy tells me it means nothing that eight years have gone by and I'm still standing. He says they'll find me when they're ready to settle the score. He says I should have taken my fifteen years and paid my dues. I'll take my chances.

When it was all over, the FBI was ecstatic. "You got any more cases for me to do?" I asked them. They laughed but said no. The day the deal went down, I flew back to Boston. The FBI made me stay at the Embassy Suites for a few days in case Alex was still around. My kids came by and used the pool and everybody ate like kings. The FBI felt compelled to again offer me witness protection, but I refused. I didn't want to move my family, and I figured I would deal with it myself. A short while later, the FBI contacted me and said *Unsolved Mysteries* wanted to do a show on Alex and me. It had been a huge cocaine bust and attracted a lot of national attention. The unsolved mystery was Alex, since no one knew where he was. I declined. It was over.

Carolyn had been real nervous when I took off for L.A., but I'd reassured her that no matter what, she and the girls were safe. One agent told me they could have blown me up when I got into that white Dodge van.

But I was committed. I was doing what I had to do to stay out of jail. That was, I figured, the only way I could be a decent father to our girls.

Sure, someday they may find me wearing a Colombian necktie. Until then, I'm going to live life to the fullest and take care of my children. As for that day in December 1991, was I scared? Not for one moment. I loved every second of it. I had a ball playing undercover cop. I can't remember having such an exciting time. Better than breaking legs for Whitey. But do I wish I'd never had to deal with the FBI and been able to do the original deal with Alex? You better believe it.

# Life after Whitey

**S**o, I beat the can. I used the juice, my Colombian connection, to help out the government and got slapped with only a four-year probation in the Whitey Bulger drug-trafficking case. It's incredible what the government can do for you if you're willing to cooperate. Look at Johnny Martorano, Whitey's top hit man who took care of Roger Wheeler and John Callahan in the World Jai Alai hits. That guy admitted to murdering twenty people, though his scorecard probably reaches fifty, give or take a body. The Callahan hit was carried out in Florida; if he'd been tried and found guilty, he could have received the death penalty. But, because he had information that Big Brother found of value, he's in a federal prison, working out the details of his plea bargain, instead of on Death Row. He could be on the street in five years.

What about me? It was 1992. I was a convicted felon and a rat. I made a deal that protected me from squealing on Whitey and the Southie guys, but still I ratted. And to this day, even among friends, I'm known as a rat. I'd be lying if I said I don't feel that.

Things didn't look so good then. I was poor, on probation, easy money was all around me, and I didn't even have a high school diploma. I had two daughters, Courtney and Lauren, with Carolyn, and had just had another little girl, Devin, with a woman named Kathy Puglisi. I was doing some doorman work and helping out at local restaurants, but I couldn't see a career there. The odds were against my staying above ground or out of prison. And that's the fact. Crime is a way of life, an addiction. Few break the cycle. Except for the rarest of exceptions — and I hope I am one of those exceptions — the street predator never sees the light. Even when he gets caught, he's certain it's society screwing him for playing the game the way it should be played.

Fortunately, I had friends who cared. Any progress I've made is owed as much to the people who supported me as it is to my own efforts. I will take credit for making the smart decision to accept the help that was offered.

Some people don't even get that right. I was sure of only a few things. One was that Whitey was out of my life, and I wasn't ever running with him again. I was also determined to stay out of jail. But crime was about the only living I knew.

Al Nugent and Al Shaw saved my life. What's weird is that the two have never met. Al Nugent has always been more than my lawyer. He's something of a father figure. He's always given me sound advice, both in and out of the courtroom. One morning, not long after the Los Angeles bust, I was sitting in his office, bitching and moaning, looking for sympathy. Nugent had been pushing me to get my GED, and he was asking me yet again if I had made plans to take the test. When I told him that I hadn't gotten to it, he looked at me, disappointed and exasperated, and blurted out, "Eddie, why don't you go to college?"

Me? College? "Al, I don't even have a diploma from high school," I said.

"Who gives a shit, Eddie? You'll get that, and then you can apply to college." Nugent might as well have asked me to try becoming an astronaut. "Eddie, you know what?" Nugent continued. "UMass Boston would be the perfect option for you. It's a state school with a great reputation. It's in the neighborhood. And you could probably qualify for financial assistance." He told me he was going to make some calls to some friends, but that I was on my own when it came to taking the GED.

That afternoon I ran into a friend named Al Shaw at the Boston Athletic Club. We'd met several years ago while working out at the Club. Shaw is black, and at the time was head of an organization called the Minority Business Roundtable in Boston. Shaw asked what I was up to, and I blurted out that I was going to go to college. He seemed surprised. "What school are you going to attend?" he asked.

"UMass Boston," I said.

"That's great. When did you get accepted?"

"Well, I haven't been accepted yet."

"So you've applied?"

"Ah, not really."

Shaw just looked at me for a few seconds. "Listen, Eddie, have you gotten around to getting your high school diploma?"

"Not really."

Al looked down at the ground, and made a face like he was thinking over some difficult problem. "Okay, Eddie, I want you to do me a favor. I want you to take the test for your GED. And once you clear that, I want you to come back and see me, and I might have some help for you." It looked like the two Al's were leaving me on my own to graduate from high school.

Within a month, even though I didn't study at all, I had taken and passed the GED exam. And, as promised, Al Nugent and Al Shaw were soon calling in favors for their boy, Eddie Mac. With a lot of help from a lot of people, I filled out the college application and dropped it in the mail. One of the people who pitched me to UMass Boston was Ken Foster, an MIT professor, who had a hand in the development of the atomic bomb. We also met while working out at the Boston Athletic Club. Can I network or can I network? A few weeks later, I received my acceptance notice. I was on my way to becoming a collegian.

I enrolled in the University of Massachusetts in Boston in the fall of 1992. I was nervous as all hell, but if I was going to start college, this was the place. UMass Boston was created as a commuter school for Massachusetts residents, with a focus on serving those living in metropolitan Boston. Many of the students were, like me, hoping that education was a way out of the tough streets. The first day of classes brought back memories of opening day at the Mary E. Curley School in Jamaica Plain, when I was ten years old. Everywhere I looked I saw people of different colors. White, black, purple, green — everybody was there. Color didn't matter. All I saw was a bunch of kids trying to learn and make something of themselves.

The university is in Dorchester, near the water, a half mile from the Kennedy Library, and less than a mile from the Columbia Point Housing Projects, where Frankie MacDonald and I got into trouble in the summer of 1975. When the semester started, I took a new apartment in Dorchester, directly across the street from the university. I wasn't giving myself any excuses to miss class.

That first semester was difficult. I could stare down the barrel of a gun, but in the world of academia I was scared. I took a full course load that semester, five classes. Maybe I should have eased into it, but I wanted to do it right. Still, skills that were second nature for most students were alien to me. I found much of the reading difficult. There always seemed to be too much homework. Writing a term paper was like writing a novel. For all I'd been through, being a student quickly became my most intense experience.

I plugged along, barely holding a C for that first year, but my skills grew quickly. I started to take six classes a semester, including Saturday and night classes. And I fell in love with reading. Soon, I was a fixture in the library. I read books for my courses and some for pleasure. I even began to haunt local bookstores. I may sound like a poster-child for literacy programs, but I'm being straight. To this day, reading, along with music, remains a major release for me.

When it was time for me to declare my major at the end of my freshman year, I chose pre-law — since the university didn't offer "outside-the-law" as a major. Of course, with my record, I knew I'd have trouble getting accepted to the bar, but I could still go to law school.

For the next three years, even though I lived right across the street from the school, I was a commuting student, a "muter," just like thousands of others. I worked odd jobs, I DJ'd, I worked the doors at bars. I still managed to pick up Courtney and Lauren at Carolyn's house every morning and drive them to school. But there was no denying that I was having "social" problems. During the first few years after my deal with the feds, I didn't go into South Boston much. With everything that had happened, I felt uncomfortable moving up and down those streets. Almost all the guys I'd run with were dead or in prison, out of the neighborhood, or keeping a low profile.

Sometimes, I'd see Whitey's Grand Marquis, Whitey behind the wheel and Kevin Weeks in the passenger seat. Whitey never stopped. He'd just look at me briefly, give me the Southie wave, and then turn his attention back to the road. As if none of it ever happened.

And so I studied. And I learned. I was not a docile student. I asked questions, I challenged professors, and sometimes I became, well, a bit disruptive. But I was going to get my money's worth. I wanted to learn.

One professor of women's studies, Shoshanna Ehrlich, opened my eyes. I realized that we men take so much for granted. What did I know about mothers? Nothing. All my life, I'd been a womanizer, and now I was the father of daughters, and suddenly I was being exposed to the problems of women in a man's world. For the first time, I began to see how awful my treatment of most women had been. I'm not going to say I completely changed and became the perfect gentleman, because I didn't. But my eyes were opened to an aspect of womanhood I'd never thought about, and it made me think about my daughters and their mothers differently. Here I was, a single parent, and I was developing a profound respect for motherhood, especially single mothers.

One of my favorite classes was Cultural Diversity through Literature, in which I read my favorite book assigned through all of college: *The Autobiography of Malcolm X*. Malcolm X's story spoke to me on so many levels: the poverty, the anger, the hurt, the violence, the need to assert oneself. He was talking to and about me when he wrote, "The hustler, out there in the ghetto jungles, has less respect for the white power structure than any other Negro in North America. The ghetto hustler is internally restrained by nothing. He has no religion, no concept of morality, no civic responsibility, no fear — nothing. To survive, he is constantly out there preying on others, probing for any human weakness like a ferret. The ghetto hustler is forever frustrated, restless, and anxious for some 'action.' Whatever he undertakes, he commits himself to it fully, absolutely."

Most people are so removed from the life of an urban street predator that they can't even begin to find a point of reference to understand who we are, what we are about. But Malcolm X understood that the street predator is an animal, devoid of conscience, whose primary objective is to survive and to win at all costs. And, let me tell you, while you are robbing and mugging, you're not thinking, *Ah, shit, I can't believe what a dirtball I am. One of these days, I am going to see the light and be overcome with regret for the sad mistakes I made.* No. Malcolm X knew what motivated a young thug on the street, black or white, uneducated, deprived of love, who has been beaten and neglected, and who is looked at by society not only in a patronizing and indifferent manner, but also with fear. That motivator is *rage*. Of course, Malcolm X was talking specifically about the young, urban, black predator. But he could just as well have been talking about a young Eddie MacKenzie or Ronny Watts or Frankie MacDonald.

When I wasn't attending classes and writing papers and doing anything I could to make a few bucks, I was trying to do other things that college students do. Like play football. Sure, I was thirty-five and these kids were eighteen and nineteen, but so what? I belonged, I was certain, on the football field, winning games for my college. It took some maneuvering and a little forging of medical records to make me appear twenty-two, but I got myself a uniform and equipment and a schedule. Ironically, Coach Kent, a probation officer from the Charlestown District Court, had heard of me.

In a pep talk before one of our games, he said, seriously, "Mac, if I tell you to kill the quarterback, I only mean for you to tackle him." I nodded.

During the 1993 season, I played defensive tackle and offensive lineman. Unfortunately, I could never quite get into the proper football spirit Coach Kent wanted. The minute I got onto the field, I went wild. All I wanted to do was hit the opposing player with left hooks to the body. We lost our first game against Westfield State 43–0. It made me crazy. I was thrown out for unnecessary roughness in every game, accumulating the most penalties of any player on our team. Coach Kent was determined to work with me and tone me down, but a vicious bone bruise to my left kneecap during one practice ended my football career. Too bad. I had high hopes for what I could have achieved out on the field.

Graduation day in June 1995 was the culmination of a lifetime dream for me. I felt as if I'd finally put everything behind me and accomplished something of great worth. For three years, I had thought of nothing but my studies and improving my mind. Receiving that diploma (signed, if you can believe it, by William Bulger, who had just been named president of the University of Massachusetts) proved that when I set my mind to something, I usually achieved my goal. My brother Ronnie and his wife, Maria, and Carolyn and Courtney and Lauren, along with some of my friends, were all on hand to see me collect that diploma and to celebrate afterward. Never had I felt so proud of myself.

# Women Studies

nfortunately, the awesome diploma in my hand did not alter some of the sadder details of my personal life. This is no Wilt Chamberlain story, but, to be honest, I have slept with more than two hundred girls. Me and Frankie alone must have fucked eighty apiece before we were twenty-four. In the nightclub business, you can get laid twice a night. I have no idea how many I knocked up. I used to joke that I'd never throw rocks in a schoolyard because I might hit one of my kids. I don't think that's such a funny statement today.

Nor is there anything funny about my tortured relationship with Kathy Puglisi. I met Kathy in 1990, while I was still working for Whitey. I was thirty-two; she was sixteen. She was living in a halfway house in Newburyport, Massachusetts, because her mother was a chronic drunk and fruitcake. The reason her mother was so crazy was a guy named Davey Brown, Kathy's father. Davey and Kathy's mother never married, but they had Kathy. Lucky Kathy.

Davey was a woman beater, a heroin junkie, and a crackhead. Growing up in the Old Colony Project in Southie, Kathy had the misfortune to witness the constant beatings her father gave her mother. Kathy told me that once they were all eating together at the table, and suddenly, for no reason, Davey stabbed her mother in the face with a fork. And then beat her senseless. Poor Kathy grew up in this horror, knowing that her own mother had put her father in prison by testifying to his abuse.

Davey spent half his life in the can, mostly for assaults on women. This prick had a thing for stabbing girls. Let me tell you, guys who beat women are the lowest of the low. They don't have the balls to try that on a man. Davey Brown was one of those men. He was a short, skinny coward that couldn't lick a stamp on the street. I guess that if you can't fight, or are a coward, then the next best way to feel tough is to beat women or kids. Any time I saw a guy hit a girl in my bar, I'd give him a bitch slap and throw him out. But I'm nervous about getting involved in a domestic scene. You gotta be real careful these days trying to be a good Samaritan. It's not like in the old days when people had scruples. Now, some guy will pull out a knife or gun and kill you if you come between him and his wife or girlfriend.

For reasons I could never understand, the bond of family has always been strong with Kathy. They say a father's bond is unbreakable. I didn't know that bond growing up, but now that I'm a father to five daughters, I understand exactly how strong it is. In Kathy's case, it was true. Kathy wrote her father while he was in prison, and when I visited Freddy Weichel in Walpole, she begged me to bring her with me so she could see her father.

I first met Kathy when her stepbrother Jake, a pal of mine who worked for me at Connolly's, needed a ride to the halfway house in Newburyport and I drove him there. When I saw her, I realized that I used to say hi to her on the street when she was just a girl. She was a little cutie, small and thin with huge brown eyes and short, shiny brown hair framing her heart-shaped face. She didn't have much of a body, but something about the way she acted, cool and very street smart for a sixteen-year-old, attracted me. I found out that she was turning seventeen the following week, so I said I'd come up on her birthday and take her shopping. She said, "I don't have any money for shopping," and I said, "It's on me, hon. I'd like to buy you some clothes for your birthday." Underneath her coolness, I could detect a lost soul, like a stray lamb. I knew right away that we came from the same kinds of backgrounds. I both pitied and desired her.

On her birthday, I took her shopping as promised. She was amazed at what I was willing to spend. I told her, "Hey, don't look at the price tags. Just pick out whatever you want." I was still rolling in Whitey's drug money, so it was no big deal to drop $600 that afternoon. You had to see how happy she was when she got back to the halfway house and showed off her new clothes. It made me feel great to give something to this kid who had nothing. Through her happiness, I was getting something back that I had lost as a child.

For the next year, I visited Kathy every few weeks with her stepbrother. I was developing a real thing for her. Then, one night, around ten, I was working at Connolly's bar and she came walking in the door. She told me she'd run away and was never going back to Newburyport. Her mother wouldn't let her stay at home because she had a boyfriend and there was no room for Kathy. Since she had nowhere to go, I let her stay at my house for a week until I was able to reach the halfway house. I tried to get them to take her back, but they didn't want her. They told me that she had been accused of stealing $500 won on a scratch ticket by another resident. I was screwed. When she disappeared on me one night, I said, "Fuck it." I figured she'd probably hooked up with a friend. Then I saw her at a party a couple of weeks later. She wanted to be with me as much as I wanted to be with her. We hung out and got drunk together.

They say a stiff prick has no conscience. I slept with her that night. I dropped her off at a friend's place the next day and that was the end of it. Or so I thought. I didn't see her until seven months later, when she came walking into Connolly's to say hi. I took a look at her and said, "Hey, you're pregnant, kid. Congratulations. Who's the lucky guy?"

She said, "You, you prick."

I was like, "Yeah, go fuck yourself." I was certain she was lying. Two months later, on June 22, 1992, she had a girl, Devin. I went to visit her right away, just in case the baby was mine. I was taken to court because she was looking for welfare support. The court ordered a paternity test which proved I was the father. I was in shock over the whole thing. But since the baby was mine, I tried to get along with Kathy.

Which has never been easy, to say the least. One day when I was living in Whitey's condo in Louisburg Square in Quincy, we had an argument. Nothing serious, but she pissed me off and I told her to get out of my house. She left, but, an hour later, when I went to my car — the brand new Jaguar Vanden Plas — it had been defaced; she'd scratched the words "prick," "asshole," and "you suck" on the hood. What balls. I wanted to kill her on the spot, but, for some strange reason, I also felt bad for her. I figured I'd thrown her out on the street like her mother had done, over and over, and I had to make up for it.

But, here we go with that second brain men have. I let it do the thinking, and sure enough, she got knocked up again. I heard nothing from her until nine months later, on June 16, 1993, when I got a call from Boston City Hospital. The little mother tells me, "Hey, prick, you got a kid here." I knew she'd been with other guys, so I denied I was the father. Again. Next thing I know, I'm in front of the probate judge. The judge ordered DNA tests, and when the results came in, I was the father of another little girl. The judge ordered support, and that was that.

Two years later, Kathy was living on food stamps and welfare in a Section Eight apartment, which meant the government sent a rent check to her landlord every month. Life was a party. I wanted to do the right thing for my two girls, Devin and Kayla, so I took them out, bought them clothes, paid good solid attention. And, of course, my little brain got going again, and I slept with Kathy again, and out popped another kid. I was totally irresponsible as far as birth control was concerned. I can say that a stiff prick has no conscience, but I can also say that I had no brains. So I got another call from Boston City Hospital with a slightly different message: "Hey, prick. You got a kid here. A boy." Danny.

In 1995, the Department of Social Services (DSS) stepped in and took Kathy's three kids away after they found them in a crack house in Dorchester. This was my first official notice she was hitting the pipe. And what did DSS do with my three kids? Put them in three separate foster homes. I was still in school, living in an apartment on Henderson Street in South Boston, but said I would gladly take them. Citing my extensive criminal history, DSS refused. I then brought my brother Ronnie and his wife Maria to court with me; they said they would take them to keep the family together. But because my brother also had a record, they wouldn't allow that. He'd paid his debt to society, hadn't gotten so much as a parking ticket in five years, was making $30,000 a year as a cook, his wife was a legal secretary making the same, and they lived in a four-bedroom home outside of Boston, but DSS still said no. Instead, they separated the girls, aged three and four. They went to two different foster homes. My fourteen-month-old son was sent to another home.

I did everything in my power to get my children back. DSS put me through the toughest battle of my life, allowing me to see my little girls for only one hour of supervised visits every Thursday at the DSS offices in Weymouth. I was supposed to be on my best behavior while the Gestapo she-wolves watched my every move. As if I would ever hurt my babies. The saddest part of it was that when the girls came for their visit with Daddy, they were happier to see each other than to see me. Every time I begged DSS to at least keep my girls together, they told me, "We just don't have enough foster homes."

I said, "Well, assholes, if it wasn't for your fucked-up policies, their uncle, who has a great home waiting for them, would have them together as a family." For the next nine months, DSS put me through parenting courses and psychological and IQ tests, all of which I passed. Things were starting to look up for me and my three kids, so I went out and got a two-bedroom condo and filled it with girly things like Disney pictures on the walls and sweet bedroom sets. On the day they were to arrive, I got a call from DSS saying that Kathy was in a halfway house in Roxbury and they were going to give her the girls. I was completely frustrated. Didn't what I'd been going through for the past nine months mean anything? Of course not. The laws have a bias against men and favor the mothers. No matter what.

Not long after, I got a call from a lady in another crack house in Dorchester who had my pager number, saying it had been two days and Kathy hadn't come back and she'd like to get rid of the kids, whom Kathy had dumped there. I called Kathy's halfway house in Roxbury and reported this so DSS wouldn't take my girls. I told the halfway house the girls were with me and they were safe, and then explained what had happened to Brenda, my case worker at DSS. It took a few weeks, but finally we ended up in probate court in Hingham, Massachusetts, for the custody hearing. Judge Black declared Kathy an unfit mother and gave me custody of Devin and Kayla. It took another two years, but, finally on July 27, 1998, I went before the court in the Suffolk division, where the girls had been born, and won permanent legal and physical custody of them.

But, back in 1996, there was a hitch in my custody arrangement. The only way I'd get my girls was if I gave up parental rights to my son. His foster parents wanted to adopt him, and everybody at DSS felt that was the right thing for Danny. If I didn't cooperate, DSS would declare me an unfit father. Apparently I was a fit father for my girls, but not for my son. I was so scared I'd lose my girls that I felt I had no choice but to sign Danny over. To this day, it breaks my heart to think about what I did. I can't make contact with him until he's eighteen. I'll never get him off my mind. Devin and Kayla ask about their little brother every day.

But, if by some miracle, I was suddenly able to raise my son, I wouldn't want him to follow in my footsteps. And I'm not alone in that. A lot of mobsters don't want their kids to do what they do. Take Steve Flemmi, Whitey's second in command before Kevin Weeks. Flemmi is a savage murderer who wouldn't think twice about slitting someone's throat. But one day, I was standing in front of Connolly's with his son, Stevie Jr., who was then in his mid-twenties, about five years younger than me. We didn't usually hang around together, but on that day we were just shooting the bull. Who pulled up in a big Lincoln Town Car but Whitey and Stevie Sr.? No sooner had the car stopped than Stevie Sr. was shouting out the passenger-side window to his son, "Hey, Eddie Mac is a dangerous man! Didn't I tell you that? Huh? Didn't I tell you I don't want you doing this shit? Hanging out with these guys?"

Stevie Sr. then looked at me and said with a straight face, "Sorry, Ed."

I don't blame him. I wouldn't want my Danny to hang around with me or my buddies. As for Kathy, I was convinced there were only two places she wanted to see me: in the can or in the ground. Take this insane stunt she pulled after one of our many messy splits. She was pissed out of her mind and on a drinking and drug binge. One Friday night, while she was on her toot, she phoned me and threatened to call the police and tell them I was harassing and abusing her.

Playing it smart, I went down to the area police station the next day to file a harassment complaint. The cop at the desk asked for my name. When I gave it to him he told me to hold on for a minute while he checked on something. Thirty seconds later, he returned with nine cops, and told me I was under arrest. I was shocked. "Wait, you gotta be kidding me," I said. "I came here for help. What am I under arrest for?" As the cuffs were being snapped on, I was told there was an arrest warrant out for me on the charges of kidnapping and intimidation of a witness. I didn't have to ask but I did anyway. "Who the fuck made the complaint?"

"A Kathy Puglisi. Says she's a former girlfriend of yours."

My little honey never ceased to amaze me. She then made up a sob story that the reason she couldn't make it to trial to testify against me was because I'd tied her up and had my brother Ronnie watch her while court was in session. Getting truly creative, Kathy even claimed that Al Nugent was in on the conspiracy! Apparently, the cops didn't take the accusation too seriously, because, as I found out, the only reason I was in the can was that I happened to show up on their doorstep. The boys didn't even bother to go after Ronnie and Al. But I had delivered myself on a platter, so I was being held in a Boston Police Department lockup on $50,000 bail.

This was bad enough for me, but it was a lot worse for Ronnie and Al. Ronnie had been a model citizen for two years of his eight-year parole when this happened. As for Al, what were the consequences for one of Boston's top defense attorneys if anyone took the charge seriously? Imagine how many cops he's pissed off by freeing guys they arrested. They'd be more than willing to do whatever they could to see him disbarred.

Me? I was already screwed. I was being held on a $50,000 bond. Since the indictment, I was no longer in the lucrative drug business or connected to Whitey, and that meant I was never going to make bail. I'd probably end up in jail from six months to a year fighting this thing. Monday morning came, and I was standing in the holding cell at South Boston District, along with the other dirtballs who'd been pinched over the weekend. When Al came walking up to the bars, I could see he was madder than a hornet. Before he could get out a word, I said, "Hey, haven't you been tied to this scam as well?"

Al held up his hand. "Yeah, you're damn right. I got a call on this thing and I'm already all over it. The judge knows what she's about. But, no matter, we still have charges we need dropped." Then he fixed me with his pissed-off glare. "And what did I tell you? What's the matter with you? Didn't I tell you to stay away from the psycho? Eddie, I could see if she was a fox or something, but that girl is a dog."

No sooner had Al said this than a broad from the women's holding cell around the corner yelled, "Hey, who the fuck are you calling a dog, you wrinkled old prick!"

Al looked at me dumbfounded. I laughed like hell because I recognized the voice immediately. It was my Kathy. It seemed she'd been arrested over the weekend for smashing a beer bottle over some broad's head.

A few hours later, Al and I were in front of the judge waiting for our accuser to show up. Only Kathy was twisted enough to manage to be arraigned *and* serve as a witness on the same day. When she finally came into the courtroom, she was strutting, making this pouty, bad-ass face, and wearing Walkman headphones.

The male judge was not amused by the scene, and he gave Kathy a look of disgust. She gave it right back. Kathy and I were giving each other our best "fuck-you" faces. The charges were read and the judge thumbed through a bunch of papers. And then I got a pleasant shock. The judge said that he had serious doubts about the charges and that the case would be under review and that I was released on personal recognizance.

Kathy went ballistic. "You gotta be fucking kidding me! This is a fucking joke! You call this justice?" Al and I were already halfway to the door when we heard the judge yelling for one of the court officers to get Kathy out of the room. If a guy had said these things to a judge, he would have been jailed for life. Al and I were in his car, three miles away from the courthouse, when I said, "Al, that was an unbelievable piece of work. Thanks so much."

"Don't thank me," he said with a chuckle. "That psycho piece of ass just cost you two grand. The next time you want to spend two grand, go into town and get yourself a hooker." It was good advice.

But, whacked as I know she is, I can't get Kathy out of my blood. I understand what her tough childhood must have been like and what it did to her; it attracts me to her, makes me feel sorry for her. What I felt for her was something deep, in my bones. But no matter how well I think I know her, she never fails to surprise me with her antics. I remember the Fourth of July in 1999 when she decided to take the kids camping at Myles Standish State Forest, a stretch of land in the town of Plymouth on the Massachusetts coast. You know, where the pilgrims landed.

I said I'd drive everyone down, transport all the gear, set the tents up, and then leave them to it. After I volunteered, I was told that the expedition party had expanded to include Kathy's mother and a friend of Kathy's named Denise. Lucky me. Kathy's mother has long been a ward of the state, on public relief, state health care, and public housing, a psycho on some heavy-duty medication. Sometimes, the medication even works.

And Denise wasn't much better. She was another welfare nut case whose tough life had recently gotten a lot worse. Four or five months prior to the camping trip, she was dumped by her boyfriend. As the guy was driving away, she flipped out and tried to hang herself. The boyfriend had gone a little ways down the street and must have felt bad, or sensed that she might do something drastic, so he turned around. He walked into the house to find her dangling from a rope. He managed to grab her and take her down, but not before she'd been deprived of oxygen long enough to have clipped a few million brain cells. She wasn't working with an abundance in the first place, so she surely couldn't afford to lose any. Now she's permanently disabled, walking kind of funny, and talking kind of weird. And that's before she starts drinking.

Our happy little group couldn't have been at the campground more than a few minutes when Kathy started in on her mother, the grandmother of my kids. With the girls watching and with families camped all around, Kathy was screaming, "You're the fucking reason I'm so fucked up! When I was growing up there was nothing in the fridge but beer! You didn't give a shit about us! I was sucking cock at twelve because you were taking it up the ass and had your door locked!"

Devin and Kayla stood in the distance, watching everything, showing little emotion. Kathy's mother begged me to take her home, but I told her to forget it. I was staying for my kids. I stayed all day and helped pitch the tents and made sure everything was all right before I left around nine P.M.

The next day, I went to South Boston to visit my older girls, Courtney and Lauren, and suggested that they take a trip with me down to Myles Standish to go swimming with their half-sisters. With the temperature in the nineties, and the humidity high, it wasn't a hard sell. As I was pulling into an area near the campsite, Kathy's mother ran up to us, begging me again to take her home. I held up my hand to cut her off and asked where Kathy and the kids were. She told me they were all down by the lake, and then explained to me what happened the previous night.

Apparently, Kathy and Denise had hidden a case of beer in the gear that we brought down. After I left, they took out the case and started pounding the booze. They got all messed up and went on a rampage, yelling and screaming and trashing the entire campsite, tearing down the tents. My babies were terrified and scurried over to the tent of another family to hide.

As soon as I heard that, I decided that *all* my daughters were leaving with me. As soon as Kathy's mother saw that I had no sympathy for her, she jumped in my face and said, "Hey, go fuck yourself, you cocksucker, and take me home!" Courtney and Lauren were shaken by this performance, but I just put my arms around them and turned away with them and headed toward the lake where Devin and Kayla were swimming with Mommy Dearest. We didn't even turn around as that crazy woman continued to scream.

The lake was two hundred yards away. At fifty yards, where the water lapped up against the beach, I caught my first glimpse of the mother of my two younger daughters, lying belly down in a few inches of water with her head propped up above the water on one of her arms. She was motionless and looked dead, like one of those World War II photos of a lifeless Marine lying on a beach after an invasion attempt. I gasped and sprinted over. But when I got to her side, I quickly realized she was alive and breathing but totally shit-faced.

I looked around for Devin and Kayla and saw them a little farther down the beach, splashing around and having a grand time. When they saw me, they giggled and waved, calling out, "Hey, Dad!"

There were about twenty other people around, just doing the family thing, not paying the floater or our kids any mind. My older daughters didn't know how to react. They trailed me as I walked over to where their half-sisters were playing. As I was walking over, who did I spy on the beach, passed out drunk on a lounge chair, but Denise? This was bad — even by my standards.

I walked back to Kathy, woke her up, and dragged her out of the water. For a few feet, I practically had to carry her, stupefied and mumbling, before she figured out what was going on and pulled her arm away and stumbled forward on her own. I gave Denise a shake by the shoulder to bring her back to something approaching consciousness. As a group, we headed back to the campsite.

I tried to make the best of it. I cooked cheeseburgers on the grill. Things were relatively calm during dinner. But then the peace broke. After we'd finished eating, I started to get Devin and Kayla ready for the ride home. I didn't consult Kathy. So she took a cheeseburger and threw it at the back of my head. It missed and instead hit my thirteen-year-old, Lauren, in the face. Kathy screamed at me, asking me why I was taking the little ones. About ten years ago, I would have dropped her, but I also knew if I did that I'd have every cop in the area on the hunt for me within minutes. And if Kathy's antics weren't enough, her mother had locked herself in my jeep and was demanding I take her back to Southie. I was tempted to drop Mom as well. But I just clammed up and tried to maintain my composure.

I couldn't bother with Kathy's mother, so I just left her to steam in the backseat of my jeep while I piled all the kids in. As I was doing this, Kathy was punching the windows of the vehicle, screaming at me, "You diddler! Rat! Child molester! I'm gonna fucking kill you!"

I would have laughed, except that the kids had to witness this spectacle. I kept my mouth shut and jumped behind the wheel, and me and the four girls and Kathy's screwy mom got the hell out of there. Just your normal family vacation.

In her defense, I have to admit Kathy will never hesitate to defend me or her children. Once I saw her talking to a girl in front of Connolly's bar. The girl said something bad about me, so, out of nowhere, Kathy yelled, "Hey, cunt, that's my man you're badmouthing!" Then, she slammed a bottle over the girl's head, splitting it wide open.

In her own crazy way, she shows the same loyalty to our kids. A few years ago Kathy and I were standing outside our girls' school in Beverly. Even though I had full custody of the girls at that time, Kathy had been clean for a few months and had convinced me to give her another chance to be a decent mother. I knew it wouldn't work, but the girls missed their mother so much and I was having a hard time as a single father, working and taking care of two little girls, so I decided to give it a shot. I set Kathy up in a nice apartment in Beverly, fifteen miles away from Boston and far removed from all her bad influences. Beverly also had an excellent school system for the girls. She lasted seven months, but blew her chance when she got drunk and got into a fight with a cop. For the short time the arrangement worked, I kept in daily contact with the girls' teacher and drove out from Quincy every day for the first two months to make sure the girls got off to school okay. One warm October day, Kathy decided to come with me when I walked them to school. We were waiting for the bell to ring when another mother walked up to Devin and Kayla. She was trying to be friendly and asked, "Oh, and what grade are you two little dears in?"

They told her they were both in kindergarten, and she asked them how old they were, and then said, "If you're five and your sister is four, why are you both in kindergarten?"

Kathy had had enough. So, while the girls were trying to answer the woman's questions, Kathy shouted, "Hey, you fucking nosy cunt, you got any more questions for my kids, you ask me, you fucking piece of shit!" The other mothers were shocked. The lady tried to apologize but Kathy cut her off and said, "Get the fuck away from my kids, you douche bag." I had to do everything in my power to keep from falling on the ground in a fit of laughter.

I pity Kathy more than I love her. There have been many times when I've hated her for neglecting my beautiful girls, abandoning them in her endless search to get high. It's because of that behavior that I've had complete custody of the girls for four years. But I know how much our girls love their mother and how much they want to be with her. When she's clean, she can be a loving and caring mother who loves them as much as they love her. My strongest prayer is that she will stay straight and not disappoint them ever again.

My relationship with Carolyn is a lot simpler. I always knew Carolyn and I would never remarry, but once she got over her anger at my infidelity, we worked out an arrangement that put our daughters first. I've always respected the kind of mother Carolyn has been to Courtney and Lauren. She's just about perfect. But her choice of men has not always been perfect.

One of her former boyfriends, Steve Conway, didn't understand that no is no. He's a big guy, 6' 4", from West Roxbury, and he can be violent. I've tried to make him understand that Carolyn is special to me. But sometimes Steve forgot who he was living with, and I had to remind him.

In 1994, a year after he moved in with Carolyn, Courtney, and Lauren, and I was still working for my degree at UMass Boston, I gave Steve one hell of a wake-up call. One warm spring morning when I came to pick up my two girls and take them to school, I saw Steve sleeping in his parked car in front of her house. I knew he'd been doing cocaine and drinking, but Carolyn had told me he was doing better. That morning, however, I could see he wasn't doing too good, and she must have thrown him out. He looked like a street person. I wasn't happy about that, but I decided to try to stay cool. I didn't want to upset my girls before they went to school.

Carolyn needed a ride to work that morning, so she got into the car with Courtney and Lauren. She gave me a stony look and I could tell she was upset, but I didn't say anything and just talked to my girls. After we dropped Carolyn at the medical office in Boston where she worked, Courtney, holding back tears, said, "Daddy, Daddy, I had the baseball bat. I was going to hit him."

And Lauren said, crying, "He had Mommy against the wall."

I was ready to go back right away and murder the miserable prick, but these were my babies and they were upset and I had to think about them. I told them not to worry, that everything would be okay. But they had to tell me exactly what had been going on. And they did. Every word was like a shot to my gut. "Steve's been slapping Mommy around for weeks now." "He's been calling her bad names." "Mommy told us not to tell you." "We promised we wouldn't tell you, Daddy."

"It's okay," I told them, forcing myself to stay in control. "Don't worry about a thing. I'm here. And I'll have a nice little talk with Steve and everything will be okay."

I dropped the girls off at school and went home to call Carolyn. "What in the world is going on here?" I asked her.

"Please don't do anything, Eddie," she begged me. "Please."

"Don't you worry, honey," I said, staying calm. "I'm not going to do anything to hurt Steve. But you know I'm not going to let anyone disrespect the mother of my kids. I promise I'm not going to do anything this time. I'm just going to explain to him that it's going to get very ugly if it ever happens again." She told me everything the rat had done. I convinced her I was not going to whack him, and she believed me.

When I hung up, I got back into my car. I checked my pockets and saw I had only $1.30 left. I'd given the girls a few dollars each when I kissed them good-bye. It was a rough time for me. I was still on my four-year probation with the federal government. I'd been doing odd stuff, painting and Sheetrocking, and going to school full-time, besides pissing in a cup once a week for my probation officer to prove I didn't use drugs.

Probation notwithstanding, I had to open Steve's eyes a little. I headed over to Dunkin' Donuts and bought a cup of coffee for $1.24. Medium, black, scalding hot. Then I headed back to Carolyn's place. Steve was still in his car, sleeping like a baby. The window was down and he had his head against the door, hands under his cheeks. I poured the hot coffee down the side of his face, making sure to get some on his eyeballs. He jerked awake, like he was on fire, and I leaned in, pulling him close to my face. "If you ever touch or disrespect the mother of my kids again," I said, real clearly, "I will fucking burn you alive. Remember, you motherfucker, the next time it will be gasoline." I swear if I'd had enough money to buy the gasoline that day that's what I would have done. I would have soaked him down and stood there with a lighter and let him know exactly how vulnerable he was. But I'd only had $1.30, so the coffee had to do.

As soon as I finished my little talk with Steve, I got back in my car and started to drive away. In the rear-view mirror, I saw Steve do a Starsky and Hutch. Now he was going at full speed, motioning me to turn onto Colony Avenue. He took a right on a side street, and went to the projects and stopped his car. Before I could get out of my car, he was in front of me, pulling me out of the car and ripping my tank top off. "Come on, motherfucker!" he shouted. "Let's fucking go!"

He never got the chance. I knocked him right out. Rather than give him the full rib-kicking treatment, I decided to go easy and dragged him over to the side of the road. Then I got in my car and took off.

An hour later, I was driving down Broadway in Southie and I saw his car parked outside the police station. I found out that he had pressed charges. Since I was on probation, I called my probation officer and explained it to her. She knew how hard I was working at school and said she wouldn't write me up for a violation. Then I went to the police station and explained the story. They said it was a bum rap and he was a piece of shit, but they had to take me in. They booked me and took me to the Southie court in time for the judge to make bail, or I'd have been there overnight.

I was eventually charged with mayhem, assault and battery, and attempted murder. So I sent a very loud message through some friends. They told Steve that they knew where his parents lived and that he was making a big mistake. Because any time they saw him, they'd hit him with a baseball bat. He dropped the charges, and everything was dismissed. A few days later, I called him up and said, "We've got to work this out. You made a mistake with Carolyn. You gotta understand I'm never gonna sit around and let you do these things to the mother of my kids." He said he was sorry and that was it for me.

A couple of weeks later, I was sitting in the parlor at Carolyn's house waiting for my girls to get ready. He came out to talk to me. "Eddie, I know you're a championship fighter," he said. "So why didn't you just take me out back and clean my clock? Why did you have to burn me? I still have nightmares thinking I'm waking up on fire."

I looked at him and saw how blond he was, a real Irish-looking kid. His fair skin had just about healed, but it still didn't look good. "You know I really was going to come after you again," he went on. "It wasn't those guys you sent down who convinced me not to go through with the case. It was my probation officer. When I told him I was gonna go after Eddie Mac, he said, 'Not a wise move.' And that did it."

I nodded. But all I cared about was that he wouldn't go after my ex-wife ever again. Because if he ever laid a hand on Carolyn again, I would have no problem chopping off his blond head and burying him in the Blue Hills, a state-protected conservation area south of Boston.

Steve stays out of her life now, although he still pays attention to their son, Stevie. I'm always telling Carolyn that when I get some money again, I'm going to buy a big house and she can live there with Stevie and our two girls and my other kids. She can have her own part of the house, and I can have mine. But she just laughs and tells me that will never happen.

In early 1998, a woman I was seeing informed me that she was pregnant. We married later that year and had a beautiful daughter whom we named Brittany. Sadly, the marriage didn't last and we divorced shortly after

Brittany's birth. Today, my youngest daughter lives with her mother. The two of us continue to try to work things out so that we can be decent parents to Brittany.

I know it sounds funny, but I'm a romantic at heart and still believe my soul mate is out there. Maria, Ronnie's wife, tells me I have to learn to let someone love me. She's right. I believe I am a good man, but because of my childhood and the work I did for Whitey, I'm secretive. I could never come home and talk about what I did for the day with a wife. It's in my blood to be the way I am. And even though I yearn for a normal life and a loving wife, I have no idea how to lead that kind of life or love that kind of wife.

# The Party's Over

**W**hile I was trying to get my own life together, my old boss had run into problems of his own. Whitey was running out of time. He'd outlived his usefulness to the FBI. He'd ratted on, and handed over, people for so long that Uncle Sam had milked the source dry. The FBI might still be using him if they had more Italian arrests to put in the papers, but the once-powerful New England Mafia, run by the Angiulo family of Boston, had been seriously weakened. Whitey had helped Connolly accomplish his mission of keeping the Angiulo family off the streets; Gennaro "Jerry" Angiulo, who served as the Patriarca family underboss from 1966 to 1983, had been convicted of racketeering, illegal gambling, and loan-sharking in 1986. The FBI had no one left to go after but Whitey.

Adding to Whitey's problems, Johnny Connolly retired from the FBI in 1990 and took a job with Boston Edison as head of corporate security. He moved up the ladder to the position of in-house lobbyist and was making a comfortable hundred-and-twenty grand a year. He picked himself up a nice condo at 335 West Fourth Street in Southie. Word was that the condo, valued at three hundred K, was a present to Connolly from Whitey. The condo adjoined two other condos, one owned by Whitey and the other by Kevin Weeks. Then again, it could all be coincidence.

Not that that was the first piece of property Connolly bought in Southie. Ten years earlier, in February 1980, the FBI agent had bought from Bulger bagman Bobby Ford a duplex townhouse at 48 Thomas Park in Southie — supposedly, for $63,000. I'd overheard Whitey telling a few guys that Connolly had gotten the townhouse for a dollar. You could tell by the smirk on Whitey's face that this gift was for services rendered. That he had the FBI in his back pocket. Not a bad deal considering Connolly later sold both units of the townhouse for $340,000. It also came as no surprise when Connolly decided his sons might be better off growing up farther away from Southie. He built a house, now worth more than $800,000, in Lynnfield,

Massachusetts, on land that had once belonged to Bulger's bookie, Rocco Botta.

Connolly, the real estate mogul with underworld connections, was doing all right for himself, but he was no longer in a position to protect Whitey. Time for the government to get cute — to turn on the criminal who had helped them for so many years. And you wonder why I say that I'm not sure who's worse: the law or the gangsters.

The FBI began by rounding up the bookies who routinely paid tribute to Whitey. For years, these guys had been allowed to run their rackets without interference. But in 1992, Fred M. Wyshak Jr., a hard-nosed prosecutor at the U.S. Attorney's office, began to threaten bookies with money-laundering indictments, crimes that could bring hefty sentences. Facing serious jail time, it didn't take long for the bookies to see that these indictments could be tossed in exchange for inside information on Whitey Bulger's system of extortion.

The FBI was soon in receipt of all sorts of information on our boy Whitey. In addition, other people who'd been involved with Whitey, like Timmy Connolly, were ratting on him to reduce prison sentences or beat them altogether.

But who was it that said of the relationship between Whitey and the feds that the government was playing checkers and Whitey was playing chess? It's true. The feds were out of their league. Whitey had decided a long time ago that ultimately he was going to end up with a better deal. As I've said, he was an avid reader of military history. He understood that many of the great military strategists and empires planned their initiatives years in advance. I remember reading that the Japanese studied the waters and air currents around Hawaii for close to twenty years before that December day in 1941. Whitey was like that; he planned well in advance of the day he would have to make his move. He once told Freddy Weichel, "Freddy, you have to be ready on an hour's notice to leave and be on the road and never come back." He meant it.

It was common knowledge on the street that for years Whitey had planned every detail of his escape, planting money where he'd need it, mapping out his route with the same brilliance he'd used to control the South Boston Mafia. Of course, the major ace in the hole was his agreement with Johnny Connolly that he would be given twenty-four-hour advance notice of an indictment being issued. It was an agreement for which Connolly would be convicted seven years later, on May 28, 2002, but one that was crucial to Whitey. All the planning in the world would be worthless if he ended up in custody.

On January 5, 1995, the feds issued indictments against Whitey, Stevie Flemmi, Frank Salemme, Patriarca crime family soldier Robert DeLuca, and Johnny Martorano. Whitey and Flemmi were, per agreement with Connolly, tipped off. Salemme was fed to the wolves. How would you like to have been that poor guy? He gets arrested and finds out that the guys he ran with, the guys he trusted, had been ratting him out for years. As they had Martorano and DeLuca.

Whitey had already been gone a week when the feds moved in to arrest him. He was driving around the country with his longtime girlfriend Teresa Stanley. Talk about brazen! Even as the authorities were looking for him, Bulger drove back to the area, to a restaurant in Hingham, a few miles south of Boston, and dropped off Stanley. He then picked up another girlfriend, Catherine Greig, the platinum-blond dental hygienist and part-time dog groomer he'd been seeing for twenty of the thirty years he'd been involved with Stanley, and disappeared.

Flemmi could have disappeared as well, but stupidity and arrogance brought him back to a restaurant, Schooner's, on the outskirts of Faneuil Hall, where the feds picked him up on the day of the indictments. His mistake was not taking the warning seriously. He hadn't grown up in Southie the way Whitey had, so he didn't realize that the heads-up he had wasn't going to last more than a few hours. The authorities were on their way. So, while Whitey took off for parts unknown, Flemmi headed to the Plymouth County jail where he spent five years in comfortable digs with a few hours a day in a jail cell, passing the rest of the day cooking his meals in the communal kitchen or playing cards with his fellow residents.

In August 1999, the FBI put Whitey on its Ten Most Wanted List, and even placed Whitey Bulger "wanted" ads in USA Today. It offered a two hundred and fifty thousand dollar reward for information leading to his capture, but upped it to a million fifteen months later.

Since he's been gone, newspapers have reported sightings of Whitey in the South and the Midwest primarily, as well as the Gulf Coast and California. The most recent confirmed sighting was in February 2000 in Fountain Valley, California, outside a beauty salon where Catherine Greig was getting her blond locks all dolled up. In 2002, the FBI received two thousand leads, the most leads in any year since he went on the lam in 1995, thanks to the publicity generated by Johnny Connolly's trial.

According to a story in the *Boston Globe* on January 4, 1998, Whitey and his blond girlfriend spent a good part of 1995 and 1996 in Grand Isle, Louisiana, a small resort island on the Gulf of Mexico. While they were there, Whitey and Catherine, who called themselves Tom and Helen from New York, actually had dinner every night with Penny and Glenn Gautreaux and their four kids. According to the Gautreauxs, "Tom" cried when Glenn had to shoot a dying puppy to end its suffering. He even bought eyeglasses for two of the Gautreaux kids. Whitey left the island in July 1996, but when the FBI arrived looking for him a few months later, they had a very hard time convincing Penny that Uncle Tom was Whitey. Penny was called before a federal grand jury in Boston in November 1997.

A sixteen-member task force, assigned to track Whitey in August 1997, received tips that Whitey had been spotted in New York, Wyoming, Mississippi, and even Southie. Special agent Gail Marcinkiewicz, of the FBI's Boston office, suggested Whitey might be hiding out in Canada. An August 2002 newspaper report cited FBI intelligence claiming that Whitey, who turned seventy-three on September 3, 2002, had stored millions of dollars in safety-deposit boxes in Ontario and Quebec. FBI agents speculate that Whitey might have gone underground in Canada, because of his money trail and possible links to Montreal. Agents are now preparing to print wanted posters in French to be distributed in Quebec. A new FBI poster lists Whitey's most recent alias as "Mark Shapeton."

Since Whitey disappeared in 1995, I've caught three episodes of *Unsolved Mysteries* devoted to Whitey. *America's Most Wanted* has produced at least six episodes about the man. Within days of these segments, both shows received tips of Bulger sightings in Florida, Louisiana, Alabama, Iowa, Chicago, Ireland, Canada, and Italy. Over the past few years, as the FBI, forced by court rulings to divulge information, started to make public the marriage between Whitey and the FBI, things finally began to make sense.

In August of 1999, Freddy Weichel found out that the reason he was in prison was because Whitey had sold him out in a deal with Johnny Connolly. That was a shocker to all of us, even though it shouldn't have been. Freddy's lawyer had obtained a 1980 FBI file in which Connolly had written that his informant, James "Whitey" Bulger, had told him that Freddy Weichel had murdered Robert LaMonica. Connolly had to know

Whitey was lying — after all, Connolly had been with Freddy at the time of the shooting — but that was of little concern to the FBI agent. What are friends for, after all?

Whitey had probably seen this as the perfect opportunity to rid himself of yet another Weichel. He'd done a good job of getting David Weichel off the streets in 1975 by supporting Jimmy Winn, the rat who fingered David for the death of Stevie Barron. David is still serving his sentence today. As for Freddy, he'd been party to the fight between LaMonica and Tommy Barrett hours before LaMonica's murder. Now, he just needed a little shove and he'd be in jail for the rest of his life — and far away from Whitey.

It gets better. Tommy Barrett, the dirtbag who really offed LaMonica, had an older brother named Jody who was an FBI agent. And guess who Freddy thinks sponsored Jody Barrett's application to the bureau? Johnny Connolly. There was a nice list of people who'd gain from Freddy taking the fall: Whitey, the Barrett brothers, Connolly, and the police. LaMonica was dead. He couldn't care less who went to jail for his murder.

Less than an hour after Freddy was hit with that shocker, he phoned me to tell me what he'd learned. I was stunned. Talk about treachery. Talk about selling your friends down the river. It was worse than the revelation I'd had at Danbury nine years earlier. I'd been dealing drugs. I would have been away for ten to fifteen anyway. But Freddy hadn't done anything and he was away for life with no chance of parole.

For Freddy, who believed so firmly in the code, the experience was shattering. He'd gone to jail quietly, knowing Connolly had screwed him, but believing that the code demanded his silence. But to Whitey, the code meant nothing. Freddy couldn't help thinking about all the times that Kevin Weeks had visited him in prison, asking for favors for Whitey, certainly knowing that Freddy had been railroaded. And yet Weeks continued to play the role of the good buddy, someone who was on the outside looking out for him.

I'm no crusader, but I hope these revelations will help to secure justice for Freddy Weichel. Believe me, he has stories to tell. His own story, which is common knowledge in prison, has just begun to emerge. And this is where things gets real interesting.

In October 2001, two sworn affidavits concerning Freddy Weichel suddenly surfaced. The first affidavit, given by former high-ranking Bulger lieutenant Patrick Nee, stated that Bulger told Nee, face-to-face, that Freddy never killed LaMonica, and that Connolly knew it. The second affidavit was given by Brian Goodman, an ex-con turned Hollywood actor, who landed decent-sized roles in the movies *Southie, Blow,* and *The Last Castle,* in which he plays —surprise! — a prison inmate — perfectly. Before Hollywood, Goodman used to play in Friday-night poker games with Weeks. In the affidavit, Goodman said that Weeks was always running his mouth, bragging that Whitey knew Connolly was with Freddy in Boston while LaMonica was getting offed in Braintree, and that he told Johnny boy not to say a word.

To make things sweeter for Freddy, a letter from Tommy Barrett to Freddy's mom, Gloria Weichel, in which he confesses to the murder, has been made public. "I haven't had a good night's sleep in almost a year," Barrett wrote to Gloria in March 1982, "because I know Fred did not kill. I did. Yes, Gloria, I killed Bobby LaMonica. Fred has known this. I told him a couple of weeks after it happened." Barrett had always been close to the Weichels, especially to Gloria, and, in a moment of weakness, he was obviously overwhelmed with sincere regret for what he'd done to the family.

No one can stop local television shows from sending their crews to the Massachusetts Correctional Institute at Shirley where Freddy, now fifty, resides. No one can stop them from asking questions about the case — questions that Freddy, for the first time, wants to answer. Even Stevie Flemmi and Kevin Weeks are weighing in on his side. He's the newest cause in town, and everyone wants to be on his team.

You might ask why, after twenty-one years of sitting in a cell for a murder he didn't commit, Freddy is suddenly willing to talk. The answer is simple: Gloria Weichel died on January 4, 2000. Freddy would never release Barrett's letter to the public while his mother was still alive. Freddy knew only too well what Whitey, or his guys, would do to his mother if that letter got out. She was safe as long as he played the game right. But once his mother died, he let the letter fall into the right hands. He was finally willing to let the truth speak for itself. The fact that Whitey was nowhere to be seen, and no longer a threat, made his decision even easier.

Twenty-two years ago, Bobby Ford, who was running Whitey's South Boston bookmaking office, gave Freddy the message from Johnny Connolly that he was going to be arrested in three days for the LaMonica murder. Unlike Whitey, Freddy never ran. "I was innocent," he said when a reporter recently asked him why he hadn't taken off. "Why would I run?"

In January 2002, Freddy's attorneys filed a motion for a new trial based on the new evidence, but the state is dragging its feet. On September 3, 2002, Norfolk County DA William R. Keating filed a fifty-page motion opposing Freddy's new trial, questioning the reliability of Nee and Weeks's testimony. But if the DA needed Weeks or Nee for testimony in one of his cases, they would then become reliable witnesses. Fucking hypocrite.

Freddy has quite a bit of support though. There's a committee called Freedom for Fred Weichel, headed by Donnie Lewis, a Southie kid who was once a pretty good boxer and has always been involved in the community. I'm not sure what the relationship is between Donnie and Freddy, but I'd guess that Freddy touched him somewhere in his life, very possibly with his judo talent, just as he did me and other youths in the neighborhood.

But in an election year, no DA wants to take a chance on setting a convicted killer free, innocent or not. Not that any of them have qualms about leaving guys in prison to rot, spinning their wheels to prove their innocence. I remember once sitting next to a young black kid while we were both awaiting trial. The kid turns to me and says, "Hey, man, you come to court looking for Justice, and that's all you find: JUST US." He captured it perfectly.

There's not too much I can do for Freddy, but hope that he gets his day in court. If the *Boston Globe* hadn't beaten me up two years ago when I went on *60 Minutes* to talk about working for Whitey, I'd be testifying for him right now. Not that I regret appearing on *60 Minutes*. I was grateful for the chance to say in front of a national audience what I'd wanted to say for a long time.

That whole scene started when John Wells, an investigative reporter for the *Boston Herald*, approached me. He was looking for an inside player who would come forward with a story on Whitey. John used to work as a producer for *60 Minutes* and, after he heard my story, he introduced me to Michael Radutzky, a *60 Minutes* producer working on a story about Connolly. I agreed to meet with Radutzky, who spent some time investigating that I was indeed an insider, and was blown away by what I told him about Connolly and Bulger. He returned to Boston a few months later, in December 2000, with Ed Bradley and a *60 Minutes* crew.

For five hours that cold day, Ed Bradley and the crew followed me to the mob graveyard in Dorchester, to John Connolly's townhouse in Thomas Park, and on a tour of South Boston. Within five minutes, Ed Bradley and I were calling each other "Ed." He was warm, very attentive, and seemed like a regular guy who was interested in my story. I answered all his questions about Whitey, Johnny Connolly, and the FBI truthfully.

The twenty-minute segment ran the following April. It was scary watching it, knowing that I was talking to a nation of viewers about a rogue FBI agent. I stressed that I understood the whole FBI wasn't rotten, just a few of its agents, but worried that the FBI might figure out a way to set me up and charge me with something.

I'm glad I did what I did. It was a story I knew well and I thought someone who knew it ought to have the balls to step up to the plate and tell it like it was. The idea that Whitey was a Robin Hood gangster was absurd and needed to be shot down. But, more than that, I was grateful for the chance to admit what I was for all those years. When Ed Bradley asked me what I called myself when I worked for Whitey, I answered, "You could call me an enforcer. But you could also call me a scumbag." It felt good to get that off my chest and tell the world that I knew exactly what I was. After the show aired, I got a lot of calls from friends who respected me for my honesty and for being straight.

After the *60 Minutes* segment ran, a story written by Shelley Murphy and Judy Rakowsky in the May 9, 2001, *Globe* questioned whether I was as close to Whitey as I said I was. The paper used Timmy Connolly as a source, who must have phoned in from whatever rock he's hiding under in the Witness Protection Program, frothing at the bit to unleash his hatred of me. "Whitey wouldn't do anything in front of MacKenzie that he could repeat," Timmy told the *Globe*. "I was down in the dirt with those guys. I know." Oh, yeah, the only people Timmy was down in the dirt with were the FBI. As the *Boston Herald* countered in my defense, according to law enforcement sources and court records, Connolly's involvement with the Bulger group was not as an "associate," as he claimed, but as one of their extortion victims.

The *Globe* also dug up retired Boston police detective Kenneth Beers, who said he never saw me talking to Whitey. The *Herald* came to my defense again by interviewing another former Boston police detective who worked on that same surveillance with Beers. This detective said he never even saw Bulger with his FBI handler, Johnny Connolly, whose scores of meetings with Bulger have since been documented in court records. So much for surveillance.

Ironically, a March 1995 piece on Whitey Bulger, written by the *Globe*'s own Dick Lehr and Gerard O'Neill, who then went on to write *Black Mass,* about Whitey's unholy relationship with the FBI, confirmed that I was part of Bulger's organization. The article said, "Only one of the South Boston 51 flipped — Ed MacKenzie, who managed a notorious local bar called Connolly's Corner Café. But he insisted on cooperating with the FBI, not the DEA. As it appears to be playing out, MacKenzie gave the bureau nothing usable about Bulger or anyone else in South Boston. He helped make a major cocaine case against a Los Angeles–based cartel that had several major dealers in Greater Boston. But to the DEA's dismay, MacKenzie — a New England kick-boxing champion and ex-Marine, which made him a Bulger favorite — has delivered nothing that meets the eye about the South Boston drug operation." Too bad Murphy and Rakowsky didn't go through their own paper's files before calling me a "wanna-be gangster who was never part of Bulger's inner circle."

When the *Herald* put together its definitive piece on Bulger on September 1, 1998, Peter Gelzinis wrote, "Boston police never knew that one Eddie MacKenzie, who hustled coke and dabbled in a host of other nefarious activities out of a bucket of blood called Connolly's Corner Café, had his own romance with the FBI. The cops learned of Eddie's true allegiance after he was spirited away to 'help make a case on the West Coast.' Both the Boston cops and the DEA felt MacKenzie could've yielded a mother lode of info regarding Whitey Bulger's drug operation. But his 'deal' with the FBI shielded him from ever having to face a grand jury in a case involving Bulger." No doubt my seven minutes with Ed Bradley on April 8, 2001, and my four-part interview with the *Boston Herald*, which ran from April 3 to April 6, 2001, stirred up a hornet's nest of anti-Mac feeling. And before I could even read the reviews of my TV appearance or my interview in the paper, I was being indicted for workman's comp fraud in Suffolk County — or should I say Bulger County — for a case that had been asleep for five years. And to think I'd been worried that it would be the FBI that would come after me following the *60 Minutes* story.

Wonder who I pissed off by destroying the belief that Whitey was a Robin Hood? Wonder who I enraged with the truth about Whitey's unhealthy appetite for young girls and boys, his swinging both ways, his cross-dressing? Could it have been Whitey and Billy's brother Jackie Bulger, who was himself charged with perjury and obstruction of justice for allegedly lying to federal grand juries regarding his big brother's activities and disappearance? (Jackie recently "retired" from his job as clerk magistrate of the Boston Juvenile Court.) Or maybe it was Connolly, or even Billy himself. Hard to tell which of my "friends" made the call.

As for Kevin Weeks, Freddy's faithful visitor, there was not enough evidence to arrest him with Whitey and Flemmi in 1995, so he went free. But in 1998, both Johnny Martorano and Frank Salemme cut themselves sweet deals with the feds. The information they provided all but ensured that Weeks was living on borrowed time. In November 1999, when the feds charged Weeks with racketeering and shaking down dealers and bookies, it took him only two weeks to decide to cooperate, earning him his current nickname, Two Weeks.

Freddy and I have never doubted, however, that Whitey did all he could to protect his boy Kevin before he took off. Whitey knew it was just a matter of time until the finger pointed at his most loyal lieutenant. The best Whitey could offer his favorite deputy was a map of the bodies, at least five, maybe as many as ten, he'd buried during his reign. (Of course, there's an excellent chance Weeks had done some of the burying himself and so wouldn't need directions.) Each body could buy Weeks a year or so off the twenty-plus he was staring at. And what did Whitey care? He knew he would never return, never be prosecuted for those murders. So Weeks began to talk.

The first three of these bodies were uncovered by the Boston police on January 14, 2000, in Dorchester — what I'll call the other Big Dig, after Boston's infamous billion-dollar construction project. I got a real eerie feeling as I drove by the dig site on that brutally cold Friday morning. One of the skeletons they exhumed had had its teeth ripped out. That poor prick was Tommy McIntyre, who had been missing for fifteen years. The dentistry had Whitey Bulger's name all over it. McIntyre signed his death warrant in November 1984, when he ratted to the Quincy police and then the FBI about Whitey's involvement, a few months earlier, in an operation intended to run stolen guns and ammunition aboard a Gloucester-based fishing vessel, the *Valhalla,* to the Irish Republican Army. But an IRA commander turned informer, Sean O'Callaghan, betrayed the shipment to the Irish police and the Irish vessel, the *Marita Ann,* was seized by the Irish navy off the coast of Ireland with the seven tons of arms it had received from the *Valhalla.*

Whitey didn't give a damn about the IRA. Yeah, rumor had it that he held dual citizenship in the United States and Ireland. He may have gotten misty-eyed listening to what his relatives had to put up with in the old country. And there are some who think, right at this moment, he's having a beer in a Dublin pub. But Whitey ran arms to the IRA because he was receiving, in exchange, tons of pot that he could sell on the streets of Boston. Whitey never did something for nothing. As with everything else in his life, his devotion to the IRA was merely a front for lining his pockets.

And the broad they dug up along with McIntyre? That was Deborah Hussey, the daughter of Marion Hussey, a woman Stevie Flemmi began romancing when Deborah was just a toddler. Flemmi moved in with Marion and eventually had two sons and a daughter by her. He also began to bang Deborah when she was a teenager. Nice step-daddy. This went on until Deborah, by then messed up on drugs, threatened to tell her mother about it. Whitey got wind of this and decided that she had become a loose cannon who probably had some knowledge of Flemmi's criminal acts. He didn't want the heat from her and told Flemmi that she had to go. Flemmi, evil as he was, couldn't bring himself to off her. According to testimony provided in early 2000 as part of his plea bargain, Kevin Weeks said that in November of 1984 Whitey strangled Hussey to death with his bare hands. Deborah Hussey was twenty-six years old.

The other guy in the pit was Bucky Barrett. His mistake? Sitting on a million and a half dollars netted during a bank heist in 1983. Whitey and Flemmi figured that if they killed him, they could take the money. So poor Bucky was relieved of both his money and his life.

Barrett, McIntyre, and Hussey were murdered separately between 1983 and 1985 in Joey Murphy's basement on East Third Street in Southie. Their bodies were cut up and buried there as well. When the house was sold in 1985 by Murphy's relatives while Joey was in jail, Whitey and Weeks dug up the three remains, transported the bodies in trash bags, and reburied them in a gully alongside the Southeast Expressway in Dorchester.

Where was the FBI during the search alongside the Expressway, and after? Conspicuously absent. Then again, after the deceit and stupidity with which the bureau has conducted its Boston business for the last twenty years, no agent would have been allowed anywhere near the dig. It is worth noting, however, that five months after the Bulger "Big Dig" began in January 2000, the Boston office of the FBI got a new boss. Charles Prouty, a Vietnam vet and Navy Seal, insists the FBI really is looking for the Southie mobster, even if it embarrasses the bureau if they find him.

But there were more killing fields to unearth. Kevin Weeks had only just started to talk. By September 2000, investigators were on the hunt for more bodies. It didn't surprise me that the new gravesites named by Weeks were within a mile or two of Whitey's condo at 144 Quincy Shore Drive. Whitey spent a lot of time in the area.

I'd spent a lot of time at that condo, too. I'd actually vacated it one day before the feds arrested me in August 1990. Whitey had let me stay there, but as soon as I heard about the indictments, I took off for Gold Street in Southie, where I also shared an apartment with Tommy Dixon. After all, I didn't want to embarrass Whitey by being arrested in his home.

Ten years later, I felt a real jolt when, in September 2000, they pulled what was left of Tommy King out of a hole a hundred yards from that condo. King hadn't been as lucky as me. In 1975, he'd done something unforgivable: gotten the best of Whitey in a barroom brawl at Triple O's. King, a big bruiser, well over two hundred pounds, had killed Francis "Buddy" Leonard, a Southie thug, a few days earlier. Something about that kill had obviously caused the flare-up at Triple O's. The end result: Flemmi and Johnny Martorano, very possibly with Weeks's help, took care of King. What I find amazing is that the DA had Weeks under police surveillance in that Quincy condo and they never saw him bury King under the Red Line Bridge a hundred yards away. What the hell were they looking at? Or not looking at? Tommy King wasn't the only body Weeks told the authorities to look for near Whitey's Quincy condo. Debra Davis, another of Flemmi's girlfriends, had disappeared on September 17, 1981. She made the fatal mistake of telling Flemmi their nine-year gig was over because she'd met another man. Some sources say Flemmi had to kill her because she knew too much. Bullshit. Flemmi and Whitey never talked business around women. Flemmi was a pretty quiet guy anyhow. Quiet but lethal. But he was weak and pussy-whipped and couldn't take it when women left him. Davis's remains were dug up on October 19, 2000.

Meanwhile, bodies were springing up elsewhere in the city. On September 14, 2000, investigators dug up yet another pile of bones, this one from under the sands of Tenean Beach in Dorchester. That was all that was left of one Paulie McGonagle, the leader in the early 1970s of the Mullins Gang, a faction that rivaled Whitey and his followers — for a while. McGonagle disappeared on November 20, 1975. Four days after he vanished, his station wagon was found in the waters off the docks of

Charlestown. With Paulie's wallet floating nearby, authorities figured that he'd been "retired" from the rackets.

Using DNA evidence from the bodies of Barrett, McIntyre, and Hussey, the feds were finally able to make their move. A federal racketeering indictment charged Whitey with eighteen murders, eleven of which he committed as an FBI informant. The sweeping indictment didn't leave out Stevie Flemmi, either. It indicted him as a codefendant in ten of the eighteen murders, including Debra Davis and Deborah Hussey. Poor Flemmi was yanked out of his digs at the Plymouth jail and bundled over to maximum-security Walpole, where he was locked up in a tiny cell twenty-three hours a day.

Another recent turn of events in the saga made things even worse for Flemmi. When Johnny Martorano pleaded guilty to executing John Callahan in Miami in 1982 on orders from Whitey and Stevie, and Joey Murphy talked about Roger Wheeler's murder in Tulsa, Bulger and Flemmi were charged with both those murders. Now Flemmi was looking at a death sentence in Florida or Oklahoma. Amazing how that can loosen your tongue. Flemmi's tried to tell his stories but the government doesn't seem interested. The feds have to bury someone and it looks like Flemmi's their corpse.

Johnny Connolly has been having a pretty rough go of it himself. It took the government less time to get its act together when dealing with him than it did with Bulger and Flemmi. The big blow for Connolly came at a 1998 court hearing when former FBI supervisor John Morris exposed the relationship between the FBI, Flemmi, and Bulger, and that Brian Halloran's ticket had been punched by none other than Special Agent Johnny Connolly. If you recall, when Halloran went to the FBI in 1981 to cut himself a deal by revealing the killers of Roger Wheeler, the president of World Jai Alai, the bureau connected him to Connolly. This was ironic in that Connolly surely already knew more about Wheeler's execution than Halloran. Connolly and his colleagues told Halloran there could be no deal because his information about Wheeler's murder was not reliable, even though Halloran was dead-on. Or, more accurately, dead-soon. Connolly then went to Whitey and told him he had a problem, in effect signing the death warrant of a guy who had offered to help the FBI solve a murder and put away some very bad people.

On December 22, 1999, the government indicted Connolly on four counts and charged him with racketeering, racketeering conspiracy, con-spiracy to obstruct justice, and obstruction of justice. Of course, if anyone else had done what Connolly did, he'd be charged as an "accessory to murder." You have to love those FBI perks.

On May 6, 2002 — a day I'd looked forward to for a long, long time — John J. Connolly Jr., the former star of the FBI's Boston office, who had earned his wings in large part because of the information fed him by Whitey Bulger and Stevie Flemmi, went on trial in federal court on charges that he had protected the duo for decades by tipping them off to impending investigations, deliberately overlooking their crimes, and warning them about potential witnesses against them, an act that allegedly caused three murders.

The racketeering count charged Connolly with associating with the "criminal activities of James 'Whitey' Bulger and Stephen 'The Rifleman' Flemmi." To be specific, Johnny was accused of "giving information to Bulger and Flemmi about two FBI informants and one grand jury witness, who were later murdered; accepting a diamond ring as a bribe from Bulger and Flemmi; delivering bribes of wine and cash from Bulger and Flemmi to FBI supervisor John Morris; aiding Bulger and Flemmi with the extortion of South Boston liquor store owner Stephen Rakes; and aiding Bulger and Flemmi in evading arrest by warning them in advance of their 1995 indictment and tipping them off about the investigation into their activities."

Reading the obstruction of justice charge brought an even bigger smile to my lips. Here, Connolly was charged "with thwarting efforts to arrest Bulger, Flemmi, and New England Mafia boss Francis 'Cadillac Frank' Salemme; providing confidential law enforcement information to the three; sending a letter containing a false statement to a federal judge; persuading Flemmi to give false testimony in federal court; lying in court." The key witnesses ready to testify against Connolly were Salemme, Kevin Weeks, Johnny Martorano, and his former FBI supervisor, John Morris.

The trial continued until May 28, 2002. It was a circus; one rat after another ratting on each other. I read my *Boston Herald* daily, fascinated, repelled, and often delighted by the daily parade of thugs who sat in the witness chair. While veteran U.S. District Court Judge Joseph L. Tauro presided over the courtroom, the government witnesses, including killers, leg-breakers, and extortionists once faithful to Bulger and Flemmi, sang their stories.

Right up there was Johnny Martorano, who admitted in his plea agreement to offing twenty people, most of them on order from Bulger and Flemmi. Johnny talked when the government agreed to recommend that he be sentenced to twelve to fifteen years for his murders. Since he's been in the hole since 1995, and the murders in Florida and Oklahoma could have brought him the death penalty, that wasn't too bad a deal for the former hit man. He also shook the courtroom when he revealed that Whitey had told him Connolly owed Billy Bulger a favor for helping him to stay on the straight road and go to college when he was a young man. According to Martorano's story, Johnny went to Billy after the bureau sent him to Boston in the 1970s and said, "What can I do to help you in return?" Billy replied, "Just keep my brother out of trouble." That's Billy. Always thinking of his big bro.

Martorano avoided the death penalty by confessing that, in 1982, he was forced to kill John Callahan, a Boston accountant with ties to Whitey who was hired as World Jai Alai president in the 1970s before Roger Wheeler, a millionaire telecommunications manufacturer, bought the company. Connolly had tipped off Bulger and Flemmi that Callahan could bring them all down for the 1981 murder of Roger Wheeler. Tips from Connolly, he explained carefully, had also resulted in his handling the 1976 hit on one Richard Castucci, a Revere, Massachusetts, nightclub owner and Winter Hill Gang associate-turned-snitch. Dressed in a dark double-breasted suit and tinted glasses, Johnny M. kept himself center stage. He told the court that, in 1976, he helped secure a stolen two-carat diamond ring for Whitey, who in turn gave it to Connolly, who was shopping for a present for his wife. Martorano explained he rewarded Connolly in any way he could, following Bulger and Flemmi's orders to take good care of Johnny.

Kevin Weeks added his own two bits. Faced with extensive jail time for his twenty-five years as Bulger's top leg-breaker, "Two Weeks" had cut a good deal with the government after his arrest in 1999. Feeling a lot more comfortable about his future, Weeks told the court he'd served as a lookout when Whitey gunned down Brian Halloran and Michael Donahue in front of the Topside bar on Northern Avenue in Southie in May 1982, a month after Connolly warned Whitey that Halloran had implicated him and Flemmi in the murders of Wheeler and Callahan. In testifying, Weeks was only following his old boss's instructions to do everything he could to save his own skin.

How ironic it was to see Connolly stand in front of the television cameras and ask why anyone would believe these men. He called them scum, murderers, drug dealers. "All of them, top echelon informants, are murderers," he said. "The government put me in business with murderers." Yet, the FBI was perfectly willing to put others away by listening to the words of the same scum, murderers, and drug dealers. So, now the tables were turned and the rats were ratting on Connolly. Small difference.

When I see guys like Weeks and Martorano cooperating with the government, probably doing less time in jail after everything they've done than Freddy Weichel, the original stand-up guy, who's served twenty-one years for a murder he didn't commit — I just shake my head and stop trying to figure any of it out. You see why I don't trust anyone. I'm not crying. I got everything that was coming to me, and cut a good deal myself with Uncle Sam. But I don't trust the crooks. And I doubly don't trust the government. My faith in what we call justice was shattered long ago.

I did, however, have a few moments of satisfaction. On May 28, 2002, Connolly was found guilty of racketeering and obstruction of justice for warning Bulger, Flemmi, and Salemme about the imminent indictment, and trying to help them even after their arrest. You gotta love the words of U.S. Attorney Michael J. Sullivan, who said Connolly "abused his authority and crossed the line from crime fighter to criminal" in his treatment of Bulger and Flemmi. "Today's verdict reveals John Connolly for what he became: a Winter Hill Gang operative masquerading as a law enforcement agent." Welcome to the club, Johnny. You've officially been outed.

But the lucky bastard was acquitted on what prosecutors called the "most distressing" charge against him: leaking to Whitey the identities of the three men — Richard Castucci, Brian Halloran, and John Callahan — who were talking to authorities about the crimes committed by the Winter Hill Gang and were subsequently killed in retaliation. While prosecutors alleged that Connolly had committed fourteen separate acts as part of the racketeering count, jurors found him guilty of only five, including accepting a case of fine wine and $1000 from Whitey to give to his former supervisor, John Morris — who, of course, was also given immunity for his testimony. According to one of the jurors, "This was a case of the bad, the badder, or the baddest. How do you know they're telling the truth when their whole life has been a lie?" How indeed.

What really stunned me was that Connolly was allowed to sit with his wife and family in the front row of the public gallery, rather than being made to sit with his lawyers, at the defense table, as most defendants are required to do. For opening arguments, he actually brought in his three sons to sit with him and the missus in an obvious play for sympathy. Guess I was mistaken in thinking that the former FBI agent was another ordinary defendant.

When all the smoke cleared, however, Connolly was convicted of one count of racketeering, two counts of obstruction of justice, and one count of making a false statement to the FBI. On September 16, 2002, Judge Tauro sentenced Connolly, sixty-two, to more than ten years in prison for protecting Bulger and Flemmi and tipping them off to their upcoming indictments. He said he imposed the maximum sentence under the guidelines because he wanted to show that he has "zero tolerance" for anyone who obstructs justice.

Connolly didn't speak at the sentencing hearing, and he blew a kiss to his relatives in the front row as he was led, without handcuffs, from the courtroom to a federal holding facility. Judge Tauro did agree to recommend that the former FBI agent, who has had two hip replacements and is prone to skin cancer, be allowed to serve his sentence at the federal medical facility in Ayer, Massachusetts. Funny, but I never got that much sun in prison. Though I don't know how comfortable Connolly would have been living in the same joint as former New England underboss Jerry Anguilo, who he helped put away. As it was, Connolly didn't last long in Ayer and was quickly shipped out to a federal prison in Kentucky.

The most Connolly will serve will be ten years, which is more than I originally thought he would get. But I still have my doubts. His appeal might even work. And I have to admit, as hard as I've been on Connolly for playing both sides of the street, I actually have mixed feelings about the former FBI agent. He was always respectful to me, though I understood he would sacrifice me at any time to get a star on his forehead. But I believe the FBI was as much to blame as he was. After all, where did they stick him? His old neighborhood! That's entrapment as far as I'm concerned. How could he betray his childhood buddies? The bureau should never have put him in that position. Sure, it might make sense to put an agent in the world he knows best, but because of the high possibility of conflict of interest, it is rarely FBI policy to do so. But the Boston bureau was so hell-bent on nailing the Italian Mob that they would have set up their own mothers.

And you have to wonder if those sunglasses the FBI likes to wear aren't really blinders. Because there's no way Connolly's behavior could have gone unnoticed in the chain of command. How do you buy three houses and a custom-built Sea Ray boat on an FBI salary? The FBI audits its agents every six months. Don't tell me no one noticed something strange during Connolly's twenty years of service.

Connolly had many friends and still does, no matter what he did. Even though they're making him the scapegoat, I still think that, behind closed doors, he made a deal with his superiors. They probably said, "John, you take the fall and do some time. We'll let you keep your pension and your three houses." Of course, if it was one of us, you can bet your life they would have seized the properties already.

Another friend of Connolly's was veteran *Globe* sportswriter Will McDonough, who died of a heart attack at age sixty-seven on January 10, 2003. McDonough grew up in Southie and knew Whitey, Billy Bulger, Connolly, and just about everyone else of importance, good or bad. Before the sentencing, McDonough wrote a letter to Judge Tauro. Calling Tauro simply, "Judge," he declared, "All of us would be better served with John in our community raising his children."

McDonough's letter, which was reprinted in the *Globe* and the *Herald,* stressed that he — not little bro' Billy, whose 1960 campaign for the state senate McDonough managed — had gotten Whitey his first big job as a janitor at the Suffolk County courthouse after leaving Alcatraz. "I got him the job to get him out of prison, when his brother didn't have the clout to do it," McDonough had written proudly. How nice. Now I know who to thank for my job with Whitey. If McDonough hadn't gotten Whitey out of prison, think how much worse off we'd all be today.

McDonough always had a fascination with the darker side of his boyhood home. To listen to him talk, you would have thought he had just stepped out of a vintage 1940s cruiser after pulling off a "job" someplace. And he was not alone. There is something sexy and seductive about the streets. We love our mob movies and our PT Cruisers and rap music with all the anger and sex and jewelry bouncing hard. Connolly loves it, McDonough loved it, and I loved it. We all want to play with it now and again, even if, after we get a taste, most of us go home to the suburbs and our boring lives.

I once read a column that tried to get to the root of America's fascination with mob culture and, specifically, the HBO series *The Sopranos.* That column hit on something I understand better than most people — that we all would love the chance to live life without any restrictions, without any fear of consequences. You want that car? Take it. You like that liquor store? You now own it. You don't like paying taxes? So, don't. That guy down the street, the show-off with the loud mouth and hot wife and big paycheck? He gets a beating the first time, and if that doesn't quiet him down, he gets whacked.

Take Sammy "the Bull" Gravano. I had to laugh when I read the comments at the end of his book, *Underboss*. He wrote, "How I could have put Cosa Nostra ahead of loyalty to my wife and kids is something I will always have to live with. All my life, growing up, I thought that people who went to school and put their noses to the grindstone were nerds, taking the easy way out. I know now that I was the one who took the easy way, that I didn't have the balls to stay in school and try. That was the tough road that I didn't take."

What a bunch of bullshit. Yeah, the sentiment is true. But Gravano sure as hell doesn't believe any of it. He's too much like the person I was to pull that shit over on me. If he hadn't been caught, he'd still be living the life of La Cosa Nostra and loving it. I've never met Gravano, but I have a good idea what the man is thinking. Because, believe me, I fight the fight every day to keep myself from believing that crime pays. Complicating the matter is the fact that gangsters are revered by so many. The crowds that gathered outside the federal courthouse in Manhattan when John Gotti was on trial weren't there to mock or curse him. They were there to show their support. Reverence and hero worship is what got Connolly in trouble in the first place. He wanted to be like Whitey, but he wasn't as smart as Whitey. That's why Whitey is free and Connolly is in the big house.

Stevie Davis — the brother of Debra Davis, one of Bulger and Flemmi's recently unearthed victims — came unglued when he read McDonough's letter defending Connolly. "I know what they say about Johnny Martorano and (Cadillac Frank) Salemme, and the deals they made with the government," he said. "But in my mind, Connolly is the worst of 'em all. What about the kids my sister will never have?"

Before the world came crashing down around his feet, I had a conversation with Connolly I'll never forget. It was at Boston's FleetCenter on Martin Luther King Jr. Day in January 1999. I was there with Courtney for a Boston Bruins hockey game. We had great seats, in the second or third section up from the boards and near center ice.

Whenever I'm in a crowd, I'm on alert, especially if there is a lot going on behind me. My life experiences have me hardwired to scan and detect. Courtney cared only about the action on the ice. She was screeching like a true Bruins whacko, waving her arms and pumping her fists. I was following the game a little, but mostly I was people-watching, turning from side to side. Ten rows up, who do I spot but Johnny Connolly, sitting with two kids, probably his sons. He didn't see me, but I made a mental note of him and kept scanning. A few minutes later, I looked back again and caught his eye. He gave me a big smile, leaned forward and did the Southie wave. I smiled slightly, gave Connolly a nod and my own Southie wave, then turned back to the game.

I didn't look back for the remainder of the first period. Not looking back is all about respect. We knew each other from the neighborhood, but the fact was, at least in terms of putting up a front, we were supposed to be on opposite sides of the fence. I didn't want to make him feel uncomfortable by eyeballing him or shouting out to him or waving and acting like he was a big buddy of mine.

But I hadn't seen Connolly in more than a year, since I'd run into him at the Boston Athletic Club. I knew he and his family were living in a big house in Lynnfield, rather than in Southie. I wondered what he had been up to, besides what I read about him in the press.

When the buzzer sounded to end the first period, I took the opportunity to stand up and stretch and look back to where he was sitting. He caught my eye and pointed to the landing a few rows behind him. I nodded, gave Courtney a few bucks, suggested that she wave down the hot dog guy, and told her I would have her in sight from the landing.

My favorite FBI agent seemed happy as hell to see me. He was leaning against a railing and smiling, allowing me to come to him. Johnny Connolly's full head of hair was, as always, immaculately coiffed, but, hey, what happened to the Don-wanna-be? With Big Brother watching, Connolly was now dressing J. Crew: a ribbed cotton sweater, tan chinos, and penny loafers. He looked like a preppy grad student in Harvard Square.

"Hey, Eddie Mac, what's going on with you?" Connolly asked as he shook my hand with one hand and grabbed my shoulder with the other.

"Nothing much, Johnny. Not nearly as busy as you, from what I read."

He laughed, his eyes darting from the people walking past to those sitting and standing in the row just below us. Then he grabbed my arm lightly and pulled me out about a foot or two away from the railing. "Eddie, it's all a bunch of bullshit. I've been fucked over big-time. Screwed by people who I thought I could trust."

"It's fucking sad," I said. "They used you when they needed you, and now that they don't need you anymore, they're coming after you. What is with justice in this country?"

"Justice? Fuck justice." Connolly spat as he took a step back and put up his arms like a revivalist preacher in a Southern Baptist church. Johnny Connolly loved to hold court. He caught himself quickly, though, and lowered his arms as he warily scrutinized the crowd moving past us. He then stepped in close and leaned forward. "Let me tell you, the U.S. Attorney's office is a bunch of bigger fucking liars than I thought."

"They screwed you over, huh?" I asked, real sympathetically.

Once again, the eyes moving back and forth, missing nothing. "Yeah, screwed me over. Let me tell you, Eddie, this is so much bullshit and nothing else. Those fuckers knew about it all along. O'Sullivan [federal prosecutor Jeremiah O'Sullivan, who was heading the Justice Department's New England Organized Strike Force from 1979 to 1989] was in on Whitey working with us. O'Sullivan was ground zero. Why the fuck do you think he had a heart attack a week before he was to testify about what he knew? C'mon, he didn't have a heart attack. It was a fake to get him out of testifying and having to perjure himself."

"You gotta be shitting me," I said.

"Not shitting you at all. That's just the way it is."

"Johnny, it's all gonna work out. They can't make anything stick."

"It's all bullshit. One hundred percent bullshit." I kept silent. Connolly smiled again. "But, hey, Eddie, you know that Whitey was very appreciative about what you did with the FBI. He called it a masterful move."

"I wasn't rolling on any of my boys. No fucking way."

"Yeah, you played it like Whitey," Connolly said. "Work it but don't sell out Southie."

I couldn't let this go. "C'mon, Johnny, I heard from Junior Patriarca himself that Whitey ratted on his own, and that our indictments were set up by information Whitey provided the FBI."

"That's a fucking lie!" Connolly hissed, and I could see the anger growing again in his eyes. "That motherfucker Patriarca is a bold-faced liar! Whitey never, ever, ratted on any of you guys! He was stand-up. He was a killing machine, but stand-up. You know that, Eddie."

I didn't know anything of the kind. "And he didn't peddle drugs, Johnny?"

"Eddie, Whitey was a lot of things, but he wasn't a drug dealer."

Okay, now I was sure that Connolly figured that I took too many head punches in the ring. By this time, the action on the ice had begun to heat up and it was difficult to hear. Besides, I'd heard all I wanted to. I nodded and headed back to Courtney. I only wish I had known then what I know now about Freddy. Or that I'd known at the time how Connolly's ship was sinking. Not that he's the only one. Everyone is going down one way or another.

Except one guy.

People ask me if I worry about Whitey coming after me when this book is published. Hell, there are a ton of people ahead of me on Whitey's hit list. When Southie boys start getting popped left and right in the penitentiaries of Massachusetts, then I'll worry.

Anyway, Whitey has it too good to seek vengeance. While former mobsters, and even an FBI agent or two, pad around in jail cells or wait to be convicted, there is a seventy-three-year-old man in some warm climate, unobtrusively going about his business. And every so often this man takes a break from reading *Hadrian: The Restless Emperor* to track on the Internet an ongoing story that is almost beyond belief in its day-after-day revelations. No doubt about it, James J. "Whitey" Bulger is out there, somewhere, enjoying a sunset and a glass of carrot juice, one step ahead of the rest of us.

# My Little Chicks

**W**hitey might be out of the fray, on some remote island, but I'm still in the fight. I wish it were over, but I know it's going to continue for a long time. Some rounds I'll win; some I'll lose. Every day I face a choice: continue to change or fall back to the comfortable, darker ways of my predator side. Yet to fall backward would mean not only to fail as a person but to destroy two little girls. Without me to look after them and keep them in school, they could end up like their mother.

When things get bad, it's easy to ask myself what's the sense of trying. I went to school to try to change my life. I took in my daughters to do something good. Yet all too often I get slapped down. To overcome my past I have to be yards better than the average guy. I'm under perpetual scrutiny, which is not a bad thing because no one, not even me, knows what side I'm going to be on.

Too often, I retreat to scams and doing "collections" for people. The money is good and easy, and the accompanying rush of adrenaline is probably close to what one gets in closing a legitimate business deal. But the money is tainted and easily thrown away. In any new situation, I look at it from my old side and my new side, and decide which to use. My old side will never be gone. Try as I might, I can never change who I was.

People may never forget my past, but so what? If I was once a feared, tough guy in my neighborhood, the challenge is whether I can be a tough guy with myself and not let my past be an excuse for future failure. If there is one noble mission I have, it's to help kids. I recognize a kid going bad; and I recognize the world doesn't need one more young Eddie MacKenzie.

Especially one that has my blood running through her veins. I confess that because of the life I've lived and the mistakes I've made, my five daughters are not living the idyllic life. But they each have a mother and father who loves them, nice clothes, and a roof over their heads. They are safe and well fed, and are constantly badgered and encouraged about doing their homework. There will be no high-school dropouts; hopefully, only college graduates.

But the truth is I get scared. I am frightened that I may have passed on something bad, and that this badness, combined with a bad environment, can amount to serious trouble. Like what happened with Courtney recently.

Courtney was at fault, totally. She was pulled over in Southie for driving an unregistered car. Stupid, but not as stupid as trying to drive the car home after the cop told her to walk home. He caught her again, a few blocks away, and this time she was arrested, cuffed, and stuffed into a police cruiser. At the station, he fingerprinted her, took her mug shot, and ushered her into a holding cell. Like father, like daughter?

When Carolyn told me what had happened, I was freaked out that Courtney had spent the night in the slammer before Carolyn bailed her out, and that, when Carolyn got there, our daughter wasn't crying like most eighteen-year-old girls would have been. Rather, she seemed hardened to life, like a gang member who had just "made her bones."

When I went with her to court the next day, she was still sporting that bored and tough attitude. My reaction says a lot about the battle I fight to stay legitimate. On one hand, I was sad, thinking how good life would be for her if she were more innocent and living in the suburbs with money and two parents under one roof. And if her father wasn't a felon with a violent criminal history. Yet, I admit, I admired her guts and the way she toughed things out.

Don't misunderstand me. I was far more scared for, and angry at, Courtney than I was proud of her. I was disappointed in her for doing something so stupid it could jeopardize her hockey career. I told her it was okay to screw up, but not okay to keep screwing up and expect her mother and me to accept responsibility for her actions. I had thought that telling her the truth about everything in life would instill a healthy attitude and prepare her to take on the world. Now I'm not so sure.

With the little girls, it's a lot easier — for now. I try to read to Devin, who's ten, and Kayla, who's nine, every night. Last night's story was *Beauty and the Beast*, about a young girl who gets lost trying to find her father. She comes upon a castle with a huge ugly beast within. Once Belle gets past the ugliness of the beast, she falls in love with the kind and gentle person inside. I told them, "You can't judge people on their looks," and they listened.

Every night after my story, my two dark-haired little beauties fall off to sleep. And I sit there, watching them, certain no one will hit them tomorrow and they will have enough to eat and no one will poke fun at their clothes because they don't fit. They are so peaceful lying there, knowing their daddy is close by to protect them and hold them and tell them how much he loves them. I never forget that I have no choice but to make Devin and Kayla my whole life.

Every morning, I give each girl a "smoochie" kiss on the cheek to wake her. Once they're up, I make them breakfast. Devin likes her eggs over easy; Kayla likes them scrambled. No one ever made me an egg when I was their age, which makes it all the sweeter for me to do it for them. Once my girls' bellies are full and each school pack is full of snackies and juice boxes, we're off.

As I let them out of the car at their school, I take another moment to marvel at their innocence. I watch my precious little chicks, their every move, each little step. I know, without question, that I would gladly give my life for my daughters.

Being a father is a gift from God that gives me the chance to make up for what happened to me as a child. I've made a lot of mistakes, but this much I know for sure: my babies will always have a loving father; I will never let them down. Their lives have to be better than mine.

As for my future? I hope that when Kayla and Devin are grown, they can understand the truth about their daddy. That he was a bad man, but he wasn't the worst man; and he even managed to improve himself and do some good.

The best part of this morning is my little Kayla, just as she opens the door to enter school. For one last second, she turns back to look at her daddy, and blows me a kiss. I melt, as I blow her one in return.

# Where Are They Now?

**Stephen "The Rifleman" Flemmi.** In Massachusetts Correctional Institute at Walpole, a maximum-security prison, awaiting trial for the murder of nineteen people.

**John Martorano.** Serving a twelve-year sentence on federal racketeering and murder charges. Thanks to his plea bargain with the government, he could be free in 2007.

**"Cadillac Frank" Salemme.** Released in January 2003, with twenty-six months shaved off his 136-month sentence, a thank you for his help in John Connolly's conviction. He slipped into the federal witness protection program and divorced his wife, Donna, so she wouldn't have to assume a new identity with him.

**Timmy Connolly.** Rumored to be selling cars in California while in the Witness Protection Program.

**Kevin Weeks.** Awaiting trial, but has already made a deal to cooperate that will net him no more than five years behind bars.

**John Connolly.** Recently moved from federal prison in Kentucky to the Hamden County Jail in western Massachusetts, maybe to entice him to cough up some dirt on the FBI, Whitey, and Billy in exchange for staying in a jail closer to the wife and kids.

**David Weichel.** Recently released from Walpole, right to the streets. He has moved back to his hometown of South Boston.

**Freddy Weichel.** At Massachusetts Correctional Institute at Shirley with no chance for parole, praying for his chance at a new trial.

**Ronnie MacKenzie.** Working his fifty hours a week, and supporting his family.

**Raymond J. Patriarca Jr.** In private business, having dropped out of all Mafia activities and not wanting any part of them.

**Carmen Tortora.** Still serving the thirteen-year sentence he received in 1992.

**Kevin O'Neil.** Made his plea agreement and still awaiting trial.

**Tommy Dixon.** Out now and putting it all behind him while trying to do the right thing in parts unknown.

**Al Nugent.** Practicing law in Boston and maintaining his reputation as a top criminal lawyer.

**William Bulger.** President of the University of Massachusetts.

**James "Whitey" Bulger.** On a rocking chair on a porch in Southie, dressed like a woman, congratulating himself on the chess game I always knew he'd win.

# Acknowledgments

This memoir is the result of a lot of hard work by many people who not only cared deeply about the book but about me as well. Some of these people deserve special acknowledgment.

If it weren't for Al Nugent, my attorney and good friend of over twenty years, today I would probably be dead or behind bars. Al helped put me on the right path and, as a result, a story of my life became possible.

In terms of the book itself, Billy Nixon, the president of Willwork Inc. Exhibit Services, first got the ball rolling in encouraging my early efforts at chronicling my life. Not only did he inspire me to get serious about a memoir but he also introduced me to Ross Muscato, a writer who became my collaborator and friend.

Working closely with me, Ross and Phyllis Karas helped mold and craft the experiences of my life into a polished narrative. Ross and his ability to capture my voice, get inside the head of the gritty street personalities of South Boston, and relate to the harsher aspects of my life, sometimes amazed me — especially since he grew up in the leafy suburbs. Phyllis, a writer of immense talent, continued to impress me with her attention to detail and devotion to the art of storytelling. I can never thank her enough for her fierce devotion. She never gave up, not even when almost everyone else did. If I ever needed a reason to become a better person, she gave me that reason, along with the chance.

My brother Ronnie has always been my world. There's no stronger brother's bond. I love you, bro.

Joel Kurtzman, a good friend, brilliant author, and one of the world's most respected intellectual property consultants, guided me, made introductions, and generally held my hand as I went about the business of trying to publish my story. Joel introduced me to superstar literary agent Helen Rees, who immediately believed in the potential of my memoir and knew how to get it published.

Mike McGoff, my friend, encouraged me to follow in his tracks and rise above the past and embrace the future. His success will always be the motivation that helps me close the doors to my past and move forward into the light. I love you, buddy.

Joe Bartel, my best friend and mentor, has been my mental strength for over twenty years. He has always been there for me with a loyalty I can never forget.

George Warshaw is not only the best real estate attorney around, but also the best source of advice in my life. He understands exactly who I was and who I am and who I want to be, and shows me the way to get there. I love you, too, man.

Chip Fleischer, publisher at Steerforth Press, understood from the very beginning what I was trying to say and made sure I had the chance to do just that. His integrity and intelligence convinced me that his way was the right way, a decision I never once regretted.

Nicola Smith, my editor at Steerforth, requested more where more was needed, cut out the superfluous, and fine-tuned and massaged the manuscript into the finished product. She was tough, tougher than me, and a hell of a lot smarter.

EDWARD J. MacKENZIE JR.